LESBIANS AND LESBIANISMS

Claudette Kulkarni's study of lesbianism explores lesbian experience from both a feminist and Jungian standpoint. Her feminist interpretation challenges the heterosexism embedded in Jungian theory, yet Kulkarni is able to demonstrate that there are links between theory and experience and common ground between Jung and feminism. Using a methodology anchored in Gadamer's hermeneutics, Kulkarni bridges theory and experience by grounding theory in experience rather than by trying to make experience conform to theory.

A major feature of this work are the insights which emerge via the interviews conducted by the author with women who see themselves as lesbians or who are in a lesbian relationship. Asked what it was like to love another woman, their responses indicate a motivation to act in spite of internal conflict and external opposition. The pursuit of their lesbian desires constitutes a significant opportunity for individuation and self-understanding.

Lesbians and Lesbianisms is not an attempt to prove a hypothesis, nor does it present findings as concrete facts or conclusions. Instead, through the use of interviews and her own narrative the author directs the reader to a better understanding of same-sex love by demonstrating where lesbian experience and Jungian theory meet, where experience challenges theory and where theory sheds light on experience.

Claudette Kulkarni is a clinical therapist in private practice and at Persad Centre, Pittsburgh, a mental health center serving the lesbigay, transgendered, and HIV/AIDS communities and their families. She is a Contributing Editor to *The Round Table Review of Contemporary Contributions to Jungian Psychology* and an active member of the Association for Women in Psychology.

'This book presents new material and does away with some very tired clichés in the field on the topic of homosexuality, particularly in women. It is a welcome text for teachers and students as well as professionals looking for an intelligent treatment of a too-neglected subject.'

Lyn Cowan, Jungian analyst, Minnesota

'Claudette Kulkarni has written a powerfully vivid account of women's experiences of being women sexually. With intellect and rigour she offers us new methodological tools for criticizing Jung's heterosexism while expanding the theorizing of sexuality within analytical psychology.'

Noreen O'Connor, co-author of *Wild Desires and Mistaken Identities*

LESBIANS AND LESBIANISMS

A post-Jungian perspective

Claudette Kulkarni

London and New York

First published 1997
by Routledge
11 New Fetter Lane, London EC4P 4EE

Simultaneously published in the USA and Canada
by Routledge
29 West 35th Street, New York, NY 10001

Typeset in Garamond by
Ponting–Green Publishing Services, Chesham, Buckinghamshire
Printed and bound in Great Britain by
Hartnolls Ltd, Bodmin, Cornwall

British Library Cataloguing in Publication Data
A catalogue record for this book is available from
the British Library

Library of Congress Cataloguing in Publication Data
Kulkarni, Claudette
Lesbians and lesbianisms : a post-Jungian perspective /
Claudette Kulkarni.
Includes bibliographical references and index.
1. Lesbianism–Psychological aspects. 2. Lesbians–Psychology.
3. Jungian psychology. I. Title.
HQ75.5.K85   1997
306.76'63–dc21   96-52975

ISBN 0–415–15510–X (hbk)
ISBN 0–415–15511–8 (pbk)

To all the lesbians who have gone before me – with appreciation for their example, vision, courage, and stamina.

To all who travel this path with me – with gratitude for their companionship, support, and willingness to share.

To all the women loving women who certainly will come after me – with hope for the future.

The love of one woman for another evokes a deep cellular remembering of woman's origins, her darkness, her beauty, her power, her wisdom, and her limitless desire. At the same time, old longings are satisfied and new longings, never before experienced, are created.

Karin Lofthus Carrington (1990: 65)

CONTENTS

ACKNOWLEDGEMENTS

I thought these would be the easiest pages to write, but they are not. There are too many people to thank for too many things. I fear missing someone important and I feel frustrated by my inability to do more than say an insufficient "thank you" to everyone mentioned here and to anyone I may have overlooked.

There are, first of all, many intellectual debts to acknowledge. I am deeply obligated to the many thinkers and writers whose ideas are scattered throughout these pages. My most profound thanks, however, must go to the two men whose ideas have guided me and whose spirits have given life to me and my work: C. G. Jung and Hans-Georg Gadamer. I think I can honestly say that everything in this book is built upon their shoulders. There are no words to express the depth of gratitude I feel toward them.

I also want to acknowledge here my appreciation for "those women" who surrounded Jung and created a kind of *thiasos* out of their deep friendships with each other and their dedication to Jung's depth psychology. (This phrase is borrowed from the title of Nor Hall's very moving book *Those Women* (1988), Dallas: Spring Publications.) Foremost among these women, in the context of this book, is M. Esther Harding. Although Harding's independent spirit is often camouflaged behind her determined devotion to Jung, she somehow manages to convey the intellectual acumen and originality which characterized these extraordinary women. They clearly did not settle for merely living out the *anima* of the men around them – not even Jung's – and they left us an amazing trail to follow.

Then there are the many heartfelt thanks I owe to a number of mentors, all of whom have played both an intellectual and a personal role in my life: To Andrew Samuels for everything he has been to me, but especially for his special friendship, encouragement, and kindness – and for making me feel welcome at the Jungian margin: his ideas, and his courage in expressing those ideas, have set an example I can only hope to follow. To Elizabeth Minnich – my "core" at the Union Institute, whom I miss immensely and who impacted me in every conceivable way – for thinking with me and questioning everything I wrote: she has informed my thinking, deepened my commitment to feminism, and ultimately helped me understand myself and what I was trying to do. To Lyn Cowan who, as a lesbian feminist Jungian analyst, has been an inspiration and, as a longtime friend, has always challenged me to be myself and to follow my dreams: her penetrating critiques of Jungian theory merit more widespread attention and I hope this book helps serve that purpose. To Demaris Wehr for being there in the very early days of my intellectual explorations and for helping me see that it is possible, really, to be both a feminist and a Jungian. To Catherine Anderson, my supervisor at Persad Center, for guiding me in all matters relating to lesbian life and for teaching me how to find what I need within myself as I do the work of therapy: she has generously shared with me her experience, her knowledge, and her intuitions. To Richard Palmer for providing me – first through his book and now through the wonderful world of online communications – a sense of belonging to a community of people interested in hermeneutics and Gadamer.

And there have been many others who have encouraged me along the way and helped me to focus my learning, especially: Stan Marlan, Jungian analyst and teacher, whose classes have provided a foundation for much of my Jungian and post-Jungian thinking and for my work as a Jungian therapist; Christine Downing, who influenced me long before I had ever met her and who has been a gift in my life in more ways than she will never know; the members of my Jung Study Group (Annie, Doris, Linda, Mary, and Wendy) – all of whom cheered me on and patiently put up with my various anxieties all along the way; Dolores Brien, an editor of *The Round Table Review*, who provided kind and constant support – from a distance, through the miracle of e-mail; and several folks who encouraged me in various and sundry meaningful ways in the earlier days of my learning: Autumn Cole, Robin Connors, Pat Hargest, Randi Koeske, and Felissa Rose.

I owe a very special thanks to Mickey Landaiche, friend, colleague, and critic, who read the almost-final text and made many suggestions which significantly influenced the final version of this book. I would make him an honorary lesbian except that I think he's just fine the way he is.

I wish there was some way adequately to describe the profound sense of gratitude I feel toward the women I interviewed. Without them, this would have been a much different book – one seriously lacking in lesbian soul and vitality.

And, finally, my sincere appreciation to everyone at Routledge for their equanimity and guidance, especially Edwina Welham and her very responsive staff, all of whom have led me through the mysteries of this process.

INTRODUCTION

Like many first books, this one started out as the dissertation for my Ph.D. The initial working title for the dissertation was "Lesbianism as a Metaphor of the Feminine." I was convinced at the time that I was on to something with this idea, but as I read and thought and talked with others, I started to question my belief in this thing that I, as a good Jungian, was calling "the feminine principle." I came to realize that use of the categories "masculine" and "feminine," as if they were innately psychological or archetypal, was based on huge assumptions and that these categories are problematic for women and men alike. Even the terms "male" and "female" became somewhat ambiguous for me, especially as I began to work as a psychotherapist with transgendered clients. I had to ask myself: Are there really only two sexes, two "complementary" and "natural" polarities with nothing in between? Eventually, it became obvious to me that if so-called feminine values are missing from our culture, it is not because these qualities are necessarily inferior in men and their animas, but because they have been culturally assigned to women whose lives are then ritualistically ignored, trivialized, and discounted. Only what is socially acceptable for women to do or be gets reified and labeled "feminine" while everything else is credited to "the masculine." It then became inescapable that the notion of "the feminine," like the construct of "the animus," is simply irrelevant to women, lesbian or otherwise.

Paradoxically, calling attention to the "feminine" and allowing women access to "masculine" qualities via the animus, has been a somewhat redeeming contribution of Jung's thinking. But it was only a step in the process of challenging "genderism" (a term borrowed from Lyn Cowan (1994)). As my views slowly became more and more radical, I came to the same conclusion as Andrew

1

Samuels (1989b): we must get beyond concepts like "the masculine and feminine principles." Otherwise we will be stuck forever with concepts like "contrasexuality," stuck with projecting onto each other socially constructed expectations of what an "Other" is supposed to look like. Needless to say, I changed the title, and the focus, of my dissertation.

In addition, as I went along in this project, I found myself irresistibly drawn to the study of philosophy which, along with spiritual studies, seems to me to be the wellspring of psychology and an area of study which mainstream psychology typically disregards to the detriment of psychology and psyche. The particular area of philosophy that got my attention was hermeneutics. Although hermeneutics has a long and rich history as "the art of text interpretation," most readers will be, at best, only vaguely familiar with the term and most likely unaware of its use as a research methodology. For some, it might seem unsuitable to research since it does not represent a "scientific" or traditional method of inquiry. I also expect that even fewer will have heard of Gadamer's "philosophical hermeneutics." Hopefully, all of this will change over the course of reading this book. Ultimately, I hope to make a case for why I think "other Jungians and feminists should know more about hermeneutics, and Gadamer in particular" (a challenge posed to me in a letter from Elizabeth Minnich in late 1993). Those who prefer to have some prior foundation for reading might skip ahead and read Chapter 11 first in order to get acquainted with hermeneutics and Gadamer.

My discovery of hermeneutics was synchronistic. It occurred at a seminar on research methods where the instructor dealt with hermeneutics almost as an aside – as often happens to what is marginalized. At first, I simply was struck by the many associations I noticed between hermeneutics and Jung's way of working, but as my study of hermeneutics progressed, I was drawn in deeper and deeper. Then, when I came across Gadamer's hermeneutics, I was hooked. I was taken by Gadamer's sense of mission, a mission that Lawrence has poignantly encapsulated: "it has been Gadamer's lot to return to the yet more basic practical and political question about the right way to live" (Lawrence 1981: xiv). Although Gadamer never suggests that there is only one "right" way to live, he is not afraid to challenge himself and the rest of us to find our own "right" way. He is convinced that our survival depends on it. Gadamer's idea of the right way is embodied in his hermeneutics and serves, in many ways, as the philosophical backbone of this book.

I truly regret that it has not been possible somehow to broaden my scope in order to include the experiences of other kindred groups (e.g. gay men, bisexuals, and transgendered persons). I feel very strongly aligned in a common struggle with these folk. I can only hope that the deconstruction of constructs like gender and sexual orientation, contrasexuality and animus, will make the world a safer and friendlier place for them, too.

QUESTIONS OF TERMINOLOGY

In this book, I take up the question of whether "lesbian" is an identity and how it might be defined, but I have chosen not to take up a full discussion of two other interrelated questions of terminology: (1) the question of which term is preferable: "lesbianism" or "female homosexuality" or "same-sex love" and (2) the question of whether the use of "lesbian" as an adjective is less problematic than its use as a noun. In the end, these questions and any possible solutions are complex, both philosophically and grammatically. At a personal level, I have chosen generally to use the term "lesbian" because I prefer it. A part of me favors using it as an adjective because that seems more politically correct in some ways and more inclusive, but another part of me likes using it as a noun and as a statement of identity because that feels more empowering, as if I am bearing witness to something meaningful. After all, I am still a Jungian in search of meaning. In the end, I decided to use whichever term seems to best fit a particular context.

There is one other issue of terminology: the use of the term "woman" (as in my interview question: "What is it like for you to love another woman?"). I am aware that "woman" is a construct, but I prefer it to the more biological term "female" which, as Judith Butler (1993) has taught us, is no less constructed. For me, the use of the term woman is a way of recognizing that human beings consist of more than their anatomy and physiology.

A TRULY BRIEF INTRODUCTION TO HERMENEUTICS

Hermeneutics is usually defined as the art or science of text interpretation. As an intellectual tradition, hermeneutics has an

INTRODUCTION

old and fairly continuous history, though certainly not a monolithic one. The procedures of text interpretation that are the hallmark of hermeneutics had their origins in antiquity, however, the earliest use of the term "hermeneutics" as meaning a theory of text interpretation was in 1654 when it was used in the context of biblical exegesis (Palmer 1969: 34).

The term "hermeneutics" is derived from the Greek verb *hermeneuein* which is usually translated as "to interpret." However, it has three nuances of meaning, all of which are generally associated with Hermes, the wing-footed messenger god of the Greeks, who was thought to mediate between the gods and humans, translating the speech of the gods into language that would be intelligible to mortals. These three meanings are explained by Palmer (1969: 13, emphasis in original) as follows: (1) *"to express aloud in words"* – which implies an oral re-presentation or interpretation of what the hearer has understood (not unlike what occurs during an interview); (2) *"to explain"* – which involves constructing an explanation of what the hearer has understood and is another act of interpretation (not unlike what occurs in creating a narrative from the transcription of an interview); and (3) *"to translate"* – which is the act by which the interpreter makes "something meaningful" out of what seemed "strange, unfamiliar, and obscure" (ibid.: 29) (not unlike what occurs when reflecting on the text of an interview). Translation is not simply a "mechanical matter of synonym-finding," but an act of mediation or interpretation between the world of the translator and the world of the text; it is here that we are confronted with the fact that language itself already "contains an overarching interpretation of the world" (ibid.: 27).

The initial impulse for hermeneutics arose from the desire to find reliable and definitive systems, theories, standards, and methods for interpreting the meaning of texts. Scholars from many fields (e.g. religion, law, literature, philosophy, linguistics, philology) have made significant contributions to this effort over the centuries. Sometimes, the objective was to get at the "hidden meaning" (e.g. of an obscure text); at other times, it was to remove impediments that blocked understanding (e.g. by identifying the historical context of a text). Sometimes the emphasis was on trying to understand the author's intention; at other times it was on transposing oneself into the author's "lived experience." In any case, at the risk of oversimplifying an extremely complex and

4

evolutionary process, one might say that the focus of hermeneutical thinking has shifted over time from a desire to establish rules by which one might assure a correct interpretation of a text to a greater concern for achieving "a deeper understanding of the phenomenon of interpretation itself, an understanding that is philosophically adequate both epistemologically and ontologically" (Palmer 1969: 38). In any case, there is no definitive version of hermeneutics. Instead, we are faced with a "conflicting array of possible forms of hermeneutics" (Bleicher 1980: 4).

The hermeneutic circle

The concept of the hermeneutic circle is probably the most fundamental principle in hermeneutics. It has its roots in the search, born of the Reformation, to find a way to interpret the Bible on its own terms rather than through church doctrine. Formulations of the hermeneutic circle and its workings have evolved and matured over time, but the underlying idea throughout has been basically the same: a recognition that understanding has "a circular and self-correcting character" (Lawrence 1981: xix).

Current understandings of the circle propose that, in order to understand a text, we must first project onto the text a certain meaning based on whatever preknowledge or "preunderstanding" we bring to the text (whether from previous experience or from the tradition/prejudices which inevitably inform us). This part of the process is often called the anticipation or forestructure of meaning. Upon further reading, this initial or partial understanding is altered and corrected by new understandings. The hermeneutic circle is thus both "an inevitable part of our efforts to understand human phenomena" (Packer and Addison 1989: 22) as well as the actual condition of that understanding. That is, understanding is made possible through this circular movement, though never a perfect or certain understanding. Gadamer acknowledges that there are various tensions present in the circle (among and between our anticipations of meaning, our tradition, the text, our interests, etc.). Without these inner tensions "there would be no questions at all" (1981: 107). Some have suggested that all of this makes the hermeneutic circle a "vicious" circle. Packer and Addison point out that this is a profound misunderstanding. The circularity of understanding is not a vicious circle at all. It is "an essential one" (1989: 275).

INTRODUCTION

SOMETHING ABOUT THE INTERVIEWS

> The sexologists may have been the ones to name us, but we
> can, and do, create ourselves. Out of a mishmash of dis-
> information, misinformation and outright lies, each Lesbian
> constructs some story about who she is and who she might
> someday be, and she approaches her literature ... looking
> for additional pieces of her story.
>
> (Penelope 1992: 36)

> The voices speaking in this book are ... those who are
> willing to follow an interior maze to its core to shed some light
> on the unknown thing that dwells there in the close darkness.
> Imagination is as important a tool in this work as reason.
>
> (Hall 1980: xiii)

Each of these interviews was for me an entirely unique experience,
dependent sometimes upon my previous relationship with a particular participant, sometimes upon the particular responses, sometimes upon whatever prejudices I brought with me into that
particular interview. I make no excuses for any of this. It is part of
what made each interview unique and strikingly individual, both in
terms of style and of content. I must emphasize my sense that none
of these accounts truly does justice to the lives of these women
or to the complex feelings and thoughts they attempted to express
to me and that I attempted to understand. I think we all just did
our best.

I went into each interview "unprepared." That is, I began each
interview by posing my question: "What is it like for you to love
another woman?" Beyond that, however, the conversation proceeded spontaneously. The first interview, because it was conducted
as a "practice interview" and as part of my learning about research
methods, was conducted with a conscious, perhaps self-conscious,
attention to procedure and "method." The later interviews were
conducted after extensive reading and thinking about hermeneutics and after my discovery of Gadamer. In these later interviews,
I was much less concerned with methods and correctness than with
engagement and with the hope of somehow creating an atmosphere in which "Being" would disclose itself.

I have not attempted to make each account look as if it were "all
of a piece," so to speak. That is, I have not tried to make each
narrative appear as if it were a simple and flowing account of the

6

participant's experience. Rather, occasionally there are breaks (signaled by a horizontal line dividing one section from the next). This seems only fitting to me and in keeping with how life actually works. Also, the profile for each interviewee describes her as she was at the time of the interview.

AN OVERVIEW OF WHAT IS TO COME

All of the odd-numbered chapters contain essentially my own narrative – created out of my personal, philosophical, and theoretical horizons. In Chapter 1, guided by Jung's concept of confession as the first stage in a therapeutic process, I reveal my personal "prejudices." In Chapter 3, guided by Gadamer's concept of foregrounding, I attempt to outline my philosophical and theoretical horizons, both of which are permeated by my personal prejudices, but also represent the main conscious elements of my particular tradition. This is not to say that these efforts will do away with the influence these factors (or others) have on shaping my every word. My intent is only to make the reader aware of them so that they will be visible as they inevitably but sometimes subtly surface throughout the book.

Chapters 5 and 7 contain what might traditionally be called literature reviews. Just as the selection of a topic is never a neutral act (according to Gadamer), neither is the identification of "the literature" relevant to a topic, particularly in these technological times when we face the impossible task of trying to keep up with constantly expanding and evolving literatures. With that in mind, I chose to focus on two pairs of questions which seem central to my subject matter: (1) Is "lesbian" a category of identity? And how can we meaningfully define the term "lesbian"? (2) How have Jung and Jungians conceptualized same-sex love? And have there been any recent contributions from psychoanalysis relative to this topic? I address the first two questions in Chapter 5 and the latter two in Chapter 7.

In Chapter 9, I describe the rationale for my overall research design. This is followed, in Chapter 11, by a fairly detailed discussion intended to reveal the *coniunctio* of hermeneutics and Jungian practice.

All of the even-numbered chapters contain the narratives of my interviews. I considered various sequences for presenting these interviews, each of which offered some advantage. In the end, however, it occurred to me that to present them in chronological order and woven into the narrative of the book itself was a way to invite the reader into the process with me. The interviews are presented without very much commentary, except for some brief reflections at the end of each interview about my experience of the interview itself.

In the final chapter, I try to bring everything together by reflecting on my "findings" and revisiting the hunches with which I started out.

1

PERSONAL CONFESSIONS

Every psychology – my own included – has the character of a subjective confession.

(C.G. Jung CW4: 774)[1]

ON CONFESSION

According to Jung, the first stage in psychotherapy is confession – the act by which we rid ourselves of the secrets which, "like a psychic poison" (CW16: 124), alienate us from others. The goal is to undergo a cleansing that will free one from the burden of carrying such secrets. Jung insists that this must be a total confession, "not merely the intellectual recognition of the facts with the head, but their confirmation by the heart and the actual release of suppressed emotion" (ibid.: 134). That is, confession requires some passion. Jung was not the only thinker to recognize that confession is an essential starting point. Ray Monk writes that for Wittgenstein, "*All* philosophy, in so far as it is pursued honestly and recently, begins with a confession" (Monk 1990: 366). In keeping with this tradition of valuing confession, which is common to both analytical psychology and philosophy, I will begin with mine.

MY CONNECTION TO MY SUBJECT MATTER

I am a lesbian.

(Downing 1989: xvii)

These are the opening words of Downing's book. When I first read them, I felt excited and touched that she could be so direct and open about who she is. I feel the same way today, but my understanding of what it means to "be" a lesbian has gotten very complicated.

9

When I started my "coming out" process many years ago, I did not initially identify myself as "a lesbian." I did not have to since I continued to be involved with men for a while as I explored my attraction to women. When I did later claim a lesbian identity for myself, it felt right and true and, most of all, compelling. To declare myself "a lesbian" seemed like a relatively simple matter back then. I did wonder about the question of definition, but I had not encountered the various postmodern critiques, I knew nothing yet of the debate over "identity politics," and I had never even heard of deconstruction. Little did I know what was in store for me.

Today, I am better informed. This means that I know more than I did before – but it also means that I have come to realize how much we really do not know about all of these matters. So, while I might say that an entirely new world of understanding has opened up for me over these two decades, I also must admit that the cost has been high: my previous world view, simple and uncomplicated in so many ways, has been shaken. I can no longer settle back and feel sure about many things. Although I would not have it any other way, I am aware that holding to this path of uncertainty is not easy. So, while I do not know how it is that I came to appropriate or construct my lesbian identity (whatever it means), the fact is that being a lesbian is a central part of me whether I like it or not (which I do). I feel pride in the community of women which I claim as mine and I have come to believe that it is this sense of identity which also provides me with a sense of community. I am not out to 'prove' anything about lesbianism nor to discover its "essence." I reject any concept of "causes" relative to lesbianism, nor do I wish to explain or defend it. Rather, it has been my intent from the beginning to explore lesbianism both as a legitimate path toward individuation and as playing some role in collective life. I suspected that this would be a formidable and enormously complex task. I was right.

ON BEING POST-JUNGIAN

I am tired of people studying [Nietzsche] only to produce the same kind of commentaries that are written on Hegel or Mallarme. For myself, I prefer to utilise the writers I like. The only valid tribute to thought such as Nietzsche's is precisely to use it, to deform it, to make it groan and protest. And if commentators then say that I am being faithful or unfaithful to Nietzsche, that is of absolutely no interest.

(Foucault 1980: 53–54)

Little more than a decade ago, Andrew Samuels ushered in a new era in Jungian thought when he coined the term "the post-Jungian" in order "to indicate both connectedness to Jung and distance from him" (1985: 19). Foucault's quote seems to express much the same thing: a desire to ground oneself in the thought of a particular thinker while refusing to be limited by his or her vision.

I discovered Jung in 1980 at a time when I was in personal crisis. It was something like love at first sight for me and it signaled the beginning of the restoration of my psychological life. Today, having familiarized myself with many other psychological theories and therapeutic approaches, I can say with unreserved enthusiasm that I still find Jung's way of seeing to be the one most compatible with my soul. And, in spite of Jung's admonitions to the contrary, I generally am comfortable with acknowledging myself to be in the community of those who call themselves "Jungian." However, while I always start from Jung, I almost always deviate from him on various and numerous points, especially those related to his ideas about women.

I have been asked many times why I bother to try to explain or correct Jung. Why not just take what I like and leave the rest? Why not just acknowledge that he made some truly awful and absurd generalizations about women (and various ethnic and racial groups), and then get on with it? Why not just admit, sadly, that Jung was a product of his time? For years my only response to this had been to say that a simple dismissal of particular aspects of Jung's work did not feel satisfying or sufficient. It would not help me mine the gold and silver of his thinking. It would be just an easy way out – and would somehow feel dishonest. That was all I could say. Then, in 1989, I heard Andrew Samuels lecture on "Jung, Anti-Semitism, and the Fuehrerprinzip" (1989a).[2] Samuels' way of working with this topic has had a profound impact on me in many ways and it has helped me both to understand my reluctance to simply reject certain of Jung's ideas and to develop a consciously post-Jungian position.

In this particular lecture, Samuels attempted to make some meaning out of the debate over whether or not Jung was an anti-Semite, an accusation that has parallels in the charges that Jung was sexist, even misogynist, heterosexist, and racist. Like most debates involving intensely emotional issues, the question of whether or not Jung was an anti-Semite has constellated two opposing camps: the defenders and the attackers. Samuels refused to get bogged down in this debate since doing so would only continue to fuel it – and it has already been going on for half a century! He also rejected the focus on personality: both sides sitting in judgement of Jung, both sides "looking for a final solution to 'the Jung problem.'" Samuels argued that the question is *not* whether Jung was really an anti-Semite. He was. That is irrefutable. However, focusing on this question has only kept us entangled in a pointless dynamic of arguing opposing opinions. Even efforts to reach some kind of "balanced point of view" have not been either successful or fruitful.

Samuels reviewed a couple of the frequently offered defenses of Jung, both of which are often used in attempts to defend Jung against charges of the other isms. The first one, "that he was only expressing the attitudes of his time," is undermined when we come to realize that Jung in fact did have other options and could have made "other choices." Citing examples of such choices made by others of the same period, Samuels effectively disposed of the idea "that there was nothing else" that Jung could have done. The second defense attempts to dissociate words from actions by arguing that: "Though Jung wrote stupid and offensive things about Jews which he should have corrected he didn't do anything that could be regarded as really destructive in the real world." Samuels pointed out that even if we could make such a separation between life and work credible for a psychologist, there is still the problem of considering how Jung's words influenced others. Although no writer can prevent someone from exploiting his/her writing, s/he can protest such use, but "Did Jung?" Those who attempt to minimize the effect of Jung's other views – for example, his views on women – offer a parallel argument, something like: "Well, at least he offers women legitimate access (via the animus) to their 'masculine' side, to qualities that Western culture usually does not otherwise allow to women." This position has some validity as a transitional idea, but it is time to recognize that it *is* a transitional idea and its time has passed.

So, what do we as Jungians do with all of this? Samuels proposed that we begin to put things right by asking ourselves what implications this controversy holds for us today. He challenged Jungians to "employ psychological reflections" . . . for the purpose of "renewing" analytical psychology "from within."

Can analytical psychology learn from its founder's errors? I suggest that we will not progress unless and until we get on with the work of mourning for Jung leading eventually to our giving him up. Only when we have mourned Jung can we learn from his experience and then proceed to learn from Jung, the social and cultural phenomenon, rather than from Jung, the man, the flawed leader.

Samuels also insisted that we abandon that "type psychology" which targets minority groups and advances stereotypical definitions of them. This is an "abuse of our authority as psychologists." Instead, he argued, we should ally ourselves with, and listen carefully to, these "so-called minority groups, for that is where we belong." People often do not know how "to talk about what it feels like to be whatever they are" – but, after all, if Jungians are good at anything, are we not good at eliciting descriptions of psychological experience, at helping others "express the inexpressible"? So, why not do what we are good at and apply ourselves to helping such groups achieve their goal of dismantling "the defensive stereotypes imposed by threatened dominant cultures"? Why not get involved in the "subversive work" of exploring "the nature of difference itself"? The world "urgently needs a pluralistic, psychological model or vision in which difference is truly valued" and where difference and diversity are seen "as normative and as mutually enriching" rather than as an excuse for division and repression. And, since we do not yet know what our differences are, any exploration of difference must be done "experientially, not in a definitory or essentialistic way."

Samuels maintained that many of Jung's ideas "can be converted." We can follow up on the "subversive possibility that Jung opens up" if we can get to the core of Jung's ideas and apply them in non-conventional ways – ways that Jung himself could not imagine, given his flaw. For example, we can "make new and creative use of Jung's protest about leveling" and of his "rejection of the imposition of the spirit of one group upon another." Ultimately, Samuels wants us to focus not on Jung, the flawed man, but on the flaw itself. Only in this way can we dedicate ourselves to the job of repairing wounds and promoting healing at the point where the injury was inflicted. Samuels' approach, extended to other similar debates, challenges us to acknowledge our responsibility in relation to Jung, our "leader."

I am reminded here of a passage from *Memories, Dreams, Reflections* in which Jung is reflecting on his place in his family tree:

> I feel very strongly that I am under the influence of things or questions which were left incomplete and unanswered by my parents and grandparents and more distant ancestors. It often seems as if there were an impersonal karma within a family, which is passed on from parents to children. It has always seemed to me that I had to answer questions which fate had posed to my forefathers, and which had not yet been answered, or as if I had to complete, or perhaps continue, things which previous ages had left unfinished.
>
> (1961: 233)

This is where I find myself on the topic of Jung and lesbian experience: wanting to make some contribution toward continuing Jung's work by attempting to explore questions he could not even pose, especially in the context of the harm his work has done to lesbians. In doing this, I hope to begin repairs on the wound caused by one of Jung's flaws.

ON BEING A FEMINIST JUNGIAN

In a sense, there is no such thing as feminism. That is, there is no monolithic enterprise that can be called "feminism." Rather, there are any number of feminisms, each with its proponents and theories. For me, feminism is basically an attitude or perspective. Pellauer captures the essential elements of this attitude in language which foreshadows some of Gadamer's emphases:

> Feminism is not, in my view, a set of *a priori* answers, nor a commitment to a particular ideology. It is rather a willingness to follow questions wherever they lead us. Feminism insists upon a commitment to listening with open ears to women's experience in order to reformulate our actions and thought. It is thus more a method for creative inquiry than a set of predetermined points. Feminism *is* a commitment to women's well-being, to pursuing justice instead of patriarchy, but the substance of women's well-being is not necessarily known in advance.
>
> (Pellauer 1985: 34)

Jung's theory as a whole is in desperate need of feminist

14

revisionings. Although there are a variety of self-identified feminists in the Jungian world, their impact on Jungian theory has been fairly minimal, partly because Jungian theory has been so stuck in the androcentric mold of its founder and partly because there is a certain elitism in Jungian circles that shows itself as a split between the official Jungian community of "insiders" (i.e. analysts and analysts-in-training) and the broader but unofficial Jungian community of "outsiders" (i.e. non-analysts). The work of outsiders, often the most provocative work being done today, typically goes unacknowledged in the official Jungian world. As a result, most feminists consider the revision of Jungian theory to be a hopeless cause. I do not. In fact, I made the decision at some point to call myself a "feminist Jungian" rather than a "Jungian feminist" – that is, I made a choice between nouns and adjectives. I did this consciously because I hope and believe that by putting Jung at the center of my work in this way I might attest to the centrality of his ideas for me and that by making an adjective out of feminist I might attest to how feminism is a world view for me, one which filters everything else.

MY SECRET HOPE TO DECONSTRUCT JUNGIAN HETEROSEXISM

Many feminist researchers have acknowledged that feminist research is committed to the goal of transforming society in a way that will free women from the various dominations of men. That is, feminism has an agenda that is avowedly "politically value-laden" (S. Harding 1987b: 182) and not driven by "that dog-eared myth of intellectual neutrality" (Kolodny 1980: 21). Of course, what counts as meaningful social change is usually dependent upon a researcher's point of view and values. Since my principal ties are to the Jungian world, I have focused my efforts on trying to change that world by setting my sights primarily on the dismantling of Jungian heterosexism. The heterosexist bias of analytical psychology is so enmeshed and embedded in the Jungian framework that nothing short of total deconstruction of the concepts which support it (e.g. complementarity and contrasexuality) will even begin to rectify the situation.

In the last few years a few books and papers on lesbian and gay issues have appeared in the Jungian world, but the basic problem remains: "mainstream" or "official" Jungian thought continues generally to ignore the existence of lesbians. Those who have attempted to address lesbian/gay concerns have done so generally by trying to adapt traditional Jungian structures and theory. For example, they continue to speak the language of "feminine" and "masculine" principles. I believe this is a fundamental mistake.

It is time for those of us who care about Jung and who care about women (and men) to take up the challenge of re-visioning him not by discrediting his work altogether, but rather by liberating his concepts from their patriarchal and heterosexist moorings. I want very much to make a contribution toward "a vision of the Jungian project worldwide" (Samuels 1989b: x), especially toward those few efforts attempting to transform Jungian theorizing on lesbianism. Lesbians (among others) have suffered for too long from the heterosexist bias of Jungian theory and practice. I believe that this is very urgent work for anyone who feels in any way a part of the Jungian community, as I clearly do. Jung's ideas have been hurtful to people who identify as lesbian or gay. *This must stop.*

Of course, it is virtually impossible to talk about lesbians without examining and impacting the topic of gender as well, not because the construct of gender is literally relevant but because any definition of lesbian inevitably immerses us in the language of gender. That is, it is gender which effectively "creates" sexual orientation. Without the concept of gender, the concept of sexual orientation is meaningless.

MY QUEST FOR A THOROUGHLY FEMINIST JUNGIAN METHODOLOGY

Jungians do not have a research methodology as such because Jung was not particularly interested in either research or "methods." I came to realize this when I turned to the General Index of Jung's *Collected Works*, looking for relevant entries, and found only references to isolated passages scattered throughout the *Collected Works*, often embedded in unrelated contexts and displaying varying degrees of thoroughness and contradiction. Jung never really systematically addressed the issue of method. My search uncovered fragments of case studies, explorations of archetypal, mythological, and alchemical motifs, some development or application of theoretical material, and inquiries into various inner experiences (dreams, active imagination, etc.) – but no "research methodology" and not even much on his therapeutic method. I soon realized that I had a problem: how and where to find a methodology that would be thoroughly Jungian, that is, one which would embody the spirit of Jungian investigation, and that would simultaneously fit with the feminism of my understanding.

In addition, I wanted a methodology which would not confine me and my subject matter to rigid and meaningless categories, one which would allow me to bridge theory and experience by grounding theory in experience rather than trying to make experience conform to theory. It struck me eventually that this ability to hold the tension between experience and theory/knowledge is precisely what a Jungian methodology is ideally all about. Roger Brooke has noted that this clash between experience and theory caused Jung to continually revise his various formulations. While Brooke considers this to be an expression of "an apparent conceptual eclecticism" (1991: 3), I would argue that it is closer to the pluralism described by Andrew Samuels (1989b), which I will discuss in Chapter 3.

2

"PAULA"

PROFILE

Paula is a 44-year-old white woman who identifies as lesbian and who has been "out" for about twelve years. She is in an eleven-year-old relationship with a woman with whom she shares her home. She works in the area of social services and is in the final months of her doctoral program.

INTERVIEW SETTING/PROCESS

This was my first interview. It occurred while Paula and I were attending a seminar on qualitative research methods, the focus of which was phenomenology and heuristics. Since the interview was an exercise, it was not recorded. Therefore, I had to rely heavily on my notes and on my memory to create this narrative. The purpose of the interview was to get some practice in conducting an interview. As it turned out, however, this is not all that happened. I was profoundly moved and astounded by the experience of this first interview. The depth of Paula's response was unexpected. It had been "luck" that another lesbian was even there and willing to be interviewed. Among other things, our conversation confirmed for me the "rightness" of my question and the importance of what later came to be my commitment to "just" listen to what lesbians had to say about their own experiences.

Since this was a practice session, I made some attempt to "construct" it in such a way as to try out the things I had been learning. I already knew at that point that I somehow felt drawn to hermeneutics, though I did not know why exactly. Our instructor had presented the material as a kind of "add on" to phenomenology and heuristics and as a methodology that occupied a middle

18

ground between those two, but he really did not spend much time explicating it. However, the little he did say put me in mind of Jung. Hermeneutics sounded like a methodology which could bridge, methodologically, the world of experience and the world of symbol while it also attended to language and description. I wondered how one would "do" research using hermeneutics. What would a hermeneutic interview look like? Would the interviewer do the self-disclosure typical of heuristics or the *epoche* required in phenomenology?

I decided to divide the interview into thirds in order to try out different things I had learned. In the first third, I proceeded in a relatively phenomenological manner. That is, I was curious to see how Paula would answer the question entirely on her own, without any direction or interventions from me (other than my asking the question or asking for more description). So, once I had asked my question, except for requests for clarification, I simply listened.

I conducted the second part of the interview in a more heuristic style. That is, as Paula was talking about how and why she made the decision to come out to her family, I was reminded of my own situation. I thought this might be "a heuristic moment." So I made a deliberate decision to "join" with her by sharing a little of my own experience. My intent, I think, was to draw her out more. I believe this was successful.

As we went along it became clear to me that Paula was really struggling to articulate her feelings about women. So, I made another deliberate decision to "intervene" from a heuristic place, but in a different way. As I listened to her, I found myself thinking about how my experiences with women have been different from my experiences with men. It occurred to me that I might be having a moment of projective identification with Paula. I decided to risk it and asked her whether that had been her experience too: "Absolutely!" she replied. Then she admitted that she'd been struggling to not compare women to men, that she had wanted to be able to describe her experience without doing that. However, from that moment on, her descriptions became more vivid, enlivened, and articulate.

In the final third of the interview, I decided to try something hermeneutical, to the best of my understanding at the time. I thought I would have to make that happen. That is, I knew I could attempt to be conscious of my engagement in the hermeneutic circle, but I did not believe that a moment suitable to symbolic interpretation would occur. But it did – and, more importantly, I was present for it. It was this turn to language and the symbolic that ultimately produced the most interesting material from this interview.

THE INTERVIEW

It was clear at the outset that Paula felt moved by being asked this question that no one had ever asked her before. Her eyes filled as she acknowledged how "nice" it was "to sit down and talk to someone about this," especially to another lesbian. It also seemed important for Paula, in order to answer the question at all, that she provide me with some context. She could answer the question only by telling me about a particular woman, not women in general. She wanted me to know about M., her partner: under what circumstances they had met, how they had connected, what drew them together, the everyday-ness of their relationship. She wanted to tell me about their beginning together: how it was "not romantic" in the usual sense (because of many external forces that were at work). But she wanted me to know the significance that their coming together had for her: "Now I was real clear what I was about." This was not just another relationship with another woman while she was looking for "Mr. Right." "This was a real relationship . . . a real core thing."

From the beginning, Paula realized that this relationship signaled for her the end of "living a duplicitous life." Not only did she stop "looking for Mr. Right," she wanted recognition and legitimacy for her relationship with M. So, she came out to her family in the context of this relationship. She did not want it to be seen as if it were "an affair."

Being in a lesbian relationship has provided Paula with a setting within which she feels free to be herself. She does not feel encumbered by "all the trappings of [role] expectations" she has observed and experienced in heterosexual relationships. She experiences a sense of security, commitment, and respect with M. Loving her is "absolutely" different for Paula from her previous experiences of loving men. With M., Paula has felt touched "at a very core level."

I noticed that Paula had used the word "core" a number of times during the interview and asked her to say more about this word "core." She went on to talk about it as "a match." "In loving a woman, there's a different kind of a match or a fit." This is something that she had never experienced before with men. As I listened to her talk about this, I decided to take a risk; there seemed to be potential for what I have come to call "a hermeneutic moment," i.e. the move to interpretation. I commented again on her repeated use of the term "core" and asked her something like: "When you talk about 'core' it seems connected to a sense of self – is that how you mean it?" This, of course, came from my Jungian frame: core and self seemed like a natural "fit" to me and seemed to be a way of appreciating the symbolic depth of Paula's term. Whether or not that is true, her response was wonderful and inspiring. I wrote frantically as she spoke, wanting to get it all, verbatim.

> "With loving a woman it's like I'm more integrated and at peace with myself – like having more core available. There's more of me – more me to myself. There's more of me in a way that is just not there with men, not because they weren't nice, sensitive, etc. There's a kind of self-knowledge. To love a woman as a lesbian is integrating – that's the most "matched." For so long I was split off – now I'm inside myself. I'm more connected with my own core when I am loving a woman. So, of course, there's more core available."

MY EXPERIENCE OF THE INTERVIEW

As noted above, I was struck by Paula's repeated use of the word "core." Later on, after the interview, when she and I were discussing our experience of the interview process, Paula informed me that it had been precisely at the moment when I made the connection between "core" and "self" that she knew that I had understood what she was trying to say. This remark became formative for me in two ways. First of all, it gave me a sense of confidence about wanting to take a more active role in interviewing than I would have been allowed in a more phenomenological procedure, thus solidifying my attraction to hermeneutics. Second, it got me thinking about lesbianism in the context of Jungian ideas such as individuation and Self in ways that I had not anticipated.

Much later, I went to the dictionary to see what I might learn about the etymology of the word "core." While its origins are uncertain, I found some of its meanings to be quite amplifying:

"1. The central or innermost part of a thing; the heart or essence. 2. The fibrous or membranous central part of a fruit, containing the seeds" (*Reader's Digest Great Encyclopedic Dictionary* 1975). Though I was not looking for "the essence" of lesbianism as such, I thought there was something here, perhaps something that was central to this particular lesbian's experience, that this word was an attempt to express something so deep that its origins were unknown.

3

FOREGROUNDING MY HORIZONS

[We must] distinguish the true prejudices, by which we *understand*, from the *false* ones, by which we *misunderstand*. Hence, the hermeneutically trained mind ... will make conscious the prejudices governing our own understanding, so that the text, as another's meaning, can be isolated and valued on its own.

(Gadamer 1960/1993: 298–299)

ON FOREGROUNDING

Gadamer argues that we cannot escape the effects of our "tradition" or our "prejudices," and so he attempts to find some way to "rehabilitate" our views of these concepts. Tradition, as Palmer describes it, simply "furnishes the stream of conceptions within which we stand" (1969: 183). That is, we live in the flow and matrix of our collective tradition, ideologies, history, customs, beliefs, etc. – all of which permeate and condition us and, therefore, affect our interpretations. We cannot merely step outside our tradition in order to find some "neutral" standpoint from which we might determine the "real" meaning of what is being observed. The same is true of our prejudices which, as Linge explains, necessarily demarcate "a particular starting point" from which we begin our attempts to understand something (1976: xxx). That is, our prejudices comprise everything that we bring with us to a situation. Understanding, therefore, is not possible without making constant reference to all of these elements of our situatedness which, if foregrounded, not only make possible our ability to experience, but provide us with the "biases of our openness to the world" (Gadamer 1976: 9).

Obviously, Gadamer's concept of prejudice is not limited to what we commonly understand by this word – at least, in English where it refers to pre-judgements, bigotry, preconceived and irrational biases or opinions. Gadamer does not deny this aspect of prejudice. He merely points out that we cannot simply ignore, escape, dispense with, or set aside the presuppositions of our situatedness since understanding itself is literally impossible without them. Rather, Gadamer's intent here is much like Jung's insistence on reclaiming the "shadow." Both ideas challenge our tendency to operate as if we were "above" such things or as if we could make a conscious decision to step outside of our situatedness. As I see it, Gadamer's intent is to deconstruct prejudice in order to make us more accountable for ourselves.

Gadamer is painfully aware that our prejudices can be problematic. After all, this is what is often called "the problem of hermeneutics:" how does the interpreter avoid distorting the meaning of a text while realizing that its meaning is inevitably mediated by her/his own preunderstandings and subjectivity? Gadamer's "solution" is to "foreground" our "horizons" so that we can achieve a "fusion of horizons" with the text/other. (This latter concept will be discussed in Chapter 11.) In order to understand Gadamer's thinking, we must start with his conceptualization of horizons. For Gadamer, to have a horizon is to have a "range of vision that includes everything that can be seen from a particular vantage point" (1960/1993: 302). A horizon, therefore, is not a limitation; it is the very thing which allows us to see beyond whatever is closest to us so that we can actually see something "better," that is, we can see it "within a larger whole and in truer proportion" (ibid.: 305). A person who cannot see the horizon cannot see very far and is likely to overvalue whatever is close at hand and thus to be able to "understand" only through his/her preunderstandings (tradition, prejudices, fore-meanings, biases, etc.). Gadamer suggests that through "foregrounding" we can become aware enough of our preunderstandings "that the text [or the subject matter or another person] can present itself in all its otherness and thus assert its own truth against one's own fore-meanings" (ibid.: 269). In other words, there is no such thing as "presuppositionless" understanding. We always understand from some point of view, from within some context, and with constant reference to our previous experiences and preunderstandings. Although we can and must make our prejudices visible and examine them, we cannot – and need not – eliminate them since "a hermeneutical situation is determined by the prejudices that we bring with us" (ibid.: 306).

Gadamer takes the hermeneutic circle as "the starting point" for his attempts to understand how understanding itself is possible (ibid.: xxxv). He credits Heidegger with grasping the idea that understanding is always made possible by the anticipatory movement of the interpreter's preunderstanding which in turn, according to Gadamer, is shaped by the interpreter's "tradition" and "prejudices." That is, the interpreter can never be a neutral observer in this process because her/his interpretations are always produced from "within a horizon of already granted meanings and intentions" (Palmer 1969: 24). Gadamer stresses that what occurs in this circle is "neither subjective nor objective" because the anticipation of meaning that one brings to the task of interpretation is never simply a personal or subjective anticipation, but one that is "constantly being formed" in relation to one's tradition (1960/1993: 306). Gadamer concludes, therefore, that the hermeneutic circle "is not a 'methodological' circle," but an ontological one (1960/1993: 293). It relates to "the structure of Being-in-the-world itself" and is directed toward overcoming any idea of a subject-object split (1989e: 23). Of course, all of this again gives rise to "the problem of hermeneutics:" how can one can arrive at genuine understanding if everything one is understanding is necessarily filtered through one's horizons and foreknowledge? Using a phrase borrowed from Heidegger, Gadamer's solution begins with a call for "coming into the circle the right way." This is not about methodological certainty, but about adopting an attitude that will allow us to approach the text without imposing "in advance our own categories upon it" (Palmer 1969: 121). Although Gadamer does not propose a systematic way of achieving this, it is clear that foregrounding is the pivotal concept.

Foregrounding, as I see it, is a very conscious decision, akin to but distinctly different from the idea of the *epoche* or "bracketing" used in phenomenology. Bracketing is an attempt to set aside our presuppositions in order to keep them from interfering with understanding, thus assuming that such a thing is even possible. Foregrounding, by contrast, assumes that "neutrality" is impossible and that "the extinction of one's self" is inadvisable (Gadamer 1960/1993: 269). Understanding rests instead on our ability to stay open to the other. In foregrounding, we are asked precisely not to forget or discard our own ideas because understanding, according to Gadamer, cannot even happen without the filter of our "preju-dices" and our interpretations.

In foregrounding, we attempt both to situate the other (text/person) "in relation to the whole of our own meanings" and to situate "ourselves in relation to" the meaning of the other (ibid.: 268). Thus, foregrounding "is always reciprocal" in that "whatever is being foregrounded must be foregrounded from something else, which, in turn, must be foregrounded from it" (ibid.: 305). Fore-grounding thus allows something to become visible which might otherwise have been hidden from view. Gadamer acknowledges that it is very difficult to suspend our prejudices since a prejudice can operate "unnoticed" until it gets "provoked" by an encounter with the text (ibid.: 299). That is, our prejudices may be unconscious. We may be able to uncover them through a rigorous process of self-examination – or they may be induced as we conduct our investiga-tion. In other words, we must recognize that our conscious inten-tions are not innately superior over the unconscious forces which surround us. Foregrounding, therefore, like most other processes in hermeneutics, is an endless task of "hermeneutical con-sciousness." In addition, as we will see later, this requires that we set out not to prove that our ideas are "right" but with a sense of doubt about what we think we know.

Jung on preunderstanding

Jung is very clear on this matter: no knowledge can exist "that is not already caught and limited by the *a priori* structure of cogni-tion" and "subordinate to" the personality (i.e. the personal presuppositions) of the individual. Therefore, in all areas of study, "psychological premises exist which exert a decisive influence upon the choice of material, the method of investigation, the nature of the conclusions, and the formulation of hypotheses and theories" (CW9i: 150). This "inborn, preconscious and un-conscious" structure of every individual's psyche is a factor in every aspect of human activity (ibid.: 151). Although Jung and Gadamer might differ on the "inborn" nature of preunderstanding, they are certainly in agreement on the outcome.

In another essay, Jung argues that psychological understanding is always "subjectively conditioned" and, therefore, there can be no such thing as an "objective" interpretation (CW3: 397). In the context of dream interpretation, for example, he notes that interpretation is dependent primarily on the intentions, expectations, and presuppositions that the interpreter brings to the task (CW10: 320). That he takes this seriously is shown in the following passage:

> Theories in psychology are the very devil. It is true that we need certain points of view for their orienting and heuristic value; but they should always be regarded as mere auxiliary concepts that can be laid aside at any time. We still know so very little about the psyche that it is positively grotesque to think we are far enough advanced to frame general theories. . . . No doubt theory is the best cloak for lack of experience and ignorance, but the consequences are depressing: bigotedness, superficiality, and scientific sectarianism.
>
> (CW17: 7)

In other words, Jung shares Gadamer's complex understanding of the nature of prejudice. On the one hand, he acknowledges that theory (read "prejudice") gives us a point of view that orients us toward our subject matter so that we can heuristically learn something about it. On the other hand, what we think we already "know" can interfere with our ability to see something different. Jung's offhanded comment that theories can simply be put aside "at any time" merely echoes the idea of the *epoche* and so is not particularly helpful, although it does speak to his awareness of the problems involved. Also, by referring to theories as "the very devil," Jung implies that setting aside our prior assumptions is not such an easy task. Our theoretical orientation is always embedded somewhere in the unconscious background of our psyche and even a thorough analysis is no guarantee of uncovering our unconscious presuppositions. In other words, translating into Gadamer's language, we cannot override the conditions of our situatedness simply by increasing the amount of consciousness to which we have access.

MY PHILOSOPHICAL HORIZONS

Choosing the margin

It is worth considering that revolution is best practised precisely from the margins, rather than from the mainstream where the temptations of assimilation, of keeping one's head down and "getting on", are so much greater. . . .. Feminists should subject even half-desires to join [mainstreams] to careful scrutiny.

(Stanley and Wise 1990: 44)

We must enter the arena of public discourse without vanishing. Strategies of simple assimilation are unacceptable.

(Phelan 1993: 779)

In the context of compulsory heterosexuality, lesbian existence, by definition, is an act of resistance.

(Zita 1981: 164)

To be honest, I am attracted to things marginalized and I tend to distrust anything that even appears to be mainstream. My selection of a methodology (hermeneutics), my choice of subject matter (lesbianism), my theoretical perspective (post-Jungian), and even my feminist perspective – all qualify for a space in the margin. Yet, I do not choose the margin casually or light-heartedly. Like bell hooks, I feel called toward "Choosing the Margin as a Radical Space of Openness." Although hooks addresses herself primarily to the issues of racism and sexism, I understand her to be attending to matters of oppression and exclusion, and so I believe that her analysis has deep meaning for all marginalized groups.[1] And I take her advice (which is addressed to "Black folks . . . who are unwilling to play the role of 'exotic Other'") to be particularly relevant to lesbians (1990a: 148).

Hooks aligns herself with "the politics of location," which she sees as "a radical standpoint" because it summons those who want to be active "in the formation of counter-hegemonic cultural practice" to come together and "identify the spaces" – or sites of resistance – from which we can begin to work for change and within which we can "stand in political resistance with the oppressed" (ibid.: 145). This choice of where to stand is for hooks a crucial one. It shapes our reactions to current practices and our ability to envision alternatives; it conditions "the way we speak" about issues that affect us; and it determines "the language we choose" (ibid.).

Everywhere we go there is pressure to silence our voices, to co-opt and undermine them. . . . Those of us who live, who "make it," . . . invent spaces of radical openness. Without such spaces we would not survive. Our living depends on our ability to conceptualize alternatives, often improvised.

(ibid.: 148–149)

28

Hooks conceptualizes these spaces of radical openness as "a margin – a profound edge" (ibid.: 149). She is careful to make a distinction between a marginality "imposed by oppressive structures" and one that is chosen "as site of resistance" (ibid.: 153). A marginality that one has chosen will not be given up or surrendered in order to move to the center. Rather, it is "a site one stays in, clings to even, because it nourishes one's capacity to resist" and because it helps us attain a "radical perspective" that allows us "to imagine alternatives" (ibid.: 150). We must do this "if we are to survive whole, our souls intact" (ibid.: 148).

As a lesbian, I can identify with this scenario, with the struggle to create alternative communities, and with the need to find ways in which to resist the heteropatriarchy. It is not that I am without feelings of ambivalence about living in such an invented and visible space. Sometimes it feels exhilarating, but at other times, it feels lonely and even dangerous to live openly as a lesbian in a culture which is without tolerance and permeated with hate. Always, however, it feels like the only authentic choice available to me. That is, it seems to me that hooks is right, that only from some site of resistance can lesbians (and others) hope to sustain "our subjectivity," to be "transformed, individually, collectively," and to "articulate our sense of the world" (1990a: 153). This affirmation of subjectivity certainly will find its critics. I am not one of them. Subjectivity, for me, is another site of resistance. As a process, not a goal, subjectivity identifies my beginning point and provides me with a place from which to experience the world.

Some writers have argued against the politics of location. Diana Fuss, for example, while not referring to hooks specifically, argues against what she calls "inside/outside rhetoric," attacking it as arising from some "misplaced nostalgia" about the outside being "a privileged site of radicality" (1991: 5). She claims that "most of us are both inside and outside at the same time" and that, to idealize the outside, one must be to some extent, "comfortably entrenched on the inside." Yet, she describes the outside as "a position of powerlessness, speechlessness, homelessness" (ibid.). Though I am sympathetic to the deconstructive tone of Fuss' remarks, I find this position to be contradictory. (For example, even outsiders who are white can rarely feel "comfortable" on the inside if they get there by virtue of hiding their sexuality.) In any case, Fuss goes on to insist that "a position of perpetual or even strategic outsiderhood" is not "a viable political program" because, for many gays and lesbians, this "is less a question of political tactics than everyday lived experience" (ibid.).

It seems to me that Fuss' concept of a marginality is confined to a marginality "imposed by oppressive structures." Of course, that *is* the everyday lived experience for many. However, hooks' politics of location does not ignore the experience of being "both inside and outside at the same time." Instead, it challenges the very idea of "a" center. That is, my site of resistance can be quite "central" to me without my being "in" the cultural/power center. To confuse these two understandings of "center" is, I believe, to miss the point, to ignore political context and reality, and to reduce all marginality to imposed marginality. In addition, Fuss seems unwilling to conceptualize marginality as anything but a strategy. I would argue, however, that the power of choosing marginality as a site of resistance is precisely that it is *not* a strategy. It is the site of being, not in the heavy metaphysical sense but in the sense of "everyday lived experience," that place from which we bear witness. Courage is required both to resist pressure from the political power center and to cross over, daily, into an unsafe world. This is not a strategy. Nor is it comfortable.[2]

Patricia Williams, author and law professor, describes her own experience of choosing the margin in a way that clearly implies the ontological dimension involved in making such choices. She conceptualizes the issue as a question of crossing over the boundary between the margin and the center, between the outside and the inside, between the unconventional and the acceptable:

> I think that the hard work of a nonracist sensibility is the boundary crossing, from safe circle into wilderness: the testing of boundary, the consecration of sacrilege. It is the willingness to spoil a good party and break an encompassing circle, to travel from the safe to the unsafe. The transgression is dizzyingly intense, a reminder of what it is to be alive.
>
> (1991: 129)

For me, this is a description of lived experience and speaks to the courage and dangers involved in deciding, daily, to cross over the threshold from the margin into the center as a disruptive strategy. It is in sharp contrast to Fuss' accusations of entrenchment, comfortable or otherwise. Williams also notes that this way of moving across boundaries is not rooted in pessimism or powerlessness. Rather,

It is a sinful pleasure, this willing transgression of a line, which takes one into new awareness, a secret, lonely, and tabooed world – to survive the transgression is terrifying and addictive. To know that everything has changed and yet that nothing has changed; and in leaping the chasm of this impossible division of self, a discovery of the self surviving, still well, still strong, and, as a curious consequence, renewed.

(ibid.: 129–130)

Finally, it is important to realize that to choose lesbianism as a site of resistance is not to insist that it is also a site of identity (although those questions may arise and will be discussed in Chapter 5). Rather, as de Lauretis points out, lesbianism is a "critical vantage point" (1990: 136; quoted in Phelan 1993: 776) from which we can attempt to present possibilities other than heterosexuality. This is not to claim, as Phelan reminds us, that lesbians are "outside of, or against, or safe from the network of compulsory heterosexuality" since even opposition to a prevailing system can be conceptualized as "participation within a system" (1993: 776). Phelan instead uses Ferguson's description of lesbian cultures as "potential cultures of resistance *within* historically specific patriarchal cultures" (Ferguson 1990: 84; quoted in Phelan 1993: 776, Phelan's emphasis). This is a way, Phelan points out, of seeing ourselves as *not* "simply outside" (ibid.: 777). In other words, we can hold the tension between being inside and outside without surrendering the power of conceptualizing lesbianism as a site of resistance.

In the end, I would argue that we do not need to choose between "inside" and "outside," as if they were a pair of opposites or literal locations. Instead, we "have to stand where we are" (ibid.: 786) and hold the tension between them in order to acknowledge the complexity of real life – thus practicing the ideology of pluralism that Andrew Samuels has described. In this way, we can do precisely what Fuss ultimately admits we "urgently" need to do in lesbian theory making: we can formulate "a theory *of* marginality, subversion, dissidence, and othering" (1991: 5). In the end, Fuss seems to settle for this with a sense of resignation, saying that perhaps, at this moment in time and just for now, the best we can do is "to exert sustained pressure from/on the margins" (ibid.: 6). This is a half-hearted call to theorizing, one that in effect buys into the very position of "strategic outsiderhood" which she has criticized as

31

being not viable. I would argue that to choose the margin as a site of resistance is anything but expedient. It is a declaration of revolt and a refusal to go along with whatever is happening in the center. In that sense, it is not a strategic move. It is an authentic one.

In any case, it is hooks' call to choose the margin as a site of resistance that inspires and challenges me. I believe it is both an invitation to assert and elaborate on "subjugated knowledge" (Foucault 1980: 82) and an opportunity to follow Williams in testing and crossing boundaries. I hope this book contributes toward inventing the kind of space hooks describes, a space of radical openness and resistance (even if it is a small one). I will not be trying to formulate "a" theory of marginality, but I do hope to subvert, at the least, the dominant Jungian discourse.

Embracing the spirit of pluralism

The term "pluralism" has been used in many contexts and defined in many ways. My use of the term is shaped almost entirely by the work of Andrew Samuels as contained in his book, *The Plural Psyche*. Samuels applies this complex ideology across all layers of life: political, social, personal, psychological, theoretical. Eventually, I came to realize that Samuels' focus on holding the tension between the one and the many was, at heart, really an argument in favor of a hermeneutical process and marked by an attitude of openness and receptivity that I later came to find in Gadamer.

Samuels' underlying concern is expressed in a question which echoes Jung's repeated warnings against "one-sidedness:" "what happens when a single part out of many begins to act as if it had the force and weight of the whole?" (1989b: 2). Jung's own take on this is somewhat sarcastic but instructive: "The moment one forms an idea of a thing and successfully catches one of its aspects, one invariably succumbs to the illusion of having caught the whole" (CW8: 356). In actuality, this is a kind of self-deception which some choose because it brings them "peace of mind: the unknown is named, the far has been brought near, so that one can lay one's finger on it" (ibid.). In other words, according to Jung, efforts aimed at achieving certainty often produce misleading results. The psyche is not so easily pinned down.

Samuels argues against certainty and one-sidedness, and sets out instead to find a way of accommodating the differences which arise when we have divergent points of view. He wants to do this "*without* imposing a false resolution" and without "losing sight of the unique value of each position" (1989b: 1). He proposes a pluralism which can "hold the tension between the one and the many" (ibid.), somewhat in the spirit of Jung's transcendent function. While Samuels is sensitive to the very human "wish and need to feel integrated and speak with one voice" (ibid.: 2), he encourages us to take note as well of our tendencies toward diversity (e.g. fragmentation, splitting, multiplicity) and to value these as much as we value our strivings for unity. He points out that the multiplicity of the psyche shows itself through our differing points of view and that the most productive way of proceeding is to genuinely engage with each other "without having unity as a goal" (ibid.: 6). This requires an attitude of open exchange "in which different world views meet but do not try to take over each other" (ibid.). The challenge, he says, is to hold this tension without always framing things as pairs of opposites and "*to combine passion and tolerance*" (ibid.: 4). He reminds us that "we are morally enriched by contrast and diversity" (ibid.: 8).

It is important to note that Samuels' pluralistic vision must not be confused with "'eclecticism', 'synthesis', 'parallelism', and 'perspectivalism'" or relativism (1989b: 1). Each of these methods attempts in some way to subvert or avoid the idea of difference. By contrast, "in a pluralistic endeavour," an entire theory is used, as a whole, and "as faithfully as possible, and together with other theories until inconsistencies lead to" a breakdown which then "becomes the object of study" (ibid.: 13). In other words, under pluralism we are not required to choose between two positions which may be equally desirable (for example, between truth and meaning), nor are we expected to hold that all explanations are equally valid or to be indifferent to the differences between them. Rather, a pluralistic attitude tries to "make space" for all points of view and "to believe in and use apparently antithetical ideas . . . without losing the specificity of each" (ibid.). Samuels asks us to do something very difficult: "to feel passionate about being tolerant, to be a radical centrist in depth psychology" and to express "animated moderation" (ibid.: 6). Samuels reminds us that depth psychology is "about preference and relevance," concepts which help us negotiate difficult problems by holding a position that is simultaneously "from a distance" and "filled with intensity" (ibid.: 227). In the same way, he argues, pluralism holds that there are no rigid rules for judging a situation, no pre-established hierarchy, no definitive canon – and yet judge we must sometimes, not between "right" and "wrong" but according to "preference" and "relevance." We do this by using the criteria of "specificity and intensity of emotion" which might not make one "right," but is definitely not relativism since it does not refrain from making judgements but also challenges us not to be one-sided (ibid.).

Samuels recognizes that it is no easy task, either emotionally or ideologically, to maintain a pluralistic attitude: one must suspend "the simple and reliable mechanism of right or wrong" without entirely discarding it and without giving up our passionate convictions or excitement at new ideas (ibid.: 6). In other words, a pluralist is someone who engages in this process while admitting that s/he "does not know everything" and who "is prepared to listen to a more informed source (as well as being aware of those aspects of his or her personal psychology that hinder that)" (ibid.: 7). (As we will see later, this description nearly paraphrases Gadamer's description of the "partners in conversation" and his insistence on self-understanding.) Samuels describes three other features essential to pluralism which are particularly relevant to my methodology: its link to metaphor (which roots it in Jung), its opposition to hierarchy (which connects it to feminism), and its reliance on spontaneity (which allies it to Gadamer).

Link to metaphor Samuels argues that pluralism "resonates" with the idea of metaphor. The basic function of metaphor is to communicate with others through multiple and "even contradictory" perspectives (ibid.: 179). To engage in metaphorical work then is to acknowledge that there is no need even to try to get at a unitary "truth" or to "prove" that one meaning is more "true" than another. We simply arrive at differing understandings (another echo of Gadamer that we will meet with later).

Opposition to hierarchy Pluralism incorporates an attitude that is specifically "anti-hierarchical" (ibid.: 11). Samuels realizes that we cannot entirely avoid constructing hierarchies since we have been conditioned by Western tradition to "search for structure" (ibid.: 14). So, instead of attacking this tendency as such, he makes a careful distinction between "an *ad hoc* hierarchy" and "a preconceived hierarchy," explaining that "the former is capable of seeing itself as one version among many possible versions" while the latter is not (ibid.: 13). Samuels objects to the preconceived hierarchies because they organize things into "positive" and "negative" categories. In such hierarchies where everything is "graded" and "calibrated" in advance "diversity will perish" (ibid.: 11).

Reliance on spontaneity Spontaneity is a challenge to hierarchy because it generates "the novel and unpredictable" (ibid.: 228). To be spontaneous is to put one's trust in the "revelatory capacity of images and experiences, without stressing any presupposition that these are derivatives of an unknowable absolute" (ibid.). Samuels argues that this aspect of pluralism also introduces a new way of understanding subjectivity psychologically, a way which does not assume that subjectivity is "a pathological skewing of the evidence," nor that it is necessarily a flaw. Pluralism conceptualizes subjectivity as "a valid dimension of theory-making" (ibid: 229) – much as Gadamer conceptualizes prejudice.

In the end, Samuels declares that "the *telos* or goal of pluralism is 'reform'" – a kind of reform that is not distinguishable from revolution. "Reform has its moral connotation and that," he says, "is deliberate" (ibid.: 230). The moral component "has to do with *involvement*" (ibid.: 231). This idea of involvement, as I understand it, is Samuels' way of achieving "the recovery of the world," a phrase which Brooke has used in describing a parallel between Jung and Heidegger (1991: 57). Involvement in the world is involvement in psyche, and vice versa.

The concept of pluralism periodically gets debated by feminist scholars. Some, like Annette Kolodny, a feminist literary critic, have argued in favor of pluralism. She, too, takes note of our tendency to create structure as if it will advance us "from difficulty and perplexity to clarity and coherence," but she advises against it (1980: 17). Kolodny critiques the formulation of unitary and rigid procedures because they are stifling and unrealistic and lead us to construct oversimplified interpretations and to establish canons of correctness. She calls instead for a "a playful pluralism," one that might be "responsive to the possibilities" of various methods "but captive of none" (ibid.: 19). Like Samuels, Kolodny points out that a pluralistic approach does not require that we abandon the search for patterns and structure: "what we give up is simply the arrogance of claiming that our work is either exhaustive or definitive" (ibid: 20).

On the other hand, Kolodny and pluralism have been the targets of attack by some feminist critics. Jane Marcus, for example, refers to Kolodny's work as an example of "the current minimization of differences" (1982: 217) and quotes the following from an unpublished piece by Gayatri Spivak:

> To embrace pluralism (as Kolodny recommends) is to espouse the politics of the masculine establishment. Pluralism is the method employed by the *central* authorities to neutralize opposition by seeming to accept it. The gesture of pluralism on the part of the *marginal* can only mean capitulation to the center.
>
> (Quoted in Marcus 1980: 218n3)

Clearly, Spivak's interpretation of pluralism is not mine. I do expect that pluralism, like anything else, can be and has been used to do all kinds of things. However, the pluralism of my understanding is anything but "capitulation to the center." To hold the tension is precisely *not* to capitulate.

I will conclude this discussion of pluralism with another reference to Patricia Williams. In a discussion of the particular perspective we need to acquire in order to take up "a nonracist sensibility," Williams proposes that this is a perspective which "is at the core of . . . feminist theory" (1991: 129, 130). It is an "ambivalent, multivalent way of seeing" – "a fluid positioning that sees back and forth across boundary" – a perspective that does not envision only "either-or" sets of choices (ibid.). Williams does not give this perspective a particular name, but I would call it pluralism.

MY THEORETICAL HORIZONS

In an article entitled "New Voices, New Visions: Toward a Lesbian/ Gay Paradigm for Psychology," Laura Brown reminds us that the field of psychology has been "shaped through the distorted lens of heterosexist psychological science and practice" (1989: 447). She wonders what it would mean for psychology if we were to use a new paradigm, one that accepts lesbian and gay experience as "central to definitions of reality," and even "as core to psychological science and practice in general" (ibid.: 446, 447). Brown goes on to propose, for example, that the "merging" experienced by a healthy lesbian couple might even be seen as "more normative and functional for intimate pairs than the illusion of autonomy and distance" that seems to exist in heterosexual couplings "simply as an artifact of gender roles" (ibid.: 453, 454). Maybe lesbians really are "the model of healthy female development" (ibid.: 455). What would be the implications for psychology if we opened ourselves up to the possibility that "normalcy" lives not at the center but in/at the margins? This subversive thought, she suggests, would force us to create a new paradigm for psychology.

While I cannot embrace this appealing suggestion of lesbian superiority, I do have some "hunches" or theoretical preunderstandings about the ways lesbian experience could impact on psychology. They constitute the outline of my own "paradigm" and my contribution toward the "program of renewal from within" discussed above (Samuels 1989a). Like Brown, I believe that a psychology which allows itself to accept lesbian experience as central to its understanding of psychological reality is a psychology that will be forever changed because it will be a psychology that is truly engaged in listening to soul.

What follows is not an attempt to provide a systematic theoretical structure, but to suggest a few ideas – some are fragmentary, some (in true Jungian fashion) are contradictory, and some are not yet fully formed. These are "hunches" that I brought with me into this process or that I accumulated somewhere along the way, and that became the framework for how I have come to interpret and understand lesbianism.

Lesbian experience as *consensus gentium*

Psychological existence is subjective in so far as an idea occurs in only one individual. But it is objective in so far as that idea is shared by a society – by a *consensus gentium.*

(Jung CW11: 4)

I came to this project expecting that lesbian experience comes in a variety of expressions, that there is nothing particularly generic about it. Yet, I did hope to find some common threads, some way of describing lesbian experience that would resonate for us as a community of women-loving-women, some way of pointing toward the meaning embodied in the desire (sexual and otherwise) for another woman. I wanted to identify something about the "essence" of lesbianism, not in the manner of "essentialism," but in the manner of beginning to identify a "*consensus gentium*" or "common ground" of lesbian experience.

I suspect that there is such a thing as a lesbian "*consensus gentium*" or what Penelope has called "a Lesbian consensus reality – a

Lesbian-centered view of the world" (Penelope 1992: 39). The purpose of such a consensus is *not* to explain ourselves to others, but rather, following Christine Downing's exhortation to women writing about women, to "dedicate ourselves to sharing with one another what we know and don't know, what we fear and hope, remember and imagine" (1992: 16–17). Through such sharing, what has had meaning for an individual at the personal and subjective level becomes part of an element of collective experience, part of our common ground.

I believe that Downing's arguments, which she puts forward in the context of trying "to articulate a psychology of women," are relevant in the present context (ibid.: 17). Downing refuses to be seduced into trying to express how different women are from men saying: "I would like as far as possible to escape formulations given their shape by the myth of difference, by the fantasy of opposites" (ibid.). I find myself responding similarly in terms of lesbians: I do not want to get caught in attempts to explain how, or if, lesbians are different from heterosexual women. Andrew Samuels (1989a) has also offered some cautionary statements about exploring "difference," noting that it is an area open to the making of mistakes which could have "disastrous consequences," especially if we fall into the Jungian trap of looking for "complementarity" (a way of seeing that is always operating at the level of wanting things to be "rounded out in a whole way").

On the other hand, I also find myself struggling against the tendency to formulate a theory based on sameness, feeling Nor Hall's warning: "Once you see that a thing is different, the tendency is to try to incorporate it or eliminate it" (1980: 128). Downing, too, recognizes this pull: "I see now," she asserts following a discussion of essentialism, "that I must question not only the myth of difference but also the myth of identity" (1992: 19).

How, in fact, do we come to understand and resist these two related fantasies of difference and identity? One way, of course, is to approach them pluralistically. Another is to understand, as Downing does, the underlying process that is being demonstrated when we yearn for a myth of identity: "What my 'we' intends to express is not an assumption of identity but a longing for a community" (ibid.). I believe that lesbians, as a subset of women and humanity, are as inclined to this longing as anyone else. My desire to give some expression to a lesbian *consensus gentium* is, ultimately, an expression of my own longing for community. In that way, I hope this work will be a contribution toward "the common ground on which ... we can create a Lesbian community that will support even those who may not want it or know that it exists" (Penelope 1992: 39).

Lesbian experience as personal and collective individuation

Any serious check to individuality ... is an artificial stunting. ... A social group consisting of stunted individuals cannot be a healthy and viable institution; only a society that can preserve its internal cohesion and collective values, while at the same time granting the individual the greatest possible freedom, has any prospect of enduring vitality.

(Jung CW6: 758)

I have long suspected that lesbianism has meaning at both the personal and collective levels and have often wondered what it is that lesbian/gay people carry for the rest of the collective. Is it something about an alternative and powerful form of sexuality, or something about "sameness" versus "difference," or something else? Then one day, a few years ago, I decided that I really "should" read M. Esther Harding's *The Way of All Women*. After all, I thought, this is a Jungian classic on the topic of women – even if it is out-of-date, having been written in 1933. I did not expect to find anything particularly significant in it, and, on the whole, I did not. Harding, a first generation Jungian, was one of Jung's inner circle of analysts. Like many others around Jung at the time, she seemed committed to providing evidence for his point of view, no matter how much it conflicted with her own experience or understanding. She, like the others, found ways to make it all fit. Harding evidently could not conceive of women wanting to be independent of men, except temporarily or because they were forced to by circumstances outside their control. Throughout this book, there is hardly a line where Harding discusses women other than in relation to men – *except* in this one chapter entitled "Friendship." I was amazed and surprised when I came across this chapter and I am not sure what motivated Harding to write it. In spite of the fact that it contains a painful mixture of insight and stereotype, it is also rather subversive in some very subtle ways.

I cannot say that Harding consciously meant to imply in this chapter what I am taking from it (though I cannot speak for her unconscious "intentions" and can only speculate, as others have, about her relationship with her longtime companion, Eleanor Bertine). Perhaps she simply meant to acknowledge the value of friendships between women, although she makes it very clear that she finds such friendships to be inferior to relationships between women and men. In any case, whatever her intent, there are some fascinating ideas in this chapter, ideas that allow us to theorize about the role of lesbian relationships in collective life.

I am presenting Harding's arguments in some detail because I believe her work illustrates both the promise and the pitfalls of a Jungian take on sexuality and sexual orientation. Harding's thinking might have pointed the way toward a new Jungian paradigm – if this part of her work had not been so totally ignored by the Jungian community. It seems to me that it is time to reconnect post-Jungian thinking to its roots via this sometimes radical thinker. My desire to do this is an attempt to acknowledge and respond to a comment made by feminist researcher Shulamit Reinharz:

> I find it surprising that few feminist researchers seem to know much about women of the past who have contributed to their own disciplines. In my search for feminist research literature, I found little acknowledgment of the continuity between the work of nineteenth-century feminist social scientists and of the current period. I hope my efforts raise the historical consciousness of feminist researchers concerning their discipline.
>
> (1992: 251)

Connecting with Harding's work in this way helps me feel firmly rooted in my Jungian tradition, no matter how far I may stray from a traditional interpretation. It is interesting to note that Jung himself wrote a laudatory introduction for this book in which he admits that "men understand nothing of women's psychology as it actually is" and praises Harding's book for its fresh insights (Harding 1933/1970: xviii). He describes it as "an important contribution" toward "a deeper knowledge of the human being" (ibid.).

Harding begins this chapter by implying, in effect, that most heterosexual relationships are "of necessity ... largely unconscious" because they are, after all, "based on the projection of the anima" (1933/1970: 91). Therefore, she postulates, something had to intervene in order to compel the further development of consciousness. Otherwise, "the progress of humanity" toward a more evolved consciousness "might have been blocked" and human relationships might "have been doomed to remain unreal" (ibid.: 92). The catalyst for change, as Harding sees it, came in the form of various social and economic forces that propelled women "out into the world" in the early part of the twentieth century. From then on, women no longer saw marriage as the only option open to them and many chose consciously to remain unmarried for a part or the whole of their lives. "These women," Harding declares, are "far from being the weaklings, the stupid or unattractive members of their generation." In fact, she claims they "may be the most vital and enterprising, the ones with greatest intelligence and initiative" (ibid.).

Harding does not see these women as consciously initiating this evolution of consciousness because, although women are "naturally" concerned with relationships, they are generally so "exceedingly undeveloped in their relationships" that they would never choose such a conscious path (ibid.: 100). Harding, in fact, goes to great lengths to argue that by and large these women simply are swept up in a cultural movement driven by social and economic forces. "It is hardly conceivable," she insists, "that any step forward could have been taken unless women had been forced to seek each other's company." That is, left to themselves, women would do as men do: they would settle for "that degree of relatedness which could be produced by the sexual bond in an unconscious or instinctive way" rather than make such a demanding effort (ibid.). Harding does acknowledge, however, that once challenged these women do respond willingly and that friendships among such women have come to occupy "a place of unprecedented importance" for them (ibid.: 92).

Harding's profound ambivalence on this topic is by now obvious and she remains plagued by it throughout the chapter. I believe this reflects the enormous effort required to hold the tension between Jungian theory on the one hand and what must have been her own observations and experiences on the other. We see this over and over again in Harding's various and very Jungian qualifiers, all of which seem rooted in the idea that relationships between women can have value only if they are "unlike" comparable relationships between men and women, and only to the extent that women are "forced" into them. For example, Harding claims that friendships between women "are often of a very high type," that is, unfettered by "ulterior motives," since they do not involve "any obligation for the mutual satisfaction of instinct" (ibid.). In other words, they are not sexual. In addition, these relationships, she contends, do not involve financial dependency, legal requirements, or social expectations, so they are based strictly on "the attraction of one personality for another, on mutual interests and on an inner psychological or spiritual accord" – all of which, according to Harding, are more indicative of friendship than of a sexual relationship (ibid.). This effort to de-sexualize women and to portray their relationships in idealized or reified ways is repeated throughout this chapter. Part of the problem seems to be Harding's difficulty in imagining women wanting to be sexual at all, let alone with each other – and certainly not deliberately! She does not deny the presence of an intensity between women that may have an emotional quality which is usually associated with "erotic" attachments, but she insists that this may occur without either "overt sexual acts or even conscious sexual impulses" (ibid.: 103).

Even when Harding eventually does acknowledge the possibility of a sexual relationship between women, she attempts to justify these relationships by noting how they contribute toward efforts to develop the "feminine values" that have been neglected by our culture (ibid.: 93). Harding takes this detour into "the feminine" in spite of her admission that "it is exceedingly difficult to define with any clarity exactly what [feminine values] are or where they may be found" (ibid.: 93). This admission of uncertainty relative to the meaning of "the feminine" is quite a departure from the usual willingness of Jungians (especially of her generation) to present definitive descriptions of, and lists of qualities associated with, "the feminine" and to locate it decidedly in the consciousness of women and in the unconscious of men. In the course of discussing this, Harding seems to feel compelled to explain that women really would much rather have such experiences in relationships with men, but men are so bored and frightened by the work of relationships – because it is so "foreign to their own instinct" – that men "can hardly be expected to be enthusiastic about" undertaking such hard work (ibid.: 100). Therefore, this "cultural task" falls to women (ibid.: 93) who, "by their very nature," are better equipped to work on relationship concerns. Yet, while women have been "forced" to undertake this new work, they must somehow "take the lead and be prepared to teach in feeling matters" for this is the area of their expertise (ibid.: 100). (Harding

42

does not explain how women can take the lead in this if they are so "exceedingly undeveloped.")

Part of the problem involved in recovering these neglected "feminine values," according to Harding, is methodological: any attempt to define "the feminine" through heterosexual relationships is likely to fail since the projection of the man's anima onto women muddles things so that it becomes nearly impossible to differentiate between "these new Eros values" of women and "the instinctual feminine of the anima role" in men (ibid.: 93). In other words, it is sex which is the problem. Therefore, "the feminine" must seek some other avenue of expression, some place where the sexual instinct might play a lesser role, for example, in friendships among women. Surely, however, if there is such a thing as "feminine values" and if women have some privileged access to it, one might reasonably expect these values to appear wherever women are, whatever their orientation, and whether in relationships with men or women. Harding indirectly addresses this by making the very curious but suggestive statement that women who are "exclusively occupied with men" may not be in a position to express "feminine values" since men are not receptive to them (ibid.: 95). Therefore, reasons Harding, these new friendships among women may be necessary for the development of new values relative to feeling and relationship. Though I do not agree with Harding's assumptions of what these new values might be, I find the implications of her idea to be very interesting: that "the feminine" (if it exists at all) can be reliably expressed only between women (a point of view which, undoubtedly, must make most Jungians pause and ponder since it flies in the face of the traditional reliance on contrasexuality). In addition, Harding seems to suggest that women who are not exclusively occupied with men (by which I do not mean to include all lesbians or exclude all heterosexual women) are free to develop values that are different from those developed by women who are exclusively occupied with men (ibid.: 118). In other words, something may emerge in some relationships between women (who generally have been socialized similarly) that is less likely to emerge in most relationships between a woman and a man (who generally have been socialized differently).

Harding goes on to remark that she has observed an increase among women of things like "masculinized dress and manner" (ibid.: 96). This signals to her "a psychological fact" which indicates a new mental attitude among women, one previously associated only with men (ibid.: 97). These changes, she declares, have necessitated an increase in friendships among women because a woman can find this new aspect of herself only by being independent of men. She notes that as women develop their own individuality and actually live out their previously unconscious "masculine values," they no longer need to project these qualities onto men. During "this phase" of women's evolution, friendships with other women might actually be "the only form of emotional experience open to" some women (ibid.: 119). In fact, some women might even have to separate themselves entirely from men in order to individuate. The unstated implication here seems to be that men have the power to inhibit a woman's individuation process. In the Jungian world, this is a fairly revolutionary argument, especially when considered in combination with Harding's previous argument that, at this period in cultural evolution, "the feminine" is best expressed between women. This is an argument that some lesbian separatists might welcome.

Eventually, after many more qualifiers and disclaimers, Harding admits that friendships among women do not always follow the theoretical ideal she has proposed; that is, they are not always nonsexual. She attributes some of this to what she sees as the "retarded [emotional] development" of young people in modern times, but she admits that this would account only for "a certain number of homosexual friendships among women, *but hardly for all*" (ibid.: 94, my emphasis). The rest of these relationships, she concludes, must be part of a larger cultural movement, much like similar friendships between men in previous historical periods. As such, these friendships between women now hold not only a personal significance, but also "a place of unprecedented importance" for the larger community and indeed "for our whole civilization" (ibid.: 95).[3]

In other words, though Harding retains heterosexuality as the norm, she is willing to concede that homosexuality may serve some purpose at the collective level. That is, being a good Jungian, she imagines psychic movement to be purposeful. So, after a brief detour through a somewhat sympathetic but pathological view of homosexuals as "victims of a changing instinct,"[4] Harding goes on to make a most profound statement: in the larger context of society, these relationships among women "must have an evolutionary significance which is both biological and psychological in its nature" (ibid.: 96, 97). She chooses to leave the question of biological significance to scientists. She is more interested in the psychological significance of relationships between women because this is where she believes women have a contribution to make toward the evolution of consciousness.[5]

Harding makes it clear that she is not talking here about women who live together as a matter of convenience. She is referring to those women who consciously choose to bond on the basis of deep attraction and mutual love. She has seen that such relationships are "likely to be very rich, attaining a permanence and a stability equalled only in marriage" (ibid.: 98). But Harding's ambivalence again surfaces here as she attempts to lift women's relationships to the status of heterosexual marriage (as if that will ensure some level of respectability) while simultaneously introducing a qualifier. As much as these relationships may be comparable to marriage, "the sexual love and mutual dependence of marriage make a far closer bond than is at all usual between friends" (ibid.: 98). Clearly, sex and dependency make a marriage in her eyes.

Eventually, however, Harding can no longer escape the fact that at least sometimes relationships among women may find sexual expression. And, to her credit, despite her apparent discomfort with acknowledging the sexual element involved in these friend- ships and her obvious reluctance to use the term "homosexuality" – because it "is hedged about with prejudices and taboos" and has a "sinister connotation" in the public mind (ibid.: 102, 103) – Harding goes on to open a door that it took the American Psychological Association another 40 years even to find:

> In judging of any sexual relationship, whether homosexual or heterosexual, it must always be borne in mind that the quality of the emotion involved is the criterion of value rather than the nature of the accompanying physical expression.
>
> (ibid.: 103)

As much as Harding seems to resist actually approving of sex between women, she also cannot bring herself to see these dy- namics as entirely unnatural. In a statement that puts me in mind of Jill Johnston's (1973) arguments that all women are lesbians, Harding notes that:

> In a friendship between women there is a natural tendency to repress the element of erotic love, a tendency which is

strengthened by the conventional aversion which is felt toward the very idea of sexual love between women.

(ibid.)

Harding believes that this repression is not something undertaken
consciously, so she attributes it to something "deeper" (ibid.).
What Harding does here, of course, is to mistake the power of
heterosexism for the "natural" tendency to repress something. In
addition, needless to say, she ignores the fact that something must
first exist before it would need to be repressed. Her statement
implies, therefore, that erotic attraction is "naturally" present in
at least some relationships between women and that it is the
repression of such feelings that will lead to psychological problems.
Though she does not have available to her the modern concept of
internalized homophobia, she describes over the course of several
pages various manifestations of that phenomenon, as well as ways
in which all of this puts additional stress on relationships between
women.

In this process, Harding writes more directly about overtly sexual
lesbian relationships. She admits that if the women involved can
accept the sexual component of their relationship frankly and
honestly, and if they can accept the problems which arise, then they
can establish "a more fundamental rapport" which will make
possible "a relationship of greater depth and stability" (ibid.: 105).
The "instinctual bond" which may occur between them, declares
Harding, may even make their love stronger. This may be one of
the kindest statements ever written about homosexuality by a
Jungian of Harding's generation – unfortunately, however, this
attitude does not last. Harding is convinced that such women
eventually will find that the physical attraction will lessen and they
will come then "to understand the true motives and purposes of
their impulses" (ibid.). In other words, they will come to realize
that "the purpose of this kind of union" is really psychological and
is intended only "to strengthen the power of the feminine element
in both women." Once this has been accomplished, she contends,
"the natural polarity of the sexes" (ibid.) will prevail and they will
each turn toward men for sexual fulfillment. So, while recognizing
a teleological aspect to sexual relationships between women (thus
implying a certain kind of "naturalness" to homosexual desire),
Harding also succumbs to the idea that Faderman (1981) describes
in relation to public perceptions of "romantic friendships" among

46

women: that relationships between women, even sexual ones, are acceptable as long as they serve to prepare women for their true purpose, i.e. marriage to men. Harding admits, however, that these friendships between women usually last beyond "this reorientation" to men and will continue to possess for the women involved "certain values which are rarely, if ever, experienced in a heterosexual relationship" (Harding 1933/1970: 105) – a sad commentary, I would say, on the state of heterosexual relationships.

Harding believes that the central difficulty inherent in relationships between women centers around the tendency to identify with each other to such an extent that they have difficulty maintaining autonomy. Yet Harding makes it clear that the path of individuation is still served here: as a woman begins to live in this close relationship with this other human being, "she is compelled to differentiate within herself *the* individual woman" (ibid.: 110). Thus, the "oneness" (ibid.) which accompanies identification is split into "a pair of opposites," namely, "*individuality* and *relationship*" (ibid.: 111). This shift from the usual pair of opposites (i.e. from the concept of contrasexuality) is quite startling in this Jungian context. Though Harding does not specifically say that this is a situation unique to relationships between women, she does state that this pair of opposites is not likely to occur in a heterosexual relationship (at least, not in one of her day). In heterosexual marriages, with their focus on husband, children, and social responsibilities, a woman has little incentive "to take up the undeveloped side of her psyche" (ibid.: 116). In other words, lesbian relationships offer a potential for differentiation and individuality which may not be available, at least not in the same way, to heterosexual women. Harding (obviously struggling here against her own previously stated opinion of "retarded development") offers, perhaps in spite of herself, a re-framing that indicates a different possibility, a way of seeing individuality without resorting to the need for something contrasexually opposite.

Next, having established that homosexual relationships can engender psychological growth, Harding does a most amazing thing. She carefully, and only a little circuitously, crafts an explanation of how homosexual desire is a natural longing. She makes note first of the connection between the yearning most people have for the "close friendship and intimacy" of a relationship and the "craving of the psyche for individual differentiation" (ibid.: 111). Returning to her earlier distinction between the biological and psychological life aims, Harding argues that psychologically an individual is always and "unerringly" urged forward toward her or his psychological goal (ibid.: 112). Thus, a longing for "companionship" can be seen as "a psychological urge comparable to the biological ones." Thus, if a woman acts on such an urge with another woman, she will have to choose between working on this particular relationship with this other woman or "regression, which is psychological death." If she chooses to be in the relationship, she will feel compelled to differentiate herself from her friend and thus will have "become the tool of one of life's purposes," namely, psychological evolution (ibid.). In other words, from the point of view of individuation, it would actually be an act of regression for a woman to repress her attraction toward another woman!

Harding believes that the two life aims (the biological and the psychological) may have divergent goals. For some (i.e. heterosexuals), both goals move in the same direction and can be satisfied simultaneously. For others, however, these "two urges are opposed" and the individual will feel caught in a devastating inner conflict, forced to make a choice between these two aims (ibid.: 113). Not having a larger frame for any of this, Harding can recognize only the intrapsychic portion of this conflict and not the role of social oppression. But she does realize that the force of the conflict must be an indication that both aims are exceedingly powerful, so powerful that there is no way to tell in any particular case "which aim will get the upper hand" (ibid.). Harding concludes that the psychological life aim must have "a validity for life" which "is paramount" in its own sphere (ibid.: 114). Harding thus effectively presents us with a new and different Jungian paradigm and a more complex view of individuation, one freer of biological determinism than Jung's.

Yet, in spite of all of this, Harding seems intent on not abandoning the primacy accorded to contrasexuality and on portraying the "increase of homosexual friendships among women" as a temporary phenomenon, "a transitional phase of civilization" and "a symptom of human evolution" (ibid.: 118). We are simply witnessing "*womanhood* . . . passing through adolescence in regard to individual development." But again she is ambivalent and cannot deny that individual women who experience love with another woman "may become mature – rounded out psychologically – through this very experience" (ibid.).

I suspect that, in her heart of hearts, Harding knew she was working hard to make her insights fit a preconceived theory, that she knew something was not quite right with her analysis. It is not difficult to hear more ambivalence in the final passages of this chapter which betray what must have been a terrific internal struggle for Harding between her own sense of a woman's potential and her desire to accommodate Jungian theory:

> These movements must be regarded without prejudice. We must seek their psychological goal and significance – their creative quota – and not regard them from the *a priori* standards with which they conflict. When we find large numbers of responsible, vigorous and adequate women rejecting marriage, which has been considered the most developed state, and "regressing" to intense relationships with other women, we recognize that they must be searching for something whether they are aware of it or not.
>
> (ibid.)

Harding argues that these intense friendships between women must be seen as examples of "a *reculer pour mieux sauter*" – a regression that is intended to give one a better start (ibid.: 119). Although heterosexual marriage may be "a mature adaptation on the biological plane," these friendships between women represent "a movement directed toward a psychological development in women" and intended to make possible "a more conscious and differentiated relationship." Harding seems forced to conclude that although this may be seen biologically as a regression, from a psychological point of view, it "has a progressive significance" (ibid.: 118).

Here Harding has linked these two life aims to Jung's idea that there are two modes of psychic energy: progressive and regressive. Psychic energy moves out into the world (progression) where it encounters obstacles which inevitably cause it to drop back into the unconscious (regression). Both directions are required. One is not "better" than the other. They operate together as a dynamic. The implications of this linking seem significant to me, though they may not have seemed so to Harding: If regressive energy is essential to psychological life as part of the "natural" cycle of energy movement, then homosexual relationships, which could be described as "biologically a regression," serve a necessary and ongoing function, not a transitional one (ibid.: 118). (And maybe it is a cultural regression to privilege the biological?)

If I were homosexist, I might even wonder whether or how heterosexuals could possibly be both biologically and psychologically "progressive." That is, how is the regressive movement expressed among heterosexuals? Although I do not want to reduce everything to yet another pair of opposites (biological versus psychological progression), I find that Harding's linking of these ideas does raise some interesting and challenging theoretical questions. For example, perhaps lesbians (and maybe gay men) "carry" for the collective the idea of embodied sexuality – not in the reductive sense that many might assume (that is, as the biological aim gone awry), but as the psychological aim otherwise embodied (and perhaps struggling to free us all from biologism?). Could this be an aspect of the "biological significance" Harding hinted at earlier?[6]

In any case, Harding sees this regression to be in service to a progressive goal: the individuation of women (and human culture). Harding notes that by refusing to submit herself to the biological aim, "many a woman in the past" has escaped from the usual demand that she live only in relation to a man, "personifying his anima." In a similar way, she proposes, perhaps "the woman of the future" may reject the psychological one-sidedness imposed on her as a result of enforced and unconscious relationships with men and thus attain a sense of freedom through which she may develop herself consciously and completely as an individual (ibid.: 119).

Harding is apparently unable to let herself end this chapter with such a radical thought. So, she attempts again to find some way to fit everything into a Jungian (androcentric) framework: the individuation of women is justified because ultimately it will benefit and enhance relationships between men and women. Thus, in the end, Harding capitulates – but not before struggling and, through that struggle, suggesting alternative ways of seeing. That she could not resolve her own ambivalence seems sad to me, though it was probably inevitable given the historical period and her privileged position in the inner circle. Yet, for me, none of this detracts from the value of Harding's work. Her pioneering and relatively audacious thinking (though often truncated to fit Jungian theory) shines through anyway.

I have been most inspired by Harding's suggestion, ambivalent as it was, that lesbian relationships represent an expression of the fulfillment of the psychological aim of the species. As such, I expect that in describing their experiences of loving another woman, lesbians will be describing an aspect of the individuation process that is not complicated by needing to satisfy "the biological aim" only. I realize that this is made more complex today by the availability of alternative methods of conception, but, like Downing, I believe that the love between women carries an energy that represents "a transcendence of reproductive love, a commitment to a different kind of co-creation" which may or may not involve children (1989: xxiv). This transcendence is not a "rising above," but rather a different kind of bridging of the biological and psychological aims of human kind.

Lesbian experience as refusal to be possessed by normalcy

What I fear greatly and suspect greatly is normality. That is something people are trained to. It is like a tight lid. That is why I am afraid of the psychologists of today who have the idea of universal validity.

(Jung, quoted in Weaver 1982: 93)

In his essay "On the Possession of Consciousness," Ponce quotes Jung's view that "what society demands is *imitation* or conscious identification, a treading of accepted, authorized paths" (Jung 1970: 174; quoted in Ponce 1988: 152). In other words, every society creates a concept of what it considers to be "normal." Anything that falls outside these societal definitions is then labeled as deviant or even pathological. As a result, Ponce hypothesizes, "it might . . . be this coercive (but albeit, necessary) societal demand that creates the medium necessary for deviant and pathological behavior to express itself" (ibid.: 153). This is in some ways a version of the social constructionist argument, but one which offers for me a more psychological frame and which is not unlike what Harding has proposed: namely, that people who are associated with "abnormal" behavior may be part of "the individuating intent," in this case, of what Ponce calls "an archetype of normalcy" (ibid.: 154, 152). Referring to Levi-Strauss, Ponce goes on to argue that individuals who, for whatever reason, fall into the gap between individual expression and societal norms are made to carry the label "abnormal" so that society as a whole can feel reassured with its perception of being "normal."

Returning to Jung, Ponce notes Jung's idea that archetypal symbols are evoked "by the process of individuation which always sets in when the collective dominants of human life [i.e. the 'norms'] fall into decay" (Jung CW12: 41; quoted in Ponce 1988: 172n44). This leads those who compensatorily identify with the "opposite" pole of the archetype (i.e. the "abnormal") into a form of possession by which they become "prophets and reformers" (Jung CW12: 41; quoted in Ponce 1988: 154) and, according to Ponce, serve "as conduits for society's individuation" (1988: 155). Ponce (like Harding) claims that this is strictly a response to societal needs rather than the result of "decisions based upon subjective analysis and self-determination" (ibid.). However, he later points out that Jung's psychology is "an individuating psychology" and that, as such, it necessarily "attends to those who do not fully meet the demands of the norm, and either cannot or wish not to be returned or included in the group – who will not sacrifice what they experience as unique" (ibid.: 165). Therefore, as I read it, this process involves both subjective and collective elements.

In the context of lesbianism, we might say that when a lesbian lives as a lesbian, she is refusing to conform to the "the terms of the heterosexual imperative" and refusing to live "within the limits established by men" (as heterosexuals may "choose") (Penelope 1992: 40, 41). "'Being' a Lesbian," Penelope declares, "means living marginally, often in secrecy, often shamefully, but always as different, as 'deviant'" (ibid.: 41). In other words, lesbians, who by our very existence disturb established categories of gender and concepts of sexuality, represent a threat to, and a defining aspect of, collective values because we challenge the prevailing collective fantasy of "normalcy." I believe this is another way of looking at the role and contribution of lesbians to the development of collective consciousness.

Lesbian experience as an expression of the transcendent function

To acknowledge that none of the ways we live our gendered lives is fully satisfying, that all of us are to some degree wounded in our sexuality, that none of us can live out all our fantasies, be all we dream of being, have all we long for, is to recognize that others who choose different paths from our own do so on our behalf. They live for us, as well as for themselves.

(Downing 1989: xvii)

In late 1992, I attended a workshop conducted by Peter Mudd at which he discussed some ideas related to the role of the transcendent function in collective life. Mudd's thinking helped me develop and give more substance to two related ideas that I had been playing with for some time: (1) that lesbianism is connected to the transcendent function because it represents a potential to "transcend" categories of gender and (2) that lesbianism need not be reduced to particular archetypes or archetypal images in order to be linked to an archetypal dimension. Before I discuss these ideas, however, I would like first to offer Mudd's ideas. This means we must first consider Jung's concept of the transcendent function.

The transcendent function, as Jung explains it, is a three-stage process which begins when consciousness, which has a tendency toward one-sidedness, chooses a particular course of action "at the cost of all others" (CW8: 136). This reflects the "progressive" or outward movement of psychic energy discussed above. In response to this one-sided movement, the psyche (which is compensatory and self-regulating by nature) produces "an equally pronounced counter-position in the unconscious" (ibid.: 138) (i.e. a "regressive" or inward movement of psychic energy.) This "resistance of the instinctual sphere" (ibid.: 178) results in a tension (or "crisis of adaptation") between consciousness and the unconscious. This tension must be "held" during this second stage in order to make possible the production of the necessary symbolic material (e.g. dreams, drawings, fantasies). Then, if these symbols are worked with "constructively" rather than "reductively" – that is, if one pays conscious attention to their "meaning and purpose" rather than trying to explain them (ibid.: 147) – the way will be paved for the third stage: the appearance of the transcendent function. This will move one "out of the suspension between opposites" and into "a new level of being" (ibid.: 189). It is through this process "of finding the courage to be oneself," that one is liberated from the tension of the opposites (ibid.: 193). It is absolutely essential to recognize that Jung's concept of transcendence does *not* imply a "rising above" the opposites. The psyche's aim is to find a satisfactory solution to the conflict by "bridging the yawning gulf between conscious and unconscious" (CW7: 121). This is "a true labor, a work which involves both action and suffering" (ibid.) and which has one overall purpose: "the revelation" of the potentially "whole" personality (ibid.: 186).

With this context in place, we may now return to Mudd who suggested at this workshop that it is time for Jungians to discard both the anima and animus because, he argued, they are only "premature forms" of the transcendent function. He proposed instead that we recover the essence of Jung's ideas about the transcendent function: namely, that it represents the *function* of relatedness and that symbols are not fixed concepts or complexes. That is, the concepts of the "anima" and "animus" should be seen as symbolic attempts to come to terms with the complexities of relationship. To reduce and reify them into rigid and gender-based concepts is to collude with Jung in losing track of his own insistence on the liberating role of the transcendent function.

In this same context, Mudd went on to propose that current political movements (e.g. the lesbian and gay rights movement) are performing a symbolic and even evolutionary role in service to some collective "task" and thus serve as indicators of collective shifts of psychic energy. Mudd described these movements as group responses to collective crises of adaptation. That is, some collective one-sidedness (e.g. heterosexuality) leads to the constellation of the counter-position or "opposite" pole of the archetype (e.g. homosexuality). This new archetypal image/symbol somehow attaches itself to particular individuals who are then brought together ("possessed") through their shared carrying of the new image.[7] As an example of this process, Mudd cited "Close Encounters of the Third Kind," a film in which people who are otherwise unknown to each other are mysteriously and powerfully drawn to (possessed by) a particular symbol (in this case, a large outcropping of rock in the middle of the desert).

In terms of connecting lesbianism to the transcendent function, we might say that lesbianism is part of the 'solution' to the problem of "gender certainty" (Samuels 1989b: 75) – not because there is necessarily a link between gender and sexual orientation, but because lesbian experience often (though not always) includes a breaking from or rejection of socially accepted definitions of gender (definitions which have been stereotypically constructed into a pair of opposites). For many lesbians, gender (and gender roles) are questionable or even irrelevant. For example, Faderman, in researching her book on eighteenth- and nineteenth-century "romantic friendships" between women, came to see that these women loved each other "for their strengths and self-sufficiency rather than for their weaknesses and dependence" (1981: 108). Therefore, when they "divided duties" they often did so according to their "natural talents or inclination or time" and not on the basis of gender-role stereotypes (ibid.: 187). Even today, many lesbians see their lesbianism as arising from a desire "to be free from prescribed roles, free to realize themselves" unbound by cultural expectations (ibid.: 387).

Unlike most heterosexuals, most lesbians are forced to face questions of role and identity without recourse to culturally sanctioned models or norms. This, in turn, conceivably can force the individuation of the collective (as individual individuation does) because it requires an ethical confrontation/decision about whether/how to live one's life: individually or in keeping with the mores of the collective. Therefore, lesbian experience can be understood in part as a carrying out of both personal and collective tasks related to the transcendent function and to the bridging of stereotypical concepts of gender and sexuality.

In terms of understanding lesbianism's connection to the archetypal realm, I will start by stating what I see to be the problem with archetypes. I do not object to analytical psychology's tendency to see archetypes as universal *potentials* or available possibilities as long as we keep in mind Jung's warnings (which, unfortunately, he himself often ignored) that we not confuse the "archetype as such" with an archetypal image. The problem, as I see it, arises from the all-too-common Jungian tendency to see archetypes as instincts which are "natural" to every individual or to certain groups of individuals (the kind of "type psychology" that Samuels critiques). The idea that I am proposing here (not articulated elsewhere that I know of) is that archetypal images and archetypes (if they exist at all) exist, metaphorically, in a "gene pool" as it were. It is *as if* all of the archetypes are floating around "out there," but, for various complicated and perhaps not entirely ascertainable reasons, both personal and cultural – *maybe* even biological – each of us "gets" (identifies with, is affected or possessed by, introjects, perceives, etc.) only certain ones. I am not proposing this reductively (i.e. as biologically inherited), but "constructively" and metaphorically, as if there is some magnetic attraction which draws us irresistibly toward something numinous. In the context of lesbianism, this is an attraction toward another woman that occurs in spite of numerous cultural prohibitions.

Lesbian experience as embodied soul

If we can reconcile ourselves to the mysterious truth that the spirit is the life of the body seen from within, and the body

the outward manifestation of the life of the spirit – the two
being really one – then we can understand why the striving to
transcend the present level of consciousness through acceptance of the unconscious must give the body its due, and why
recognition of the body cannot tolerate a philosophy that
denies it in the name of the spirit.

(Jung CW10: 195)

I have struggled with the question of biology. If, on the one hand,
"we are embodied souls, ensouled bodies" as Downing has written
(1989: 32), do not our bodies (with all their limitations and
possibilities) have some meaning? Could not our biological sex and
its physiology inform, shape, or be a part of that meaning?
Otherwise, are we not in danger of seeing the body as somehow
extraneous or incidental to the self, something to be risen above,
etc.? On the other hand, why should biological sex be any more
meaningful, psychologically, than the color of one's eyes or hair or
skin, or one's height, etc.?

I have come to the conclusion that any physical factor which has
a significant impact on a person (whether because one assigns
importance to it or because one's culture does) will have a
psychological expression with psychological intent. In other words,
the body is not separate from the self. It is both a vehicle of the self
and a mediator both between self and other and between consciousness and the unconscious.[8] I am not talking here about "body
as destiny" – nor about resorting to restrictive body metaphors, e.g.
birthing metaphors which attempt to describe female bodies or
"the feminine" only in relation to reproductive functions as if a
woman's body is capable of no other metaphors of activity. No
matter how important and symbolic such functions might be for
many women, they are not so for all women nor at all times in any
woman's life. In other words, these are not the only possible
metaphors by which we might come to understand a female body
which is capable of those functions *and* more. To privilege this
aspect of the female body is limiting, distorting, and counter-
productive.[9] Rather, I am arguing here for the body as the ground
of experience, regardless of (or in addition to) any particular
meanings one might attribute to its parts or to any of its possible
functions. I am speaking of how the body can take the lead in
showing us the way on the path of individuation. And I am
suggesting, following the lead of Audre Lorde, that the erotic is a

resource against oppression – which is why women have been made to suppress their eroticism. Women who are able to trust such power from within become "dangerous" to the oppressor (Lorde 1984a: 55).

Perhaps all of this fills in the gap that Esther Harding theorized between the biological and psychological aims by dissociating biology from reproductive functions and linking it instead to one's sexuality. I believe that this is what Downing is also getting at when she says that "for Jung our sexual feelings are to be understood as really meaning our longing for inner wholeness and integration – as being about our embodied souls, not only our bodies" (1989: 110).

Lesbian experience: "the masculine" and other irrelevancies

I believe that all close bonds between women inevitably conjure up memories and feelings associated with our first connection to a woman, the all-powerful mother of infancy. They remind us of a time in which one neither required the phallus nor rebelled against its power, when it was merely irrelevant.

(Downing 1989: 204)

Like Downing, I feel no need to conceive of lesbianism in relation to men or "the phallus" or "the masculine" – or "the feminine" for that matter. Lesbianism does not seem to me to be a resistance against men or even a choosing of women against men. Rather, a woman's decision to act on her sexual feelings toward women is an explicit and decisive move toward women. Men are simply irrelevant to it. To see it otherwise is to define lesbianism by recourse to men, thus leaving the construct of male supremacy ironically intact. So, I object rather strongly to those separatist writers who insist that lesbianism is represented primarily by its politics: women bonded against men and/or male supremacy. I certainly accept and endorse the political potential of lesbians to challenge patriarchal norms, but I find attempts to define lesbianism primarily in these terms to be simplistic and one-sided.

Along the same lines, I would argue that lesbianism can never be understood by recourse to concepts like "contrasexuality." Samuels has led the attack on this concept, noting that Jung's insistence on "innate" opposites only "hamstrings us" by leading

Jungians to posit "an unjustified psychological division" between various pairs of opposites which are then "expressed in lists of antithetical qualities, each list yearning for the other list so as to become 'whole'" (1989b: 97). Samuels takes the position that questions of gender had best be left "in suspension" for now – or, even better, "in some confusion," for only such "gender confusion" can provide the "*necessary antidote to gender certainty*" (ibid.). He goes on to argue that those who insist on a "feminine principle" are only playing into the unconscious search for "gender certainty" and thus adding to analytical psychology's preoccupation with gender.

Lyn Cowan also has taken the offensive against contrasexuality, denouncing it especially for "its insistence on heterosexuality as the norm" (1994: 71). She wonders why Jungians (and others) insist on seeing sexuality always and only as "contra" and always and only in terms of gender. She goes on to critique heterosexuality itself in a move that is humorous but to the point and she concludes that analytical psychology must rid itself of its various imbedded biases, heterosexism included, if it wishes to be a psychology that is truly concerned with psyche.

Lesbian experience as a "*coniunctio*" of likes

Women are becoming individuated through mirroring themselves increasingly accurately and fully, and through finding more comprehensive mirrors.

(Douglas 1990: 149)

Douglas is arguing here that women individuate through mirroring ourselves and each other. Unfortunately, she limits her analysis by interpreting the idea of mirroring only in asexual terms. She thus stops short of using this insight to undermine the normative power expressed through the concept of contrasexuality. She does use it to challenge the Jungian obsession with complementarity which, she points out, "fails to mirror woman herself" (ibid.: 291). While this is a step in the right direction, Douglas does not take the next logical step which would be to theorize that such mirroring might be the stuff of lesbian relationships. For example, very early in my reflections on my own lesbian experience, I came to the conclusion that what made my relationships with women significantly different from those with men was that with women I was allowed to be more of a "whole" self (what I then mistakenly called "more feminine") while with men I got to be and do whatever was left over, that is, whatever men did not lay claim to. With women, who were "like" me, there seemed to be more room for the individual me and more access to parts of myself that were previously inaccessible.

Lyn Cowan does take this step. Cowan is one of very few Jungian analysts willing to remember that "alchemical conjunctions [which she describes as 'an inherently sexual image in Jungian thought'] may happen between sames as well as between opposites" (1994: 75). That is, we can challenge the primacy of contrasexuality by using one of Jung's major sources of images and inspiration: alchemy. By recognizing that the mirroring of "like to like" relationships can include a sexual component, Jungians can open themselves to learning from lesbian experience and to repairing past harms done to lesbians. Like it or not, as Downing has pointed out, Jungians have been a part of creating the enormous amounts of "fear and hate" that have been leveled at "those of us who direct our love and sexuality primarily to others like ourselves" (1989: xvii). It is time to let it be known that those of us "who have become who we are primarily through relationships based on analogy rather than contrast, on mirroring rather than the complementation of opposites" are in revolt (ibid.).

4

"ANN"

PROFILE

Ann is a 43-year-old white woman who thinks of herself as bisexual
although she has been involved with women exclusively for the last
sixteen years and is comfortable calling these relationships "lesbian." Ann has had two children by artificial insemination. The
first child, a daughter, was conceived and raised in partnership
with a previous female lover. The decision to have a second child
was made with her current partner of eight years. Ann and her
partner parent both children jointly. Ann is a mental health
professional.

INTERVIEW SETTING/PROCESS

This was my first interview since the initial one at the seminar, the
first which would benefit from all the reading, thinking, and
reflecting I had been doing over the intervening year and a half or
so. I have known Ann for many years, though only as an acquaintance. She, too, had made a career change at mid-life and had
completed her own dissertation (in a fairly traditional program)
about a year before the interview. She was curious about my project
since it was constructed so differently from her own and made it
clear to me that she wanted very much to be helpful. I assured her
that anything she said would be helpful in some way.

THE INTERVIEW

Ann was quite adamant: she did not grow up thinking she was a
lesbian. In adolescence, she experimented sexually with other girls,

but she is clear that this was "experimentation, not love" and that it came from curiosity, not passion. She had "always thought heterosexually" and, if we lived in a society free of gender-consciousness, she probably would fall in love with a person "regardless of" that person's sex. At this point, Ann can say that her lesbianism has "become a sense of identity" though "it certainly wasn't before." But she is hesitant. To say that she is a lesbian really does not tell the whole story. "It is a part of my identity but that's not all of it." Ann will say "I am a lesbian" because she is in a lesbian relationship right now, but she adds immediately, "I can also say I'm bisexual." That is, she sees herself as a bisexual person who is choosing to act only on her lesbian feelings at this point in her life. Ann sounded sad when she expressed her sense of how hard it is within the lesbian community "to honor" her bisexual feelings. "There is a lot of pressure to not be bisexual if you're lesbian."

Ann sees herself as having made "an intellectual decision" to be with women – it was a by-product of her politics, though it was rooted very much in the context of her life experiences. There were two major factors involved in this decision: (1) her strong urge for intimacy and (2) her desire to be able "to love someone without having to struggle against roles" that were socially constructed. Ann was not unhappy with men sexually; emotionally, however, she was. She remembers a night in 1974, a time when she was dating a man. It suddenly became clear to her that she had not been able "to find men that could cross the barrier into intimacy – it was just too big of a barrier for them." Therefore, she concluded, if she wanted to have "a full and complete relationship" she was going to have to consider being in relationships with women. This would mean stepping across "the sexual barrier" that she had grown up with, but the alternatives were clear: she could spend the rest of her life "waiting to run into" a man capable of intimacy or "I could make the changes myself internally." She opted for the latter, although it was another few years before she actually acted on this decision. In the meantime, however, her view of women began to shift and she became slowly more open to the possibility of taking her libido and "re-directing" it.

As she looks back on it, Ann sees this as not such a big step. She had grown up in a politically liberal family, with a mother who was actively feminist and a father who was generally non-sexist. The interesting twist, Ann jokes, is that her mother had been so homophobic (having had a bad experience around the public "outing" of her gay father, as Ann later learned) that Ann never heard the terms gay and homosexual while she was growing up. All of this effectively created an atmosphere which allowed Ann, eventually, to come to see same-sex love simply as an acceptable option.

The other factor in choosing to be with women was Ann's sense of an "internal need to be free of roles and constraints." Although she recognizes that there are similar struggles in women's relationships, Ann sees these struggles as having "more to do with us as individuals" than with societal expectations about what makes "a sexually desirable female." Ann assesses herself honestly: she is a person who tends to anticipate the needs of the other person. Her experience with men has been that they needed and expected her to fit some stereotypical view of what a woman should be like. Although Ann sees herself as having attempted to make herself physically attractive to others, she neither desired nor attempted to meet that stereotyped standard. Yet, she still would end up feeling that she was a disappointment to men – and this left her feeling somehow incomplete and lacking: "I don't like that feeling that I'm not good enough as who I am." So, Ann sought out "people who do not buy into" such socially constructed ideas of how a partner should be. Eventually, she turned to other women with whom she could "be all of me without feeling like I'm inadequate to this other person in some way."

> "For me, one of the things that happens in loving another woman is I feel freer to be me and not constrained by certain expectations of what I'm supposed to do in relation to this other person that is determined by somebody else's ideas of what my role is. For me, that freedom to be able to be me, all of me, in relationships and not feel confined by roles is probably pretty central to my choosing to live as a lesbian."

Ann experiences relationships with another woman as involving "two individuals interacting like two whole units." As a result, Ann feels "less encumbered and therefore more comfortable" with women (which is not to say, she is quick to add, that relationships with women are always easy.) In her relationships with men, by contrast, both she and her partner were so "strongly influenced by roles and expectations" that each was somehow diminished from the outset. With women, however – regardless of how two women choose to act out in the world – at home, they can shed those disguises. In a heterosexual couple, one "can never get away from" the presence of role expectations.

For Ann, loving another woman is an "intense" experience. After all, "when you're all of you in a relationship, that's very intense. When you're only part of you in a relationship, there's less intensity because there's less risk because you're just partially invested." Ann sees the flip side of this intensity to be "some sort of reflection process that goes on in some way, or some sort of merging process that happens." Although straight couples can do this, too, Ann has noticed that there is something more obvious about how lesbians do it. There's a "sort of we-ness and a struggle to maintain the I." In lesbian relationships things seem to "blow up more" in order to maintain the I and "separate it out from the we." Ann acknowledges that this problem of maintaining an I exists for her in any relationship, but she finds it harder with women. With men, to maintain an I was "so much clearer and easier." In fact, it seemed to her that "it was really hard for them to get a we at all. It was all 'I'. By 'I' they meant them! So, if all the I is them, that doesn't leave much I left for me."

I was struck by a distinction that Ann drew between her private life ("my life with family and friends") and her public life (out among "the rest of the world"). It seemed rooted metaphorically in her childhood family system: she and her brothers were treated equally, so she came to expect that she would be treated the same way in the world. "But when I went out into the world it was a different world. Part of me is still very angry about that." She learned that out in the world she would have "to blend in." So, Ann accepts that in public she has to think twice before taking her partner's hand (for fear of "offending" others and being "judged"), but "that's not about the relationship." Keeping her relationship hidden while in public does not feel like much of a burden to Ann. She can "get away" from that. It is her life at home that is more important to her; it is at home that she must be free to be herself. "It would be nice to be able to be yourself anywhere, but if I can't be myself in my home with the people I love and my family, forget it!" As a result, Ann says, "I don't think I could live with somebody who really didn't understand at a profound level what it is like to be oppressed as a female in this society."

In discussing how she has been affected by not being able to be herself in public, Ann noted that the issues involved here were not "core." (There's that word again, I thought.) I asked what she thought the core issues are for her.

"I guess a core issue is being involved with somebody that I can be all of me with. So that in my most intimate relationships I'm not putting on some sort of mask. The ability to be myself intimately. So not being able to do that with other people I'm not friends with is not that big of a deal."

Ann realizes that she has had more experience with loving men than with loving women: She grew up in a heterosexual culture, spent 27 years thinking heterosexually, and has had sex, including a fair amount of casual sex, with a number of men. But she has been with only three women and has never had casual sex with a woman. Her experience tells her that loving a woman is not that different from loving a man. However, she is aware that with women lovers she has felt "more of a sense of responsibility" and "more respect for the intimacy" between them. Perhaps, she suggests, this has to do with feeling "more of a sensitivity" to a woman as a whole person.

"So, if I'm sexual with a woman, I can't just relate to her sexually, I have to relate to all of her. There's this whole person with this whole history. We can't just talk about a sexual attraction; there's all this other stuff that has to come with it. . . . There's a relationship that comes with it."

With men, however (even though she knows "they have all this other stuff, too"), it was different. She "could just want sex." Perhaps, she offers, this is because "they were able to keep it at a sexual level so it was OK, just kind of fun and games. I'm not able to even imagine myself having that with women."

For the first time ever, Ann is working in an environment where a number of her colleagues are lesbian or gay. She admits to liking this a lot. Ann is aware, in fact, that she experiences a different sense of fullness when she is in a group or community of women (for example, at the Michigan women's music festival, or at the March on Washington, or at the local women's restaurant) than that she feels in her one-on-one relationships. These are the times and places where she can escape from the narrow definitions of a straight and patriarchal society, where she can experience a "more global female-affirming feeling," where she senses an attitude of respect for individuality, for individual choices and differences. For Ann, lesbian culture, on the whole, offers more options and is "more fluid," more affirming, and more open, than heterosexual culture. She joked: "If straight people could act like lesbians, I'd probably like being in the straight world, too!"

On a more serious note, Ann remarked that she does not believe that either she or her partner could survive as a couple in this relationship without this sense of community. During difficult periods between them, "going out into the community and tapping into that 'God, isn't it wonderful to be a lesbian' feeling can reconnect us to each other." In fact, part of the appeal to Ann of their recent move into a new neighborhood has been that it is a neighborhood with a noticeable lesbian population. Ann loves that she runs into lesbians almost every time she walks down the street. She finds this very comforting. "We're out there in that bigger world that used to be so 'other,' mingling with the other more."

Ann made only passing references to the sexual part of her relationships with women, saying that "in generic terms" it was "not important" to her. She acknowledged, however, that sex is "critical" to her in terms of being in a particular relationship. In fact, she observed, "it feels like it is probably one of those core issues." What would be the point of having "an intimate, committed relationship if there isn't a sexual component to it?" Ann has a number of intimate relationships with close friends, many of which probably will last a lifetime. It is sex which makes her relationship with her partner meaningfully different from the rest. "Libido can be repressed, but that's not the way I want to live." Ann feels that if she is not expressing herself sexually with her partner, then her sexual energy eventually will pull her "into another relationship where it is there." She speaks from experience. "I learned this the hard way," she says emphatically, remembering how her last relationship ended.

Ann's experience of the sexual component of her relationships (with men as well as with women) has varied, depending upon the stage of the particular relationship. She smiled when she noted that her current relationship is the first (with a man or woman) in which she has been able to maintain sexual interest "over the long haul." This has helped them negotiate hard times. But, at this stage, sex is something of "a loaded subject." Both she and her partner attempt to juggle their very busy lives, the demands of attending to the children, the desire to have a joint social life, against the need to have sufficient time together. But they are not always successful. Sex and intimacy seem to be the areas which suffer most. Ann seems to wonder whether this can possibly change before the kids get older. She seems to grieve the loss of the earlier times which were more carefree and playful. But she is convinced that those aspects of her sexual feelings are only "dormant, not gone."

What Ann misses about heterosexual sex is that she could be "more passive" sexually with men. (On the other hand, she "got fed up with having to do 85 percent" of the rest of the work.) With a woman, Ann still works as hard as she did with a man, but now her partner is working as hard, too. For Ann, this is evidence that the relationship means as much to her partner as it does to her. "I know I'm not taken for granted" when everything is "fair and equal."

MY EXPERIENCE OF THE INTERVIEW

Ann's initial response to my opening question was to say that the first word that came to her was "comfortable." Then there were long silences as she pondered and wondered: Should she talk "globally" about her love of women? Could she answer without contrasting her experience of loving women to what it has been like for her to love a man? How would any of it be different from simply talking about what it is like to love a person? She seemed somewhat uneasy that there was clearly "something specifically gender-based" in the question, since she identifies as bisexual. Yet most of her reflections and experiences were framed in the context of how her experiences with women were different from her experiences with men.

All of this made me wonder at first whether there was something wrong with my question. I had not consciously intended to frame my question in such a way that it could be answered only by contrasting one's experience of loving a woman against one's experience of loving a man. But Ann's response made me realize how this idea was embedded in the question. After thinking about it for a while, I came to the conclusion that the problem is not in the question *per se*, but in a culture that can visualize only two sexes, one "opposite" the other. The problem of attempting to deconstruct the category of "woman" is far beyond the scope of this project. I decided that the phrasing of the question would have to do.

I found it interesting and instructive that Ann did not talk very much about her current relationship, saying that while talking about this particular woman would make her response more "concrete," it also would make it "less universal" and take us inevitably into a discussion which would revolve around the two personalities involved, rather than around the question of their being women. Yet it was also only in the context of references to specific relationships that Ann ever mentioned gender roles. For example, Ann described her first female lover as "a butchy woman" who served probably as "a transitional step" for her in moving from relationships with men to relationships with women. Later on, Ann initially described herself and her current partner as "fairly androgynous," but then commented that maybe her partner is slightly more "butch" than she and admitted, reluctantly it seemed, that maybe, since others have told her so, she presents as a bit more "femme." Both of these examples occurred spontaneously and entirely without any prompting from me. I am not sure what to make of this except to wonder whether the lack of non-stereotypical lesbian images at a cultural level leads women to fall back upon heterosexist images even when we have made conscious efforts to avoid these. And, finally, I must mention Ann's use of the word "core." I tried to tell myself that this was just a coincidence, but I must admit that it made an impression on me.

5

DEBATES FROM LESBIAN LITERATURE

"LESBIAN" AS A CATEGORY OF IDENTITY

But because there is no other word [than lesbian] that communicates the depth of our commitment to each other and of our bond to other women who have defined their lives by their love for women, we continue to rediscover the importance of claiming the name.

(Downing 1989: xxx)

What started out in the early 1970s as "lesbian practice" soon matured into a debate over identity and politics (Decker 1995: 71). Today there are lesbians on all sides of this still evolving debate which has become terrain for "lively exchanges which have revitalized the field of lesbian and gay psychology" (Kitzinger 1995: 150). Although I am posing this question relative to sexual orientation, the debate over identity politics typically is intertwined with discussions of gender as well since, as Sedgwick has pointed out, gender and sexual orientation are among the "available analytic axes" which "mutually constitute one another" (1990: 31). In its simplest terms, the debate generally constellates four positions:

1 the essentialists, who argue that sexual orientation and/or gender are innate, essential, and "eternal" features of individual identity;
2 the social constructionists, who argue that sexual orientation and/or gender are socially and historically constructed;
3 the interactionists/synthesizers, who argue for a concept of identity that bridges essentialism and social constructionism; and
4 the postmodernists/poststructuralists, who generally argue against the concept of identity altogether although some are

attempting to develop new ways of thinking about and theorizing the concept of lesbian identity.

The essentialists

The gender essentialists come in many forms, ranging from some of the French feminists to the hordes of Jungians dedicated to "the Feminine principle." Most rely on biology as the basis of differences. There also are lesbian and gay theorists who take a similar position relative to sexual orientation, that is, who assert that there are fundamental and pregiven differences between heterosexuals and homosexuals. They believe that a person is simply "born that way." Some lesbians and gays argue that essentialism is, in effect, an essential strategy for a politics of identity and that it is in line with the mission to end the oppression of gays and lesbians. There is some disagreement over who the essentialists are, but prominent among the authors often associated with this position relative to gay and lesbian identity are John Boswell, Mary Daly, Sally Gearhart, Simon LeVay, Janice Raymond, and Adrienne Rich. Since I already have registered my deep doubts about this position, I will not discuss it further here except to refer the reader to Squire's thorough critique (1989) and to cite Phelan's comment that attempts to prove that lesbianism is "natural" inevitably do so "by recourse to the same old metaphysic, in which nature is a privileged, unchanging, unchangeable category" (1993: 770).

The social constructionists

Those who adhere to this stance generally see sexual orientation as a phenomenon that has been constructed and/or manipulated by social and political forces. Some argue that sexual orientation is an arbitrary category, that it "exists" only because we all agree that it exists. Although some social constructionists attack the concept of identity itself, others are more concerned with examining how identity is formed and what it means, and many argue that we need categories of identity in order to organize for political action. A number of well-known writers have applied a social constructionist perspective to the study of gay men and lesbians. Most have been men (e.g. Altman, D'Emilio, Katz, Stein, Weeks), but a few have been women (e.g. Faderman, Kitzinger, Wittig). Even some psychoanalytic writers have aligned themselves with some version of this position. O'Connor and Ryan, for example, take a relatively constructionist stand on this question, asserting that they "would argue against any conception of a 'true' lesbian sexuality (or identity) that can be uncovered or discovered" (1993: 237).

One representative though radical version of the social constructionist position in the area of lesbian identity is the one presented by Celia Kitzinger in *The Social Construction of Lesbianism* (1987). Kitzinger is convinced that patriarchy is the foundation of all forms of oppression and that all men, because they benefit from the patriarchy, must be seen as the enemy. Heterosexuality is "central to women's oppression" and lesbianism is a political bonding of women against male supremacy (1987: viii). Neither heterosexuality nor homosexuality are "natural" in Kitzinger's view since both are constructed, the former as "a 'compulsory institution' (Rich 1980) into which women are coerced" and the latter as "a political challenge to the patriarchy" (ibid.: 64). Lesbians, she argues, *are* different from heterosexual women since they are subjected to oppressions which "shape and mould lesbian consciousness" and which give them privileged access to insights about male power (ibid.). In a later essay, Kitzinger points out that "to be seen demands some identity, even if culturally scripted" and she reiterates the often cited feminist position that just when it has become possible for lesbians to assert a sense of identity, "we are told that such a stance is theoretically suspect, and charges of essentialism are now used to scare lesbians and gays away from making any political claims on behalf of a group called 'lesbian' or 'gay'" (1995: 154).

In essence, Kitzinger rejects the liberal humanistic agenda and its various strategies to "normalize" homosexuality in order to prove that homosexuals are not a threat and should "be integrated into society" (1987: 49). She argues that lesbianism *is*, in fact, a threat to a male-dominated society. Liberal humanists who insist that homosexuality is just as "normal, natural and healthy" as heterosexuality, simply present a picture of homosexuality as insignificant and harmless (ibid.). Homosexuality is thus relegated to the realm of "depoliticized individualism" and personal choice, diverted from its role as a force for change, and reduced to being "an instrument of social control" (ibid.: 62). Kitzinger argues for a concept of lesbian identity that is subversive. She does not want to be integrated into society; she wants to transform it.

The interactionists/synthesizers

Some theorists have argued for the adoption of a kind of pluralistic perspective in order to transcend the dualistic tendencies reflected in the debate between constructionism and essentialism. Weinrich (1990), for example, contends that both the social constructionists and the essentialists are correct in important ways and that each should respect the points made by the other. He suggests that these positions, in fact, interact. Stein (1990) proposes that we work to create a synthesis between these two positions since he believes that neither position holds all the answers. He concludes that together they offer valuable tools for continuing the exploration into sexuality.

Although Stanley and Wise do not address the category "lesbian" in depth, they do acknowledge that it is a category parallel to "women" and therefore that the arguments they advance in that context are applicable, namely, that certain categories must be retained since, without them, "a distinctively *feminist* philosophy and praxis would no longer exist" (1993: 205). But they also maintain that these categories are both socially constructed and "internally fractured" (1990: 24), that is, these are not monolithic categories that describe universal experiences. They also contend that the concept of identity does not inherently require "an essentialist definition" (1993: 214). They favor a strategy that would "treat identity as completely constructionist in everyday practice" while at the same time attributing "essential features to it in political arguments" (ibid.).

Another lesbian theorist who attempts to define some middle ground in this debate is Julia Penelope. Penelope expresses frustration at the tendency of so many contemporary theorists to speak of essentialism and social constructionism "as necessarily opposing accounts of sexual identity" (1992: 20), as if sexual identity must be an "either-or" matter. She argues that both positions are accurate: "I was born a Lesbian in a specific social and historical context" (ibid.). Penelope refuses to privilege either side of the debate. She agrees that identity is always partially socially constructed by various factors (environment, family, geography, class, age, etc.), but she argues that social constructionism misses the fact that "Lesbianism is an active identity" and that individuals "are not simply passive objects caught up in and overwhelmed by the flow of events" (ibid.: 33, 34). Individuals are capable of acting and

71

reacting. She notes, for example, that many people had tried "to coerce" her into heterosexuality, but she resisted – "and so have a lot of other Lesbians" (ibid.). She is convinced that there is some element of "being" in being lesbian, that it is not a choice, that the only choice is whether lesbians choose to live *as* lesbians, as "*who we are*" (ibid.: 42). To identify oneself as lesbian in a largely hostile heterosexual world requires courage and it is, she explains, an act of political and ethical importance.

Penelope also calls attention to a particularly significant aspect of lesbian identity: our "invisibility," which she sees as "part of the social construction of a Lesbian identity" (ibid.: 34). Most contemporary lesbians have had to suppress their identities. If a lesbian puts herself into this "state of suspended animation" long enough, she may awake to find that she does not know who she is and she will feel forced into "a silence that smothers, deadens, sucks the life out of her" (ibid.: 35, 36). A lesbian who disrupts the silence by telling her story is crossing over "the conceptual line that separates the known" (the "safe" heterosexual world) from "the tabooed unknown of deviance" (ibid.: 41) (that is, she is crossing into the margin). In claiming a lesbian identity, she also accesses a capacity to reinterpret her own life story on her own terms and acquires a "Lesbian Perspective," a new outlook, rooted in a sense of identity, which makes it possible to challenge "male consensus reality" and to create a new "Lesbian-defined" reality (ibid.: 51).

The postmodernists/poststructuralists

Those who take one of the postmodern perspectives generally reject the concept of identity as we have come to know it. In some cases, they simply challenge our complacency about the content of these constructed concepts, in others they attempt to deconstruct them altogether. A few representative writers in this category are: Teresa Brennan, Judith Butler, Diana Fuss, Nancy Fraser, Virginia Goldner, Teresa de Lauretis, and Linda Nicholson.

Goldner, for example, questions the possibility and desirability of "an internally consistent gender identity" (1991: 250), since it would be "a developmental accomplishment that requires the activation of pathological processes" (ibid.: 258). That is, to construct a "consistent" gender identity, one would have to "disown" or "split off" everything and anything (ideas, behaviors, mannerisms) that are "gender-incongruent." Therefore, she concludes, gender is "by definition, a universal false-self system generated in compliance with the rule of the two-gender system" (ibid.: 258–259).

Fuss asserts that the categories of heterosexual and homosexual "like so many other conventional binaries" are constructed, first, in relation to each other and, second, "on the foundations of another related opposition: the couple 'inside' and 'outside'" (1991: 1). She critiques the convenient "structural symmetry" of such complementarity and notes that an identity which shores itself up using "ontological boundaries" is really working out of a defensive and protective posture (ibid.: 1, 2). That is, those on the "outside" (for example, homosexuals) are perceived as deficient in some way, not because they really are but because those who are on the "inside" (in this case, heterosexuals) want to keep their own deficiencies from becoming visible – and vice versa. So each "partner" in this symmetry "is haunted by the other" (ibid.: 3) – that is, each "needs" the other to define itself. Therefore, both are forever defending against "the very real possibility and ever present threat of a collapse of boundaries, an effacing of limits, and a radical confusion of identities" (ibid.: 6). Fuss wants to deconstruct homosexual identity on the grounds that even if we conceptualize homosexuality "as a transgression against heterosexuality," we are not "undermining the authoritative position of heterosexuality so much as reconfirming heterosexuality's centrality precisely as that which must be resisted" (ibid.). In the end, she resigns herself to the idea that the time might not yet be right to give up the idea of lesbian identity, so she suggests that, for now, we develop a capacity to tolerate all of the complexities involved in performing (versus "having") a sexual identity.

Butler is a lesbian feminist philosopher and theorist who has written extensively and very provocatively on various topics including aspects of identity. Butler does not equivocate. Her critique is always political and centered in a resistance to conventional ideas of a unified or "coalition subject" (1990a: 327). She has little tolerance for identity politics and denounces categories of identity as "instruments of regulatory regimes" (1991: 13). Butler is aware that some theorists have tried to make the concept of identity serve the goals of emancipation and she even appreciates the desire which motivates many to form a sense of "transhistorical commonality" among "us." But she wonders who this "us" can be which is constructed through such a simplified narration, one which does not incorporate "a decidedly more complex cultural identity – or non-identity, as the case may be" (1990a: 339).

Butler argues that theories built on categories of identity are caught up in the essentialist, ontological strategy of attempting "to construct a coherent female subject" based on the illusion of an inner core organized around gender (1990a: 332). This conflation of sexuality and gender effectively supports "the regulatory fiction of heterosexual coherence" which presents heterosexuality as within the person (ibid.: 336).

In Butler's frame, categories of gender identity and sexual orientation are exposed as parts of an overall fiction intended to regulate our lives. These concepts are not politically useful because they are not sufficiently radical. They cannot generate a politics that is truly new because they take the focus off the political practices which create and reinforce the categories themselves. To adopt strategies based on identity is to engage in the dominant discourse and to avoid the inherent issues of power. Butler is not oblivious to the real and grave dangers posed by homophobic forces, but she opposes allowing "such threats of obliteration" to shape "the terms of the political resistance to them" (1991: 19).

Yet even Butler admits that while the "visibility of identity" cannot "*suffice* as a political strategy," it might serve as a starting point (ibid.). In spite of her extreme discomfort with "the identity-sign" of lesbian (because there is no way to control its significations or use now or in the future), Butler comes to the conclusion that there "is a political necessity to use some sign" for now. But it is essential that this be done while at the same time ensuring our sense of its temporality. We can do this by making identity "a site of contest and revision," a site from which to disrupt constantly all notions of sexuality and gender, including one's own (ibid.) – a kind of counterpoint to hooks' "site of resistance."

In a move that I find uncommon outside depth psychology circles, Butler also critiques the concept of identity by drawing on the idea of the unconscious, arguing that any claims to a unified and stable identity which are made by "the conscious 'I'" can only be misleading and incomplete (ibid.: 15). One cannot come to know "the true and full content" of a self because in every act of disclosure there is also "a certain radical *concealment*" (a very hermeneutic description as we shall see in Chapter 11). In addition, asks Butler, "What, if anything, can lesbians be said to share? And

who will decide this question, and in the name of whom?" (ibid.).
What could lesbians possibly have in common?

Butler, like Fuss, proposes that we see lesbian identity in terms
of a performance at which one "plays." This is not to say, she
clarifies, that one is not "really" a lesbian. Rather, "'being' gets
established" in this "deep-seated . . . psychically entrenched play"
(ibid.: 18). It is not that the "I" is playing "*its lesbianism as a role*,"
but that "the 'I' is a site of repetition." That is, it is constantly and
continuously being "reconstituted" through a series of repetitions,
each of which displaces the 'I' that was there the moment before.
The 'I' is therefore never exhaustive or comprehensive. What is
produced is only "the semblance of identity" (ibid.). For Butler,
this is a way of "working sexuality *against* identity, even against
gender" (ibid.: 29). In so doing, we can ensure the "disruptive
promise" of an "I" which can never "fully appear in any performance" (ibid.).

In a more recent book, *Bodies That Matter*, Butler takes some of
her arguments even further. She wonders "what, if anything, is left
of 'sex' once it has assumed its social character as gender?" (1993:
5). She questions what the value would be within homosexuality of
theorizing "beyond the categories of 'masculine' and 'feminine'"
since doing that would "privilege sexual practice as a way of
transcending gender" (ibid.: 238). She resists "deterministic"
(ibid.) accounts which insist on theorizing sexuality within "the
rigid framework of gender difference," arguing that these are
permeated by "the heterosexual presumption" (ibid.: 239). She
denounces the psychoanalytic position that splits "identification"
from "desire" in order to attempt to conceptualize them as
"mutually exclusive" and thus to keep gender and sexuality forever
linked together. She notes that:

> if to identify as a woman is not necessarily to desire a man,
> and if to desire a woman does not necessarily signal the
> constituting presence of a masculine identification, whatever
> that is, then the heterosexual matrix proves to be an *imaginary*
> logic that insistently issues forth its own unmanageability.
>
> (ibid.)

Butler describes this kind of heterosexual logic as "one of
the most reductive of heterosexism's psychological instruments"
(ibid.) and she demands instead patience and a tolerance for
complexity:

The vocabulary for describing the difficult play, crossing, and destabilization of masculine and feminine identifications within homosexuality has only begun to emerge within theoretical language. . . . The thought of sexual difference *within* homosexuality has yet to be theorized in its complexity.

(ibid.: 239, 240)

Ultimately, as I read Butler, she consistently and relentlessly opposes all approaches that rely on causal, foundational, or reductive thinking in favor of those which strive for complexity and ambivalence. It is my experience that there is no easy way to read Butler, and no way at all to read her without feeling challenged at the level of one's every sacred belief. But that is exactly what makes her so worth reading.

Conclusion: a pluralistic "solution"

In some ways, I feel convinced that efforts toward deconstructing identity are correct and that to insist on lesbian identity (constructed or otherwise) is to get stuck in a form of patriarchal discourse. Yet, I cannot divest myself totally of the other side. In the context of discussing "Postmodern Blackness" (1990b), bell hooks addresses herself to the postmodern critique of identity, difference, and otherness. Although she appreciates the necessity and relevance of this critique, she also sees how it can undercut the struggle for racial justice. She argues that we must consider how the postmodern critique will affect struggles for liberation: "Given a pervasive politic of white supremacy which seeks to prevent the formation of radical black subjectivity," she argues, "we cannot cavalierly dismiss a concern with identity politics" (ibid.: 26). In other words, she recognizes that the issue of identity for a member of an oppressed or minority group is a very different matter from the issue of identity for a member of a dominant or majority group.

Ultimately, hooks' solution is pluralistic. On the one hand, she argues, we cannot discount postmodernism's critique of essentialism or its challenge to "notions of universality and static overdetermined identity" (ibid.: 28). A postmodern perspective "can open up new possibilities for the construction of self and the assertion of agency" and help us begin to understand (black) identity and experiences as "multiple" and "varied." This, in effect, defies "colonial imperialist paradigms of black identity" which insist on a blackness that is one-dimensional so that they can "reinforce and sustain white supremacy." To adopt a postmodern critique of essentialism would constitute, therefore, a serious confrontation of racism. On the other hand, echoing many other feminist writers, hooks points out a curious synchronicity: "Should we not be suspicious of postmodern critiques of the 'subject' when they surface at a historical moment when many subjugated people feel themselves coming to voice for the first time?" How can "those who have suffered the crippling effects of colonization and domination . . . gain or regain a hearing" without subjects who can come to voice (ibid.)? Hooks contends that there is, in fact, "a radical difference" between essentialist arguments in favor of blackness and arguments in favor of a "recognition of the way black identity has been specifically constituted in the experience of exile and struggle" (ibid.: 29). In order to continue to resist assimilation or domination, groups of oppressed people must have some "basis for collective bonding" (ibid.). That is, they must share a sense of common identity while recognizing the need for diversity as well.[1]

Hooks' analysis of the ideological struggle between essentialist and postmodern attitudes is as applicable to the identity debates within the lesbian and gay community as to those within other subordinated groups. I must admit to a very primal sense of agreement when hooks calls for "ways to construct self and identity that are oppositional and liberatory" but that also help us establish a sense of community through the bonds of a common history and through some identification of "the unique sensibilities and culture" that result from our common experiences (ibid.). She concludes that the only "adequate response" in the face of this problem is "to critique essentialism while emphasizing the significance of 'the authority of experience'" (ibid.). That is, rather than embrace or reject postmodernism, hooks takes a position which I would describe (though she might not) as a pluralistic holding of the tension between these two points of view.

A more radical, but still, to my mind, pluralistic view on the specific question of lesbian identity has been presented by Shane Phelan who argues that identity has been "the fundamental issue for lesbian feminism" (1989: 59). The issue for her is not one of "whether we are 'like' heterosexuals or not but of how, precisely, we live our lives" (1993: 776). Phelan is critical of the essentialists who by dividing the world into women and men "have accorded men the status . . . of ontological oppressors" and who by seeing

77

men as "irredeemable" have simply constellated the opposing
position, i.e. that women somehow are essentially superior (1989:
61). This position, in effect, is "male-identified" in that it defines
women in contrast to men (ibid.: 62). Phelan declares that lesbianism is more that resistance to men. It is a connection between
women.[2] Phelan proposes a separatist agenda which is not "grounded on the metaphysical difference between male and female
essence" and which does not pretend that lesbians are a homo-
geneous group (ibid.: 57). She argues for diversity and against the
idea of the politically correct lesbian. She bemoans the fact that a
"legitimate drive for community" has degenerated "into un-
mediated unity, a unity that carries as its twin an excessive fear of
difference" (ibid.).

Phelan ultimately argues for a concept of identity that can be
used as "a matter not only of ontology but also of *strategy*," one that
is not rooted in the rhetoric of liberalism, but which retains some
"liberal *sentiment*" (1989: 136, 155). Like hooks, Phelan is concerned that the postmodern attack on identity can undermine
political action and she argues that the rhetoric of deconstruction
will not, for example, remove baseball bats from the hands of
homophobes. We need a politics which guarantees that lesbian
voices will be heard. Yet she can also see the dangers inherent in
constructing lesbian identities. So, she calls for an identity politics
in which the tension is held between the striving for individuality
and the striving for community. This requires "the proper recognition of difference as well as commonality" and a capacity "to
embrace paradox and confusion" (1989: 160, 170).

Phelan argues that we must enter the arena of political discourse
"not as 'Lesbians' with a fixed, eternal identity but as those who
continue to become lesbians – people occupying provisional subject positions in heterosexual society" (1993: 779). This, in turn,
means that we must not simply describe or justify our experiences,
but must find ways of "articulating our lives, interpreting and re-
interpreting them in ways that link us to others" (ibid.). We also
must find ways of shifting our focus from questions which address
lesbian identity and serve to present lesbianism simply as an
anomaly within "heterosexual space" to questions which will
interrogate "heterosexist social institutions" (ibid.: 775, 771).

We must hold on to our sense of subjectivity while acknowledging
that it is always "part of the terrain of possible change" (ibid.: 779).
The question, she points out, is not who we "are" but "Who might

we become?" (ibid.) This is "the 'second wave' of identity politics" (ibid.: 780). Phelan, borrowing from Gloria Anzaldua, challenges us to conceive of an identity politics that "transgresses" categories rather than attempting to "transcend" them (ibid.: 783).

In the end, I find myself drawn to the idea that identity is a place, not a thing or a label. It is a complex process and a kind of moving target. It is a metaphor which allows us to have multiple and even contradictory identities. It is "a narrative of a subject's location within social structure" which gives meaning to one's experience (Duggan 1993: 793). "Collective identities," on the other hand, might best be conceptualized politically as the basis on which we "forge connections among individuals and provide links between past and present" (ibid.).

Of course, debates over identity aside, this still leaves me with a dilemma and a question: Who is a lesbian? How can this term be defined in a way that, at least, serves the purposes of this project?

DEFINITIONS OF "LESBIAN"

Even when we put aside the question of whether 'lesbian' is a category of identity and "simply" try to define the term lesbian, we are immediately thrown into yet another debate which is as complicated and full of strategic arguments and political ramifications as the debate over identity. As Phelan has noted: "Every new definition highlighting some aspect of our lives, shades another, and this is a choice with political consequences" (1989: 79). This debate, in its simplest terms, is much like the debate over identity. There are those who want to define "lesbian" and those who do not. Among those who resist efforts to define the term are those who have argued against the concept of identity and who would cite parallel reasons for this (although, since they cannot escape language, they must use the term lesbian anyway.) However, even some theorists who would defend the idea of lesbian identity have written against efforts to define it – for example, Shane Phelan and Sarah Hoagland. Phelan argues that there is no need to define who we are because that would be the equivalent of trying to prove we exist which, "in the manner of metaphysics," is related to proving "that we have the right to exist" (1989: 158). She goes on to say that to justify our existence "by defining, by ontologizing, by tracing descent, is to suggest that our present existence is open to dispute" (ibid.).

Hoagland, a lesbian separatist, points out that although she has named her book *Lesbian Ethics*, she refuses to define what she means by lesbian. She notes that the reason people feel obliged to explain the term lesbian is because they see it as not the norm. To define the term lesbian, therefore, would be "to succumb to a context of heterosexualism" and to act as if the term heterosexual need not be defined (1988: 8). Hoagland speaks instead of invoking a lesbian context – a context whose borders need not be defined or defended, a lesbian community which is "a ground of lesbian be-ing" – the context within which "we perceive each other essentially as lesbians" (ibid.: 9). She argues that this is the only true challenge to heterosexualism, and that separatism is essential to its creation. Echoing Esther Harding, she declares that only by separating from men can lesbians "withdraw from the existing ground of meaning" (ibid.: 63). Only such a separation can allow the necessary re-focusing that will allow lesbians to come to see "not that we exist in relation to a dominant other, but rather that we can create new value, lesbian meaning" (ibid.). In other words, "lesbian" is a kind of process not a term to be defined as such.

Other lesbian theorists, however, have invested much energy into attempts to define "lesbian." Most of these, however, have advised caution, noting that there is "no reason to think that there's only one kind of Lesbian, just as there's no one kind of heterosexual" (Penelope 1992: 36). Any effort to define "lesbian" must take care to acknowledge the diversity of lesbian experiences and the various paths that are followed. According to Penelope, even efforts such as that by Bonnie Zimmerman who has identified three Lesbian types ("lesbian-from-birth, lesbian-by-choice, lesbian-through-love"), do not adequately "address the complexities of Lesbian identity" (ibid.).

Given the level of complexity involved, it is likely that we may never arrive at a definition that is completely satisfactory to all or sufficiently comprehensive. But that does not stop us from trying. Among those who have tried, definitions of lesbian usually revolve around two intertwined sets of questions: (a) How central to the definition of lesbian is sexual behavior? Is a lesbian a woman who has sex with other women or simply a woman who loves other women? And does a lesbian have sex only with women?; and (b) Who gets counted as a lesbian and who does the counting? Who has the right to claim that she is a lesbian? Is someone a lesbian *only* if she says she is or *because* she says she is? Can others say that someone is, or is not, a lesbian? These questions and their potential ramifications have been tackled by *many* writers and certainly will not be resolved here. My intent is merely to acknowledge the parameters of the debate in order to establish a context for my own conclusions.

In many ways, it was the work of Adrienne Rich which really opened up all of these questions. Rich proposed the idea of a lesbian continuum as a way of beginning to understand lesbianism in a larger context not dependent on sexual behavior. For Rich, lesbianism is defined as resistance to the patriarchy. She was less motivated by a desire to define "lesbian" than by a desire to create the idea of a community of women who love each other and who have a history which can be both traced and moved forward in joint resistance to male domination. Lesbianism for Rich centers around the fact that it is, "like motherhood, a profoundly *female* experience" (1980: 650). Rich argues that sex is just one aspect of the continuum and that it is not the determining element of lesbian experience. How women bond (whether sexually or not) is less important than a woman's independence from men (sexually and emotionally). In Rich's opinion, a woman can be considered lesbian even if she has never had sex with another woman. Zita defends Rich's idea of the lesbian continuum because it makes visible "a long history of sexual/political resistance" (1981: 175) and Phelan notes that Rich's work represents "the shift from lesbianism as a sexual identity to lesbianism as a *political* definition" (1989: 72).

Ann Ferguson accuses Rich of oversimplifying and romanticizing the notion of lesbian resistance to the patriarchy and criticizes her for not distinguishing between lesbian behavior and lesbian identity. She speaks for those who argue that the historical development of lesbian identity is so explicitly "connected to genital sexuality" that to ignore this by proposing such a sanitized definition is to undermine lesbian history (1981: 149). Another problem she cites is the question of what to do with women who identify or live as bisexuals. A definition which excludes them also fails to include many women "from lesbian history . . . like Sappho, Vita Sackville-West, and Eleanor Roosevelt, whom most lesbian feminists would like to include" (ibid.: 151). And it would bar "many commonly accepted historical situations involving homosexual practices," situations in which women had same-sex relationships while also forming "economic and procreative marriages" with men (ibid.).

After considering various definitions, Ferguson settles on one which has come to receive a lot of attention:

> *Lesbian* is a woman who has sexual and erotic–emotional ties primarily with women or who sees herself as centrally involved with a community of self-identified lesbians whose sexual and erotic–emotional ties are primarily with women; and who is herself a self-identified lesbian.
>
> (ibid.: 155)

A number of other theorists have also discussed the relative importance of sex in definitions of lesbian. Marilyn Frye, for example, recognizes that sexuality cannot be reduced to sexual "preference." Sexuality "is a matter of orientation of attention," i.e. of commitment (Frye 1983: 172, quoted in Phelan 1989: 74). Penelope also argues against focusing too much on sex, as if it were "the only, or primary, criterion of who is a Lesbian" (1992: 32). This would produce a misleading definition, one that overvalues the sexual aspects of lesbian relationships while obscuring all others. In addition, she notes, having sex with another woman does not necessarily mean that a woman is a lesbian. Penelope concludes that while the definition of lesbian should not revolve solely around the question of sexual acts (or the lack thereof – as, for example, in the case of women who choose to be celibate), it should include some reference to sexuality in a way that does not make sex the deciding factor.

Lillian Faderman has followed Rich's lead to some extent, arguing that in order to establish some sense of historical continuity among women we cannot be fixated on the question of genital sexuality. She argues that it is not sexual activity that makes lesbianism subversive to the patriarchy. After all, she points out, romantic friendships "had been encouraged or tolerated for centuries" (1981: 240). Love between women became threatening only after the emergence of the feminist movement in the first quarter of this century when women suddenly began to have the opportunity, through living and working and loving together, to achieve some semblance of economic power and independence. It was then that love between women "became potentially threatening to the social order" (ibid.). Sex as such, she concludes, had nothing to do with it. She thus settles on a definition that conveys this relativization of sex, describing a lesbian relationship as one:

82

in which two women's strongest emotions and affections are directed toward each other. Sexual contact may be a part of the relationship to a greater or lesser degree, or it may be entirely absent. By preference the two women spend most of their time together and share most aspects of their lives with each other.

(ibid.: 17–18)

I find Faderman's definition, along with Rich's idea of the continuum, to be suitable for historical purposes. That is, in recognition of changing mores and views of sexuality, it would seem important to relativize the importance of sex in a definition of historical lesbians. However, it seems unsatisfactory for contemporary purposes. There I find myself persuaded by Phelan's argument that a failure to include sexual activity as part of the definition of lesbian is a failure to acknowledge that "in our time, it *is* 'the sexual aspect of lesbianism' that disturbs so many" (1989: 75). Phelan criticizes Faderman for attempting "to greatly mute the importance of sex" and thereby silencing "the voices of lesbians who have been and are still persecuted for their sexuality and/or defiance of gender stereotypes" (ibid.: 76). Phelan insists, however, that any definition of lesbian that includes sex must be willing to envision something other than heterosexual male definitions of sex.

Ferguson's definition, on the other hand, seems adaptable for contemporary purposes but unsuitable for historical purposes since self-identification is relatively appropriate and possible only in a contemporary climate of relative openness toward sex in general and toward lesbian sex specifically. That is, very few women before the past few decades ever wrote statements even approximating contemporary declarations of "I am a lesbian" or discussing their sexuality as such. For the purposes of this project, therefore, I have adopted a modified version of Ferguson's definition. Although I am drawn to the idea of women self-identifying as lesbians, I am a little uncomfortable with a definition that relies totally on self-selection. It is not that I am concerned that women who may simply be "experimenting" will claim to be lesbian (a concern Ferguson herself points out). I do not see any way to exclude such women without also excluding women who are simply newly out or without setting some impossible standards. That is, there can never be a guarantee that a particular woman will "always" identify herself as lesbian or be seen as one by others. I am more concerned that

Ferguson's definition might exclude those who refuse to be bound by the label "lesbian" or those who are unable or unwilling to vocalize a lesbian identity. Critics such as Julia Penelope have addressed this aspect of Ferguson's definition: it assumes that identity must be self-conscious and therefore it counts only "out" lesbians. Penelope concludes that: "A definition of *Lesbian* that excludes so many who live and love *as* Lesbians, yet includes so many undeserving of the name [i.e. 'bisexuals and women who claim to be Lesbians for some period of time' (1992:32)] is no definition at all" (ibid.: 32).

CONCLUSION: ANOTHER PLURALISTIC "SOLUTION"

Phelan notes that the recent work of some lesbian theorists has resisted reified definitions of lesbian while working toward a definition which would envision lesbianism "as a critical site of gender deconstruction rather than as a unitary experience with a singular political meaning" (1993: 766). In other words, these efforts contribute toward seeing lesbianism not as something essential or fixed, "but as a critical space within social structures" (ibid.) – perhaps not unlike hooks' "site of resistance" (1990a: 153). With this in mind, I have tried to construct a workable definition (for the purpose of selecting my interviewees) that employs this strategy. Therefore, I am inclined to present my definition as "a political strategy conducted within and through language" rather than as containing "the deep meaning and truth of lesbianism" (Phelan 1993: 772). My definition begins with Ferguson's definition from above (p. 82) and ends with my modification:

> *Lesbian* is a woman who has sexual and erotic–emotional ties primarily with women or who sees herself as centrally involved with a community of self-identified lesbians whose sexual and erotic–emotional ties are primarily with women or who acknowledges a commitment to a current lesbian relationship. She may or may not self-identify as a lesbian.

6

"EILEEN"

PROFILE

Eileen is a 37-year-old white woman who has been "out" for about seventeen years. Eileen was born and raised in England, and came to the United States about eight years ago. She thinks of herself as "a lesbian." Eileen would rather not think that she "was born this way." She believes that she has chosen to live as a lesbian because she likes it. Eileen lives with her partner and co-parents their two children. Eileen works in an academic environment coaching athletics.

INTERVIEW SETTING/PROCESS

Eileen was a relative stranger to me before this interview. I had met her only once, at a social event. We had chatted only a little, since she was occupied with watching over her son. At the time of the interview, Eileen indicated some interest in understanding more about my project and the interview process before we began, so we spent some time talking about "the partnership of conversation." Eileen expressed an appreciation for the underlying philosophy of this methodology and was an enthusiastic participant in our conversation.

THE INTERVIEW

Eileen seemed taken by the question and by the opportunity it offered to talk about such an important part of her life. Being gay, she told me at a later point, is such "a very integral part" of her self concept that it "pervades everything about who I am in the

world." In spite of the difficulties involved in living in a homophobic culture, her lesbian identity is a part of her life that she
would not want to change.

> "I really feel that this is so central to who I am that it's not
> something you could strip out and leave other things whole.
> It's completely fundamental to how I operate in every part of
> my life, in my existence. Sexuality is clearly a highly important
> part of that. You couldn't take it away and not leave other
> things torn and bleeding behind it."

Perhaps because her lesbianism is so important to her, Eileen
found it "hard to know where to start." Although she has had
relationships with men, Eileen felt unable to talk about her lesbian
experiences in opposition to those because "I've never fallen in
love with or felt myself to be in love with a man." She realized the
first time she became involved with a woman that there was
something qualitatively different going on. She noticed an emotional involvement that "had just not even begun to exist" in her
relationships with men. Although her sexual experiences with men
had been pleasurable, they did not "hold the same meaning for
me on an emotional level. Not at all. Not even close." Sex with men
had never touched Eileen "any more deeply than a highly pleasurable athletic activity. I mean it hasn't. It just has not." She
remembers thinking during her last sexual experience with a man:
"Boy, this is great! It's like a good game of squash." She felt no
emotional attachment because sex with men has been something
that she could not "give myself up to emotionally." She corrects
herself: "It's not that I can't, it's just not there to give it up to." She
feels no intimacy with a man. "I could sleep with a man and be
absolutely non-intimate."

Eileen's first experiences of loving women brought her "a sense
of rightness" that she had not experienced before, a sense that
there was something mysteriously "appropriate" about her feelings,
a sense that this was her "normality."

> "So, just starting out there was this whole realization not even
> of rightness but of a whole depth of feeling for me that had
> not entered my realm of experience before. And so that was
> quite a wondrous experience in a way, a sort of revelation or
> something."

Eileen thinks of herself as a lesbian. "It's an identity." It has

taken her some time to become comfortable with claiming lesbianism as an identity, not so much because of any internal struggle,
but because she is aware of how others can use it as a label to
stereotype her before they even know her. She does not want to
"become to someone else their definition of what a lesbian is"
because that may be irrelevant to her life and to who she is. The
reactions of others have not affected Eileen's commitment to living
as a lesbian (for example, she described her parents' negative
reaction to her lesbianism as "puny" against the sense of "central
rightness" that she was experiencing within her relationships with
women). But concerns about the reactions of others have kept her
from being as open in some settings as she would like to be –
although she recognizes that she is more out now than she used to
be, or ever thought she would be. Eileen has come to accept that
she can no longer try to live in a role that does not fit with who she
is. This has become especially obvious to her since the birth of the
son born to her partner, a son who calls them both "Mom" for the
world to hear.

Eileen believes that it is "extremely important" for her, both
personally and politically, to lay claim to a lesbian identity because
"it is important to name who you are." Eileen sees her identity as
"a truth in the world" and recognizes the costs to her if she were
unable to name who she is.

> "It's that thing of naming who you are that's part of maintain-
> ing one's sanity. I know who I am, but I also have a right to
> say who I am in the world. It's part of one's right to be in the
> world. This is who I am. This is an integral part – and a huge
> part. . . . I have a right to that. I have a right to say
> it. I may choose not to, out of fear, but then I am diminished.
> It's real integral to me to name the truth, my truth."

Eileen is aware that her relationship to the world is mediated to
a great extent by her physicality. That is, it is through her body and
its responses that she assesses and makes decisions about how to
proceed. For Eileen, "communicating by touch is as common as
communicating by voice." The closer she feels to someone, the
more she will touch them. For Eileen, physicality invariably has a
sexual component in that through physicality the body becomes
totally and intimately involved in life – whether in sex, sports, or
other physical activities. This is especially the case for her in
relationships. All of her meaningful friendships have "some kind

of sexual element" in them (though this aspect is not typically acted upon). As I listened to Eileen, it seemed to me that this element of sexuality serves as a kind of cement for all of her meaningful relationships.

However, Eileen was quite specific in wanting me to know that in her relationships with women there is also "clearly something that goes beyond" physicality and sex, something that relates to intimacy and bonding (words that Eileen used repeatedly as she attempted to convey to me how high a value she attributes to her relationships with women). Intimacy for Eileen involves "emotional connection" or what she sees as "almost a spiritual connection." For Eileen, body and spirit are inseparable, so the spiritual aspect of a relationship is not separate from the sexual: "If I am drawn to a woman sexually, I am also drawn to her on other levels." Even when the sexual element is the strongest level of attraction in a particular relationship, that is never all that is happening for Eileen. She invariably experiences connections at emotional and spiritual levels. In other words, Eileen's relationships with women are "not emotion neutral" as they are with men where it feels to her as if "that gear is not engaged." There is a long silence as she searches for an analogy: "It's almost like the difference between a chemical reaction and a mixture. You can mix things together and they don't bond, but if there's a chemical reaction then things are fundamentally changed in their nature." With women, something emotional is triggered for Eileen: "There's an interplay of emotions." Eileen has known straight women who have admitted to her that in choosing to be with men they know they are giving up intimacy. "I just couldn't do that. For me, that's a deal I just wouldn't be interested in." The capacity to be intimate is an essential factor in women's ability to bond. To feel a bond with someone is to have a sense that this person "would be there for you and you for them." It is a powerful feeling that gives Eileen a sense of "solidity." Again, she does not feel this as much with men. There is a "difference in intensity" with men and a lack of trust that seems to prevent this from happening.

Eileen does not believe "that women are fundamentally more good or balanced or less in error or less able to make mistakes" than men. Rather, she associates the intensity of her feelings for women and her ability to trust women more than men to her sense of "solidarity" and "camaraderie" with other women. She can feel "more empathy" for women because she really knows what it is like to be a woman in this society. This makes her feel "relatively comfortable about having a sense of what's happening for other women" and gives her "a sense of where someone is likely to be coming from." With men, she can feel sympathy, "but I don't have the same gut sense of what it must feel like." It is this sense of a shared experience with other women that makes her relationships with women so intense. With lesbians, this is emphasized all the more because of the additional factor of a shared "counter culture."

This political aspect of Eileen's love for other women also provides her with strong links to her community. Eileen is very direct in conveying that a sense of community is essential to her well-being. She traces this back to her school days in an English girls' school, a highly structured environment in which she made deep and lasting friendships. Although the lesbian community does not have such a formalized structure, Eileen finds that there is similar "acknowledgment of a commonality" which provides "some kind of cohesiveness" and creates a culture which "fosters relationships and bonding." Therefore, for Eileen, the lesbian community at large "is a structure within which loving another woman can thrive." As a result, she has been an active participant in her local lesbian community.

Eileen also spoke enthusiastically and at length about her experiences working at the Michigan women's music festival. She used a number of emotionally evocative adjectives in her attempts to describe the impact this event has had on her over the years: incredible, stunning, powerful. There is "a bonding" that can occur there because people feel so safe in that environment. For Eileen, this link between safety and bonding seems to be the product of the "amount of commonality" one can assume at that event: for example, "you can assume that 99 percent of the people you walk into are lesbians. Where else can you do that?" In this environment, one does not have to spend months just trying to assess the situation and other people. "You can cut to the chase if you like and start dealing with those people as people" without feeling paralyzed by some of the fears one might experience out in the world. That is, the amount of commonality allows for a level of communication not often experienced by lesbians.

"Anyone there is someone with enough of the same culture that we're not speaking through as thick a filter to each other.

I can say ten things and have most of them be understood pretty well even though her experience is not my experience. There's probably enough that we can hit a nerve for each other. That's highly important to me."

Eileen believes that if she does not have to strip away so many filters before attempting to communicate with someone, her ability to understand the other person is enhanced despite any differences of experience and any biases. Also, because everyone there shares "a broad commitment toward the same goal," all experience an immediate and higher level of trust with each other. This, in turn, allows for more bonding among all the women there. Eileen cannot imagine that this could happen among a group of men since men "are not the oppressed group in society" and are not faced with the consequences of oppression as a group.

When Eileen looks back over her childhood and her years in an English girls' high school, she sees a history of her forming "incredibly strong relationships with women, whether sexual or not." This re-interpretation of her previously unnoticed attraction for women provides Eileen with a way to make meaning of where she is now and how she has come to be there. The bonds she established in high school with other girls and some teachers were "pivotal and very powerful" in her life even though, "in true English fashion," nothing was ever acknowledged openly. She cannot even "conceive of falling in love with or forming that same kind of bond with a man or men." As she talked about this, there is an obvious attempt in her voice to make me understand that the feelings she has had for women simply were not there in her relationships with men. The kind of bonding she experiences with women is "just not a relevant concept" for her in relation to men, mainly because she experiences "no sexual element" in her relationships with men. Thus, she is not drawn to bond with men in the ways she can bond with women, though she generally likes men, works well with them, feels affection for particular ones, and deals with them "very happily."

Toward the end of our conversation, I asked Eileen if we could return to the original question and if she could consider it again, this time in the context of all that she had already said. It was then that Eileen expressed an awareness that she had not yet talked specifically about her current relationship. She wondered if answering from this perspective would add or change anything. She supposed that she did not talk about "the minutia" of this particular relationship because she felt it would not answer my question, it would have pulled her into the details of this relationship and away from a broader response. However, she decided that everything she had said in general holds true in relation to her partner specifically and that this relationship would serve, in fact, as "an illustration" of what she had been saying. She talked about their commonalities, the "incredibly powerful" sense of bonding she feels with J., the "tremendous amount of trust" she experiences toward her. She jokes that they actually have "a boring life together" (home, kids, work), but admits that she cannot imagine sitting here in this house with a man because she "cannot imagine having that depth of bonding with a man," a bonding that persists "whether J. and I are doing well or doing badly – and we do both."

Eileen noted that our conversation was, in some ways, nothing more than a verbal attempt "to nail down" a phenomenon that ultimately consists of "something that is just completely inexplicable – something that just is." The factors we had discussed "play into it and are important," but nothing we say can ever really "explain it." She wishes she could explain it better for me: "but there really just is a part of it that defies description. It really just is."

MY EXPERIENCE OF THE INTERVIEW

This conversation with Eileen was really delightful for me – perhaps because she brought to it a great curiosity about my question herself. She needed very little prompting and very few interventions. Although she often framed her comments in a way that contrasted her experience of women against her experiences of men, she also conveyed to me a striking capacity to describe her experiences of women in ways that were quite independent of (and not so much "in opposition" to) her experiences of men. I was impressed also by Eileen's thoughtful attention to re-examining her past in light of the present. This produced an understanding of her past that seemed to me to be less of a rewrite than a reinterpretation. She does not need to maintain a view of herself as heterosexual in the past.

Eileen's focus on commonality, mutuality, empathy, and trust as major factors in lesbian bonding and intimacy put me very much in mind of Gadamer's idea that every attempt at understanding is an attempt at finding agreement. In Eileen's experience, the common ground she shares with another lesbian promotes her capacity to understand and be understood. Eileen's frequent returns to this theme of commonality also resonated for me with images of the *coniunctio* of likes as did her repeated references to the idea of "bonding." I went again to the dictionary. The particular meaning that grabbed my attention was: "4. A substance that cements or unites" (*Reader's Digest Great Encylopedic Dictionary* 1975.) I thought about how Eileen had talked about the sexual element which is present for her in all of her relationships with women, how this is what draws her to women. I thought about her reference to the spiritual dimension of lesbian relationships and how inseparable that is for her from physicality. Finally, there were Eileen's repeated uses of words like "central," "fundamental," and "rightness." These seemed to me to be connected to ways we might talk about individuation and certainly had an echo of "core" in them. I was beginning to think this might not be coincidence.

7

SAME-SEX LOVE IN DEPTH PSYCHOLOGY

JUNGIAN CONCEPTUALIZATIONS OF SAME-SEX LOVE

But moving beyond Jung requires beginning with him.

(Downing 1995: 266)

Jung on same-sex love

In all of Jungian literature, there are only two books which deal at length with Jung's attitude and beliefs about homosexuality. Yet, between them, the task of surveying what Jung wrote or thought about homosexuality has been thoroughly and insightfully done. Both books were written by non-analysts. The first is Christine Downing's *Myths and Mysteries of Same-Sex Love* (1989), a book which can only be described as an enormous achievement from several perspectives. Downing devotes the first half of her book to reviewing and contrasting Freud and Jung – their personal lives, theories, and case studies – as these relate to homosexuality. Then, in the second half of her book, she turns to a scholarly search of Greek life and mythology still looking to find some greater understanding of homosexual experience.

Downing writes lovingly and knowledgeably about both Freud and Jung, in a way that is rare in depth psychology circles, and she manages to do this without letting either of them off the hook for their respective failures. She is one of very few scholars who are gifted at interpreting both Freud and Jung without oversimplifying them. Downing emphasizes some of the differences between them in ways that shed light on both. She highlights Jung's focus on recovering symbolic thinking rather than lost memories. She considers especially how Jung applies this "neglected mode of apprehension" by exploring "the psychical longings" that human beings try to satisfy through sexuality (1989: 107, 127). She explains that Jung regards male homosexuality as "a spiritual yearning misunderstood as a sexual orientation," a kind of longing for a "male spiritual mentor" (ibid.: 121, 122), but that his views of female homosexuality are rather different. He sees it as recapitulating "the primary attachment to the mother" (ibid.: 126). In either case, he assumes that heterosexuality is the "natural" and therefore stronger force.

Downing notes with regret that Jung was never able to consider the possibility "that to love another like oneself may represent not narcissism or immaturity, but a love directed toward the Self" and that it might express "a desire to be free of being defined by cultural gender definitions" (ibid.: 127). She underscores the problems inherent in the concept of contrasexuality (a "never seriously questioned assumption in Jung's theory") and points out how this took him in particular heterosexist directions (ibid.: 110). In spite of all of this, Downing manages to salvage something from Jung's method by appreciating what he has taught us: a way of seeing, a way through which homosexuality can carry some meaning, a way that "may immeasurably deepen our experience of our own sexuality" (1989: 127). She herself then turns to Greek mythology "in search of the lost archetypes" that might "free homosexuality from being viewed through the lens of pathology and perversity" (ibid.: 130).

The other comprehensive work that investigates Jung's views on homosexuality is *Jung, Jungians, and Homosexuality* (1989) by Robert Hopcke. Hopcke examines everything that Jung "did and did not say" on this topic (1989: 12). He does a truly superb and meticulous job of finding, presenting, and analyzing every reference to homosexuality (generally male homosexuality) in all of Jung's writings. Hopcke notes that it is difficult to construct a systematic account of Jung's ideas on homosexuality since Jung simply did not leave "very many definitive statements on much of anything, especially homosexuality" (ibid.). Hopcke attributes this to several factors: Jung's tendency especially after his break with Freud to minimize the role of sexuality as such, his "notorious distaste" for dogma pronouncements (ibid.: 13), and his perception that homosexuality is usually "secondary" to other factors (ibid.: 32).

Hopcke notes that Jung's views changed over time and he divides

Jung's life into three major periods to demonstrate this. In the first period, "The Early 'Psychoanalytic' Writings: 1908–1920," Jung's ideas are clearly influenced by psychoanalytic thinking and he sees homosexuality "as a fixation or arrest in psychosocial development" (ibid.: 18). Hopcke notes, however, that although Jung cannot keep himself from seeing homosexuality as pathological, he nevertheless assumes that there must be some kind of individual meaning involved in this phenomenon (at least for men). For example, in a letter to Freud written in 1910, Jung proposes that the moral stigma be removed from homosexuality because it is "a method of contraception" (Jung 1974: 298, quoted in Hopcke 1989: 44).

By the beginning of the next phase, "Theoretical Complexity and Consolidation: 1920–1927," Jung has distanced himself from psychoanalytic thought and is involved in the process of developing his own ideas, especially his concepts of anima/animus. Jung theorizes that the homosexual individual is someone who identifies with the contrasexual element "within" rather than projecting it onto an "outside" other. Since Jung believes that the projection of unconscious contents onto some "external" other, followed by the withdrawal and integration of those projections into oneself, is essential to individuation, the inability of the homosexual to project the contrasexual would, in Jung's view, hinder individuation. So, while Jung does not specifically condemn homosexuality as such, his perceptions of homosexuality during this period are mostly negative and filled with comments which simply perpetuate stereotypical views, for example the belief that homosexuality reflects a desire to "be" a person of the other sex. This, of course, conflates the categories of gender and sexual orientation, blurs distinctions between identity and constructedness, and is a confusion which remains with us to this day in Jungian thought.

On the other hand, Jung also continues with his efforts to find some meaning in homosexuality. For example, he makes occasional references to the important role homosexuality has played in social and cultural life, noting in one passage (and foreshadowing some of Esther Harding's theorizing) that female homosexuality "somehow acts as a stimulus to the social and political organization of women, just as male homosexuality was an important factor in the rise of the Greek *polis*" (Jung CW10: 203, quoted in Hopcke 1989: 26). Jung also makes attempts to dissociate homosexual behavior from an individual's character, thus shifting homosexuality out of "the realm of sexual perversion" and into the arena of "moral judgments" where it can be theorized in relation to its potential role in individuation rather than as being inherently pathological (ibid.: 31).

During the third and final period, "Jung's Mature Thought: 1936–1950," Jung's theoretical formulations continue to evolve, although he still really does not know what to make of homosexuality. Jung declares that for "a man to be a man" he must, during young adulthood, free himself from his "anima fascination with his mother" (CW9i: 146, quoted in Hopcke 1989: 37). However, he makes an exception for artists and homosexual men who are "usually characterized by an identification with the anima":

> In view of the recognized frequency of this phenomenon, its interpretation as a pathological perversion is very dubious. The psychological findings show that it is rather a matter of the incomplete detachment from the hermaphroditic archetype, coupled with a distinct resistance to identify with the role of a one-sided sexual being. Such a disposition should not be adjudged negative in all circumstances, in so far as it preserves the archetype of the Original Man, which a one-sided sexual being has, up to a point, lost.
>
> (ibid.)

In the next paragraph, however, Jung makes it clear that this exception applies only prior to mid-life, not afterwards. In spite of this, Hopcke finds something interesting in Jung's linking of homosexuality with the images of the hermaphrodite and the "Original Man." Hopcke describes these as images which reflect "psychological wholeness" and "the union of opposites," and he claims that through them Jung is linking homosexuality with "the Self" (1989: 37). I, too, find Jung's remarks to be very interesting, but for very different reasons. I believe that Hopcke has conflated the image of the hermaphrodite with that of the androgyne. As Downing so aptly describes it, the image of the hermaphrodite "points forward to a creative union of opposites" (1989: 115). In that sense, it suggests a connection to the self, but it is not itself an image of wholeness. It is an image of an unconscious and primordial unity of male and female, an image that *precedes* differentiation and individuation. For Jung, the androgyne symbolizes the more conscious "balancing" or union of "the masculine" and "the feminine" which is the goal of the individuation process. Any reflections on the meaning of Jung's reference to the hermaphrodite must take this into account. I believe that Downing gets closer to Jung's view when she says that Jung saw homosexuality as "a misguided attempt to actualize psychical androgyny" (ibid.: 115). That is, Jung conceptualized androgyny as a symbolic union between the outer person and the inner "partner" of the "opposite" sex. Jung theorized from this that homosexuals are misguided because they try to live this out literally and externally rather than symbolically. Unlike Hopcke, therefore, I would not stay within this gendered conversation by accepting either the hermaphrodite or the androgyne as images central to an understanding of homosexuality because to do so simply keeps us enmeshed in gendered language. In addition, I would argue that androgyny, this most sacred of Jungian ideals, is a concept that is too abstract, bland, compact, dualistic, and symmetrical (one of my major complaints against Jung) – and thus is not much of an improvement over contrasexuality.[1]

That Jung invariably thought and spoke in genderized images does not mean that we should, too. Rather, what I see in this quote is an opportunity to break out of all of those gendered categories by focusing more specifically on the concept of the self, the process that guides individuation away from one-sidedness toward "wholeness." (In spite of my skepticism about notions of "wholeness," it is a somewhat more liberating concept than the construct of gender.) What I find most interesting in Jung's quote is not just what he says about homosexuals, but what he implies about gender and heterosexuality. According to Jung, for "a man to be a man" he must be heterosexual (i.e. he must disidentify from his anima fascination). Jung recognizes that while this is the preferred path it is also "one-sided." He suggests that homosexuality is less one-sided because it preserves an attachment to the archetype of the Original Man. I would suggest that Jung thus inadvertently offers us a view of homosexuality as a kind of symbolic corrective to the one-sidedness of "man" and heterosexuality. Truthfully, however, I am not concerned with rescuing homosexuality from Jung (which I believe Hopcke wants to do). I would rather get beyond Jung's limited vision by deconstructing the usual Jungian formulations and creating a post-Jungian theory in spite of Jung.

Hopcke makes the point, inadvertently, that Jung's attitude

toward homosexuality is limited by his focus on individual meaning. Although Hopcke believes that Jung thus "lays on the doorstep of gay people a psychological task of no mean measure," he sees this as simply in line with "the spiritual task" at the heart of Jung's psychology: the task of living our meaning individually and in spite of social forces (1989: 56). As much as I sympathize with this view in some ways, it saddens me that Hopcke deliberately discounts the political dimension of this task by calling it "a task that ultimately will not be solved simply by political action or social agitation" (ibid.). It is as if he does not recognize what he himself points out only a few pages later, "that negative social attitudes . . . are actually more to blame for mental illness among gay people than anything inherent in homosexuality itself" (ibid.: 59).

Jungians on same-sex love

Considering how extremely common is the sexual orientation generally called "homosexuality," it is surprising how little relating to the subject appears in Jungian literature.

(Payne 1990: 155)

Hopcke adds to this that his review of contemporary Jungian literature for references to lesbians yielded "woefully little" (1989: 125). Given this sorry state of affairs, I have focused instead on trying to meaningfully categorize what I did find. In her book *The Woman in the Mirror* (1990),[2] Claire Douglas surveys the range of post-Jungian attitudes toward "the feminine" and suggests that there are two categories of Jungians in this context: the Conservators and the Reformulators. She describes the Conservators as those who "essentially follow Jung, systematically elaborating, deepening, and widening" his work, while the Reformulators are those who "reexamine, discard, reinterpret, or save" Jung's ideas by applying revised points of view to them (1990: 112). So far so good – but what about the radical Jungians? I knew they existed (although in small numbers). I knew that the phrase "revolutionary post-Jungian thinkers" was not oxymoronic, that there are Jungians who want more than reform, who want to overthrow official dogma and interpretations. So I wondered why Douglas had not imagined, if only intellectually, a third category for them. I decided, therefore, on a framework that would employ three categories: Conservators, Reformulators, and Radicals.[3]

The Conservators

The Conservators are those who do not really deviate from Jung's own views although they may attempt to expand on them. Many of the Conservators are well-known 'first-generation' analysts, for example: Eric Neumann, Jolande Jacobi, Joseph Henderson,[4] Anthony Storr, Marie-Louise von Franz – and even Esther Harding (whom I include here because she was so committed to conserving Jung's thought). Other, more contemporary Conservators, include Nathan Schwartz-Salant, Murray Stein, Anthony Stevens, Ann Ulanov, and Louis Zinkin.[5] Hopcke critiques some of these writers and finds that, on the whole, they disregard "the genius of some of Jung's most important insights and attitudes" and fail to "advance Jung's own thinking" in any really creative way (1989: 102). Hopcke attributes this to "the form of homophobia endemic to analytical psychology," although he claims, rather optimistically, that this is changing among contemporary Jungians (ibid.).

In general, I would also include in this category many writers (*not* all) who are involved in promoting the "return to the goddess" movement or who are calling for things like "the restoration of the feminine." Many of these writings impress me as homophobic at worst and heterosexist at best. An example of the former can be found in Jennifer and Roger Woolger's, *The Goddess Within* (1987). They have only one indexed reference to lesbians. It is in the context of a discussion of women who represent "Athena at her most wounded" (1987: 81). In a passage which speaks for itself, they write:

> In fact, in the excess of her rage against the mother, she will displace its overflow onto men and the fatherworld generally, perhaps withdrawing bitterly into poverty as a hopeless welfare mother or joining a radical feminist group or lesbian community that readily encourages her to indulge her anger.
>
> (ibid.)

Examples of a more heterosexist approach can be found in Marion Woodman's *Addiction to Perfection*. Woodman has two indexed references to lesbian relationships. The first is in the context of an initiation into femininity for older women: "Some try to find validation for their femininity through a lesbian relationship; others try to find that validation through making their lovers into loving mothers; others unconsciously step into the constricting shoes of their mothers" (1982: 122). I find the phrase "trying to find validation" to be offensive in itself, but to include lesbian relationships in the same sentence with behaviors that are controlling or otherwise unconscious makes Woodman's attitude truly insulting (though I do not believe she intends it to be so). The heterosexism of her second reference is more subtle and is made in the context of advocating that Jungians recognize the value of body work. She notes that in the course of such work:

> Strong lesbian feelings often emerge because the feminine body needs the love of a woman in order to accept itself. Sometimes that need has to be projected in order to be recognized, in which case a lesbian relationship may happen.
>
> (ibid.: 161)

Had Woodman stopped after the first sentence, she might have redeemed herself in my eyes. However, her comment that lesbian relationships just "happen" minimizes any conscious expression of lesbian love. In her later book, *The Pregnant Virgin* (1985), Woodman's references to lesbianism are clearly more carefully worded, but the implications are not significantly corrected. Many other Jungians who are interested in the goddess and/or the feminine (e.g. Jean Shinoda Bolen, Helen Luke, Linda Leonard, Sukie Colgrave) often use this material so stereotypically in terms of gender roles, etc., that lesbian relationships are simply made invisible. As a result, most do not even index any references to lesbian relationships.

The Reformulators

The Reformulators are those Jungians who try to salvage Jung's basic work by redefining it through a process of re-examination and re-evaluation. My attitude toward many in this category is in some ways parallel to Kitzinger's (1987) critique of "gay affirmative research": that its "liberal" view of homosexuality simply attempts to assimilate it into a heterosexually defined framework. I am also reminded here of Audre Lorde's often-quoted remark that we can never dismantle the master's house using the master's tools (1984b: 110). In other words, I share their distrust of effecting change through the use of existing and problematic categories and concepts. In any case, this is a somewhat crowded category consisting mainly of contemporary writers who could be organized into a number of subgroups, for example: feminist, non-feminist, and lesbian/gay. Most of these writers at least pay lip service to the legitimacy of lesbian and gay relationships, but some continue to promote rigidly defined (though not always stereotypical) gender views that support the assumption of contrasexuality. Although I do not doubt the sincerity of these writers, I do not believe they can be excused from looking at the consequences of their theories.

Among this group are a number who self-identify as feminist. Some of these refer to lesbians in their work in non-judgemental, even affirmative, but usually parenthetical ways (e.g. Claire Douglas, Genia Pauli Haddon, Nor Hall). Douglas, for example, suggests that any reinterpretation of Jungian theory and practice "must also be relevant to homosexual as well as heterosexual perspectives" (1990: 298) and she argues that the contrasexual is just one particular manifestation of "the other." Others simply ignore or neglect lesbian experience by not mentioning it in their work at all (e.g. Estelle Lauter, Carol Schreier Rupprecht, and Ginette Paris). Yet, from a strictly gender point of view, many of these writers might be categorized as relatively radical. Lauter and Rupprecht, for example, do attempt to dissociate gender-biased concepts from archetypal images produced by women "without any intent of proving or disproving gender differences" (1985: 15). Yet, on the whole, their discussions of these images are gender-linked.

Unfortunately, some feminist reformulators include lesbian experience in their writings in ways that effectively minimize or demean it. One example is Sylvia Brinton Perera who, in *Descent to the Goddess* (1981), has only one indexed reference to (male) homosexuality in which she associates addiction and homosexuality in a way that clearly conveys a negative connotation (1981: 75). Another more offensive example can be found in *Female Authority: Empowering Women Through Therapy* (1987), co-authored by Polly Young-Eisendrath[6] and Florence Wiedemann. The authors index only one reference to a lesbian client. At first, they appear to be discussing this case without singling out the client's choice of a female partner as problematic. However, the very next paragraph following this discussion begins with: "Identification with the alien Masculine Other of early childhood can be one of the most troubling aspects of a client's identity at this first stage of animus" (1987: 71). Not only does this locate lesbianism in the "first stage" of animus development (always a necessary but immature stage in stage theories), it labels it as an "identification" (a concept with

SAME-SEX LOVE IN DEPTH PSYCHOLOGY

heavy negative implications in Jungian theory). I would argue that even Harding had a more enlightened view than this.

The second sub-group of Reformulators consists of non-feminist Jungians, that is, Jungians who may resist stereotypical formulations, but who do not claim a feminist perspective. Two examples here are Charles Ponce and Eugene Monick. Ponce (1988) questions both the content and formation of the Jungian concepts of "feminine" and "masculine," but he does not seem to doubt their fundamentally instinctual nature. Monick is the author of a number of books and essays on "the masculine" and men. Though he works out of a gender-based model, he does take a strong stand against conventional Jungian views on male homosexuality. He insists that homosexuality "never has been pathological" and he argues that "it is as wrong for psychoanalysis to judge where a man should be on the continuum of the homosexual radical as it would be to judge a man's masculinity by the size of his penis" (1987: 115–116, quoted in Hopcke 1989: 121). Other essays by Monick, however, strike me as somewhat heterosexist. For example, in a recent essay (1993) he links male homosexuality, with some apologies, to narcissism. In addition, Monick seems committed to maintaining gender as a meaningful category.

Finally, the third sub-group in this category consists of a number of Jungians who have been active in trying to alter Jungian perspectives on homosexuality. In this group are openly gay analysts (such as John Beebe and Scott Wirth) and non-analysts (such as Robert Hopcke, Karin Lofthus Carrington, and Mitchell Walker), as well as a number of analysts who presumably are not gay/lesbian (such as Robert Bosnak, James Hillman, and Donald Sandner). Unfortunately, most of their work is hampered by their continued use of gendered language and imagery. For example, Beebe (1993) is firmly attached to finding some way to salvage contrasexuality; Wirth (1993a) is hopelessly entangled in "the masculine" and "the feminine"; and Walker (1991) seems immersed in gendered images of brothers, fathers, and sons. While it may be difficult to avoid gendered images when dealing with the topic of same-sex attractions, because they are already framed in gendered language, unless we try to break out of that language, we will be condemned to it possibly forever.

I had once thought that Bosnak, who has done a lot of clearly unbiased work with gay men, might be a Radical Jungian. After all, in an essay on same-sex love, he acknowledges that same-sex love is "a primal urge of creation" that "does not follow nature's path of multiplication, thus giving birth to imagination" (1993: 272). However, in a later interview with Pamela Donleavy, Bosnak discussed "a new form of feminine communication" which he calls "symbiotic communication" (Donleavy 1996: 4). Not only does he not rebuff the interviewer's remark that he seems "to be in contact with a feminine energy that even most females can't get to,"[7] but he also goes on to make the tedious and offensive link between women and "bodily, emotional intelligence" (ibid.). It was at that point that I realized that while Bosnak may not be homophobic, his thinking is still unbearably sexist.

While Hillman's work is more promising in some ways – that is, I can appreciate the pluralistic flavor of his archetypal psychology and his rebellious efforts to dismantle favorite Jungian concepts (like "the opposites" and "wholeness") – his work generally does not break with the fundamentals of Jungian gendered thinking (as evidenced by his current involvement with certain aspects of "the men's movement"). And even Sandner, who presents a very sympathetic view of homosexual relationships, still feels compelled to observe that they are "less stable over time" than heterosexual relationships because they involve partners who are "too much alike in certain important aspects" (i.e. gender) (1993: 226).

Hopcke is the only writer I know of who suggests "a coherent theory of sexual orientation" (1989: 9). He sets out several requirements that he believes must be met by a new Jungian theory of sexual orientation. It must: (1) address all sexual orientations; (2) be archetypally based; (3) incorporate a sense of "meaning and purpose" (ibid.: 131); and (4) avoid Jung's confusion of anatomical sex/gender roles/sexual orientation and correct the inadequacies of traditional definitions of masculinity and femininity. In keeping with these requirements, Hopcke proposes a theory that he describes as "both simple and elegant":

The sexual orientation of an individual or any group of individuals is determined through a complex interaction of the archetypal masculine, the archetypal feminine, and the archetypal Androgyne
(ibid.: 132, emphasis in original).

Needless to say, I was profoundly disappointed in this. I cannot see how such a gendered and heterosexually-based image is going to get us anywhere.

Carrington hopes that her essay of 1990 (which is the only

Jungian work in this category that is entirely devoted to lesbian experience) will be a catalyst for reforming Jungian theory and practice. I am not sure that she achieves her goal. Parts of her article are thought-provoking and promising, but her attempt to codify lesbian experience (into the ever-Jungian "four" patterns of lesbian love and individuation) is limiting.

In the first pattern, "I. Return to the Source," a lesbian seeks "the original source of our wholeness," not by setting "*out* to imitate the man's heroic journey of separation in which the ego is first dismembered and later rebuilt" (since "women are already dismembered"), but by setting "*in* – and back *in* further" (1990: 69). Relationships in this pattern are "in response to some cellular need to merge again and then re-emerge more complete" (ibid.: 70). She illustrates this pattern by referring to the myth of Demeter and Persephone. The second pattern, "II. Reunion with the Lost Sister Self," involves an erotic attachment between women which allows a woman to incorporate "her shadow self" (ibid.: 74). To illustrate this woman "divided against herself," Carrington refers to the stories of Inanna/Ereshkigal and Eve/Lilith (ibid). In "III. Remembering My Self: Twinning," one woman comes to love another "through the twinning of the Self" with this other woman (ibid.: 76). This idea, which precedes but is similar to Walker's idea of the "Double," involves a kind of mirroring process. The danger, Carrington warns, is of "imitating one another" (ibid.: 78). The last pattern, "IV. Re-Creation of Social Organization and Values," involves a shift from an androcentric perspective to something more "gynocentric" (ibid.: 79). There is another reunion here, but not "with a personal mother" (ibid.). Rather, this reunion represents a "remembering of the empathic bonding with the Source" (ibid.: 80) and women are called upon "to form a true partnership with their internalized masculine and with the men in their community" in order to dissolve "the boundary between masculine and feminine" (ibid.: 81).

Carrington notes that each of these patterns contains an image of "two aspects of women's selves which have been separated by the patriarchal system and are longing for reunion in an embodied merger," that is, they "yearn to recollect their dismembered selves" (ibid.: 69). This is a powerful image that Carrington undermines when, a sentence or two later, she argues that these patterns also present "an opportunity for reconciliation with some aspect of woman's internalized masculine" (ibid.) – a concept which she never explains or defines (and which I would be inclined to call "internalized heterosexism"). In any case, why introduce the idea of "the masculine" at all? If lesbians do not need men for individuation, why do we need "the masculine"? If we argue (as she does) that love between women is an attraction of "like to like," why not simply declare that "complementarity" and "contra-sexuality" are irrelevant to lesbians? And if we do not need "the masculine" . . . well, then, maybe we do not need "the feminine" either?

Although I appreciate Carrington's use of powerful mythological themes, I am very uncomfortable that there are exactly and only four of them, and that there are a number of notably missing themes, for example, more dramatic ones like "The Call of the Amazon" – the image of a strong, independent lesbian woman who might, or might not, choose to be in any romantic relationships (e.g. Athene and Artemis) or who, like Lilith, has tried men and found them wanting.

The Radicals

The Radicals are the Jungians who are intent on taking Jung in entirely new directions, beyond himself (and usually in spite of himself). They are the iconoclasts, the freethinkers, the agitators, the renegades. They are on the cutting edge, as I see it, of Jungian feminist thought. This is not a crowded category. In it are openly lesbian analysts Lyn Cowan and Caroline Stevens and non-gay analysts Peter Mudd and Andrew Samuels. These are analysts who have been vocal and unusually direct in expressing their desire to drastically re-vision Jung. And there are "outsiders" here, too, for example: Christine Downing, Naomi Goldenberg, and Demaris Wehr, all of whom have presented profound challenges to Jungian thinking on sexual orientation and gender. The strategy of the Radicals has been to focus on a number of concepts, typically considered sacred to conventional Jungians: gender, contra-sexuality, the animus, and the "feminine" and "masculine" prin-ciples. Radicals generally see these as ideas which are in desperate need of being deconstructed or even discarded if we are ever to see a change in Jungian attitudes and theories.

Naomi Goldenberg was one of the first feminist theorists to confront and critique Jung's idea of the animus. She argues that Jung's concepts of anima/animus "serve as smoke screens" and are really "descriptions of cultural conditions that are rooted in history" (1979: 60). To pretend that such "stereotypes are archetypes can only impede progress," she notes (ibid.: 61). But Goldenberg, a feminist theologian, has never had much of a hearing within official Jungian circles.

Demaris Wehr, also a feminist concerned with the psychology of religion, was probably the first feminist theorist to really engage Jung's idea of the animus while also critiquing it. She is truly intent on building a bridge between Jung and feminism, so her critique is not a very harsh one – after all, she does not want feminists to give up on Jung altogether; she wants them to find something worthwhile in him. Her critique, therefore, fails to deconstruct contrasexuality as such, but her feminist analysis and her attempt to de-ontologize the animus go far in breaking ground for that project. So, while Wehr may not be an extreme radical, I believe she qualifies for this category. Wehr's intent is to liberate or dissociate the idea of archetypes from the realm of the sacred by pointing out how this link has been 'used' to depotentiate women. For example, Wehr, making reference to the work of Doris Lessing, Mary Daly, and Jean Baker Miller, argues that women have internalized patriarchal society's definition of "woman" into an image she calls "the self-hater" (1987: 18), an image whose "voice cripples women from within" (ibid.: 20) and leaves them feeling "uniquely deficient and inadequate" (ibid.: 18). Jungians would call this the "negative animus." Wehr calls it "internalized oppression" (ibid.: 10). Wehr appreciates that, in spite of its flaws, the idea of the animus historically "has meant a great deal to many women" because it gave women access to qualities of "natural female authority, logic, and rationality" via "their 'masculine side'" (ibid.: 122). She believes this is "more liberating than not claiming them at all." In addition, Wehr points out that Jung's appreciation of "the feminine" (questionable though that may appear to us today) allowed women to "feel vindicated in a way of being that our society does not value" (ibid.).

Although I agree at the historical level with Wehr's observations, I am uncomfortable with how she then settles simply for reworking the animus. She calls for a "positive" or "integrated animus" (ibid.: 121). "De-ontologized and contextualized," she argues, "Jung's anima and animus can be useful to women and men" (ibid.: 124). I disagree. Do we still really need to call these repressed qualities "masculine" in order to reclaim them? It seems to me that feminist Jungians need to push beyond maneuvers which attempt to salvage concepts which are intrinsically harmful. However, it is important to point out that, although Wehr does not call for a total rejection of the animus concept, she does *not* romanticize the concept either (as Douglas and others have done) and she does recognize that its creation is a construction attributable less to re-pression than op-pression. That is, the animus is not simply a collection of "masculine" qualities that a woman can suddenly access and "integrate." It is an internalized reflection of patriarchal proscriptions. When women introject the animus, they are swallowing society's idea that "the feminine" is complementary and inferior to "the masculine." It seems to me that the only way women and men will ever be free to access repressed "contrasexual" qualities will be when we demolish the categories of gender altogether.

Christine Downing has written two books which are particularly significant as vehicles of a radical feminist critique of Jung. The earlier one, *Myths and Mysteries of Same Sex Love* (1989), has already been discussed. Her later book, *Women's Mysteries: Towards a Poetic of Gender* (1992), which is dedicated to Esther Harding, is aimed at articulating "how complexly body and soul are intertwined in the psychology of women" (1992: xii). Downing approaches her task rather hermeneutically, asking us to go past traditional interpretations of both Freud and Jung and to engage instead in "midrashic interpretations of the received texts" (ibid.: 45). She appreciates that we need to work "in relation to a tradition," but attests that her own thinking emerges most creatively "through a never quite ending dialogue with Freud and Jung" (ibid.).

Downing brings a radical perspective to her interpretation of Jung. There have been many "outsider" attacks on Jung, but very few engage Jung with the kind of insight, respect, and obvious affection accorded to him by Downing. Downing's critique of Jung's theories are generally in line with other feminist critiques and with the points made by other radical Jungians (although I have heard her say that she is not "a Jungian"). She notes, for example, the heterosexism imbedded in Jung's idea of contrasexuality; she insists on putting terms like "feminine" in quotation marks; she faults Jung for having derived his concept of the animus from his own experience of his own inner life (thus leaving Jungians with a psychology of "the feminine" based on male experience); and she observes "how smoothly [Jung] elides the distinction between 'feminine' and 'female'" (1992: 54). What I find most powerful about Downing's work, as much as her radical views, is the depth of personal experience she brings to it, the ways in which she weaves her self (lesbian or otherwise) into her work, and her ability to be a bridge or mediator constantly in dialogue with and between Freud and Jung, thus bringing great depth to depth psychology.

Andrew Samuels has garnered much international attention even while his radical analyses have generally been overlooked by mainstream Jungians. Samuels has virtually single-handedly led an assault on a number of Jungian ideas precious to most Jungians. He has attacked the reductive use of "opposites," proposing instead the attitude of pluralism (already discussed above), he has pointed out problems inherent in the use of the concept of "contrasexuality," he has questioned gender as a construct, and he has challenged us to look "Beyond the feminine principle" (and, by necessity, beyond "the masculine principle" as well) (1989b: 92).

Samuels, who is avowedly feminist, criticizes "the mythopoetic men's movement" for failing "to understand the traditional nuclear family as a *source* of oppression" (1992: 54), for being driven by a "fear of homosexuality" (ibid.: 57), and for promoting patterns which rather than change anything effectively only serve to "legitimize what already exists" (ibid.). He argues that society has more to learn from "the transgressive styles of family organization – the so-called marginal or deviant lifestyles" (for example, from "two lesbians bringing up a son together") than from "cliches about restoring the father's authority within the family" (ibid.: 54). In addition, Samuels suggests that it is "the existence of a thriving gay community" that ultimately will undermine "a social system that deploys heterosexism to maintain control of women" (ibid.: 59).

Samuels' analyses are consistently feminist and political. He pulls no punches in analyzing the role of men in the patriarchy and notes that "it is disingenuous to divorce 'men' from 'the patriarchy.'" (ibid.: 55). Although "men have no monopoly on the ruthless misuse of power," the fact is that "in today's world men have power *and* a power complex, whereas women have only the complex" (ibid.). Samuels ends his critique of the mythopoetic men's movement with a comment that saddens me even while it gives me hope for men as a whole:

One goal of the mythopoetic men's movement is to try to make men feel 'good' about being men. I must say that I cannot see why one has to feel good about being a man; I feel ambivalent about it.

(ibid.: 60)

Perhaps his ambivalence is exactly what is needed to undermine the patriarchal structures which have been erected and maintained by Jung, Jungians, and others in the name of psychology.

Lyn Cowan, in an unpublished paper entitled "Dismantling the Animus" (1994) has put forward the most profound, thorough, and entertaining critique yet launched against contrasexuality and the animus.[8] In this paper, Cowan argues that Jung's animus theory is more stereotype than archetype and that it forces a woman to live in a state of split consciousness whereby she must attribute to the animus what more properly belongs to her ego-identity. Cowan attacks Jung and Jungians for their naiveté in imagining that the "masculine" and "feminine" principles could be equal in a culture in which men and women are so clearly unequal and for imagining individuation "like a balancing act, two sides together fair and equal, making an androgyne" (ibid.: 48). Much like Wehr, Cowan exposes the animus as the introjection by women of patriarchal culture. Women do not create "the man's world" by projection, so, to tell a woman that she should "'take back' her 'animus projection' from the world 'out there' is like telling her to inhale carbon monoxide to cure her headache" (ibid.: 89).

Cowan recommends that we give up on trying to rehabilitate the concept of the animus. She sees "no value in coining a new word for an old concept" or in trying to reformulate the concept in order to keep the old word (ibid.: 108). She wants "to throw out the whole raggedy animus mantle. I don't like the style, the fabric is worn, the stitching is shabby, the buttons are missing, it doesn't fit" (ibid.: 20). She wants to take it apart, unravel it, and dis-mantle it in order to expose it "as a male fantasy of women that obscures and even denies women's actual experience of themselves" (ibid.). This is a truly radical departure from the usual terms of the Jungian debate over whether the concept of the animus has any value for women today and it strikes at the very heart of Jungian theory. Cowan notes, among other things, that if Jungians would stop using the term animus we might be able to "free ourselves from a chronic heterosexism that keeps us psychologically impoverished" (ibid.: 100).

Cowan links her attack on the animus to an overall attack on contrasexuality and the heterosexism of Jungian theory. She presents a stinging (only sometimes tongue-in-cheek) critique of heterosexuality and its assumption that "the Other" must always be "opposite." She maintains that the institution of heterosexuality exists only in order "to support all other male-dominated institutions by insuring that men retain power in sexual form" (ibid.: 71). Picking up on Jung's various remarks about one-sidedness, Cowan concludes that it is heterosexuality which "is the locus of one of our culture's root neuroses," that is, it is heterosexuality which is "adamantly one-sided" (ibid.: 82). In addition, because heterosexuality is taken to be so "normal," it is also taken for granted – and, thus, it is essentially unconscious. Therefore, we might even say that heterosexuality is "a compulsive neurosis" (ibid.: 85). Cowan ends her essay with a heartfelt warning:

> If we cannot extricate ourselves from the labyrinthine patterns of genderism, sexism, heterosexism, and all other confining isms, our entire species must remain psychologically imprisoned and physically on the brink of disaster. It will take many minds, and every contribution, every milligram of consciousness, counts.
>
> (ibid.: 109)

Peter Mudd's unpublished work on these topics has already been referred to and discussed in Chapter 3, so I will not repeat those ideas here. However, I will call attention to a suggestion he has made in an unpublished paper entitled "Jung and the Split Feminine" (1992) that it is time for Jungians to discard *both* the anima and animus and to question other basic Jungian constructs such as the so-called "feminine" and "masculine" principles. Mudd presents a strong case for seeing all of these constructs as products of Jung's personal psychology.

Caroline Stevens is included here with some hesitation. Her earlier writings and lectures would put her squarely in the Reformulator camp, but her more recent work (including a lecture presented in October 1993)[9] certainly exhibits dramatic movement toward the radical fringes of Jungian thought. She has begun to question, though still somewhat cautiously, the familiar Jungian concepts of gender, complementarity, the "feminine principle," etc., and she has been vocal and forthright in sharing her own lesbian experience. While she has not yet rejected the concept of the animus, she has begun challenging its "archetypal status" and questioning whether it is "inherently and exclusively masculine" (1992: 190, 189). I include her here because I believe she is still on the move.

FROM PSYCHOANALYTIC LITERATURE

Although I cannot claim a great depth of knowledge in relation to psychoanalytic thought, its early influence on the development of Jung's ideas and its power to shape current perceptions of homosexuality lead me to believe that no study of lesbian experience would be complete without some discussion of psychoanalysis' role in contemporary theorizing of lesbianism. In addition, most of the criticisms which are being leveled at traditional psychoanalytic thought are easily translatable into Jungian language and applicable to Jungian theory.

The differing tasks of psychoanalysis and analytical psychology

While the Jungian world seems to have slept through the past decades of gay and lesbian activity and theorizing, psychoanalytic writers have been busy formulating theories of gay and lesbian sexuality. The task facing psychoanalysis in this area is in many ways rather distinct from the one facing analytical psychology since each movement has been shaped by the views of its respective founder. Freud's interest in sexuality and his greater willingness to engage and accept a wider spectrum of sexual behaviors has produced a fairly voluminous body of writings on the topic of homosexuality. Jung, on the other hand, was inclined to reconceptualize sexual issues as spiritual strivings and so the literature of analytical psychology is relatively sparse on the topic of homosexuality. In addition, conceptualizations of homosexuality in both schools were born of the "complexes" of their respective founders. For example, psychoanalytic theory is characterized to a great extent by a phallocentric bias, a search for causes, a focus on early childhood experiences and the primacy to the sex drive, and the pursuit of systematic explanations. Analytical psychology, on the other hand, is distinguishable by its focus on the archetype of the Great Mother, its teleological concern with finding meaning, its focus on later life developments and spiritual explanations, and its insistence on individual facts. This is not to imply that psychoanalysis and analytical psychology do not share a lot of (usually negative) common ground, for example: a preoccupation with dualistic and polarized dichotomies, a homophobic conflation of gender and sexuality, a blindness toward the effects of oppression on an individual, and "the unreflective incorporation of social norms into notions of maturity" (O'Connor and Ryan 1993: 13).

Jungian writings on the topic of homosexuality are generally just as negative and dismissive as those of psychoanalytic authors. There are just not as many of them. So, as I see it, the task facing psychoanalytic thinkers is primarily one of undoing the rippling effects of an extensive body of theory in order to get to the work of creating new theory – while the task for Jungian writers is primarily one of creating new theory in order to present homosexuality itself as a viable and purposeful area of inquiry. I am not sure which is the easier task, but I believe that the following comment about psychoanalysis from O'Connor and Ryan might just as easily be said of analytical psychology: "Homosexuality provides an interesting case study of the perversion of psychoanalytic methods and values. . . . . it has been the site of some of the worst excesses of psychoanalysis" (ibid.: 13, 14). This suggests, they propose, "that we are at the nexus of some unthinkable anxieties" (ibid.: 14).

Contemporary psychoanalytic perspectives on lesbianism

The last few years have witnessed the appearance of many articles and essays on lesbianism written by psychoanalytic authors. Many of these continue on traditional paths searching out causes, presenting pathologized views, and generally ignoring the impact on lesbians of living in a culture which equates lesbianism with "evidence of sinful character, disturbed or arrested psychological development, socially disruptive behavior, and disordered femininity" (Magee and Miller 1996: 191–192). On the other hand, there is also a growing literature that is striking out in new directions. I will be looking at two of these, both of which are particularly outstanding and pioneering examples of new psychoanalytic theorizing on lesbianism.[10] Each of these books has a different objective and therefore different strengths. In *Wild Desires and Mistaken Identities: Lesbianism and Psychoanalysis* (1993), Noreen O'Connor and Joanna Ryan undertake an ambitious and systematic account of psychoanalytic theory with the aim of telling us essentially how psychoanalysis got here from there and where it needs to go now. In *Lesbians and Psychoanalysis: Revolutions in Theory and Practice* (1995), editors Judith Glassgold and Suzanne Iasenza have gathered together a collection of essays written by a wide range of psychoanalytically oriented writers. Their aim "is to liberate psychoanalysis from its colonial legacy" and their focus is primarily on clinical material, though a number of the essays do have theoretical implications (1995: xxiv).

Wild desires and mistaken identities

O'Connor and Ryan attribute psychoanalysis' failure to incorporate a nonpathological view of lesbian experience to the many unexamined presuppositions which underlie existing theories about homosexuality. The task, as they see it, is to determine exactly what needs to be changed in order to revise psychoanalytic views of homosexuality.

As a way of establishing a framework for their critique, O'Connor and Ryan propose that there are three categories of concern:

1 *Questions of theory* Here they identify several goals: the removal of heterosexuality from its position as the normative standard, an acknowledgment of lesbianism's diversity and complexities, and a recognition that social forces have constitutive power in the formation of lesbian identity. O'Connor and Ryan call for a critical attitude informed by postmodern thinking and for a "post-phenomenological" approach (1993: 15) which will avoid causal/reductive explanations and universal claims to truth.

2 *Language and identity* O'Connor and Ryan note that "the centrality of language to the process of psychoanalysis" makes urgent the need for new terms and a new language capable of describing lesbian experience (ibid.: 21).

3 *Textual and clinical matters* O'Connor and Ryan devote about half their book to identifying, discussing, and critiquing many of the main texts of psychoanalytic literature. It is far beyond the scope of this book even to summarize their very detailed and thorough review, but I will run through a very condensed version of the chain they follow in the next few paragraphs.

They start with Freud, presenting both his inconsistencies as well

113

as some of his promising insights, including his recognition that heterosexuality is itself a problematic in need of elucidation. Next they discuss the analysts (Horney, Jones, and Riviere) who effectively departed from Freud's more accepting views and cast lesbians in the role of "the masculine woman" who identifies with the father. This is followed by a consideration of Deutsch's mother/child view of lesbian relationships and then by a critique of Klein's very negative view of lesbianism "as oral-sadistic, destructive, fixated at the paranoid-schizoid position" (ibid.: 74). Next, they turn to two groups of more contemporary writers: first, a group of those who conceptualize homosexuality as some form of perversity (e.g. Socarides, McDougall) and then a group of French analysts (Lacan, Irigaray, Kristeva) whose works seem generally to fall short of fulfilling their promising potential. Finally, and to my great surprise, they allot an entire chapter to considering Jung's position. They give him a rather fair hearing, pointing out where his ideas align with Freud's and where they differ. They consider and challenge some of Hopcke's interpretations and criticize the work of feminist Jungians for remaining entrenched in oppositional categories and for not including references to lesbian experience. In the end, they question the Jungian concept of archetypes (especially "the masculine," "the feminine," and the "androgyne") and note the ways in which these archetypes serve to uphold ideas of "gender conformity" (ibid.: 173).

The rest of this book is devoted to an in-depth summary and critique of psychoanalytic theory as it applies to lesbianism, and most of their analysis has great applicability to Jungian theory as well. They are concerned with scrutinizing both the theoretical and the personal prejudices which interfere with the ability of psychoanalysis to meaningfully theorize lesbianism. Theoretical prejudices, they observe, have produced the two prevalent but inadequate models of homosexuality ("identification with the father/masculine" and the dyad of "mother/child"). They counter the former account by making two points: (1) if lesbianism is due to identification with the masculine, then how does psychoanalytic theory account for "the 'other' woman, the supposedly feminine one, who desires another woman" (ibid.: 174)?; and (2) sexuality cannot be reduced to the penis as if it were "the uncontestable standard" for mature sexual activity (ibid.: 176). They then move on to dispose of the "mother/child" model: (1) for its failure to envision "a mature sexuality between two women" (ibid.: 175); (2) for being so fixated on "enmeshed and pre-oedipal" versions of the mother–child relationship that it is unable to conceptualize other interpretations of any mother/child aspects of a lesbian relationship (ibid.: 188); and (3) for promoting reified interpretations whereby any woman to whom a lesbian is attracted is literalized into her mother.

In terms of the personal prejudices, O'Connor and Ryan take note of psychoanalysis' relative lack of attention to counter-transferential issues in relation to homosexual patients. They determine that this is one of psychoanalysis' "defences against lesbian eroticism" (ibid.: 179) and link it to the reluctance of many lesbian patients to talk about their sexuality. They also discuss how the tendency to take gender "too literally" limits the ways one thinks and feels about gender and how it forces a view of homo-sexuality that privileges "the sameness of gender" above all other features of homosexual experience (ibid.: 189, 190), noting that this is a reductive and overly simplified view of the experience of "belonging to a gender" which assumes that any two people have a similar experience of gender (ibid.: 191).

In an effort to locate some more dissenting voices and to further illustrate how the relationship between psychoanalysis and lesbian-ism is "fundamentally political" (ibid.: 235), O'Connor and Ryan broaden their search and invite other voices into their discussion, including a number of psychoanalytically oriented writers whose work has been largely ignored and some feminist writers. They criticize feminist theorizing in this area as "extremely limited in both its extent and its ideas" (ibid.: 209). Although they are somewhat disappointed with Horney and Thompson (who might be seen as prototypal feminists), they are much more deeply disappointed with, and critical of, a number of modern feminist psychoanalytic thinkers (e.g. Dinnerstein, Mitchell, Chodorow, Eichenbaum, Orbach, Benjamin) whose writings presuppose "a fundamental heterosexual frame" and are strikingly devoid of any substantial discussion of lesbianism (ibid.: 216). They cite a few feminist psychoanalytic writers who are attempting to theorize lesbian sexuality (e.g. Hamer and Adams), but are critical of the particular ways in which each either omits or limits considerations of how lesbian desire might impact on psychoanalytic theory in general. O'Connor and Ryan then briefly review various models of lesbian psychology. They consider the prevalence of "fusion" and "merger" theories among these, but find these to be too simplistic and homogenizing and argue that attempts to establish lesbian psychologies (even in the plural) should be abandoned since these are inherently reductive, assuming as they do that "lesbians have something in common psychologically by virtue of being lesbian" (ibid.: 234). While they concede that lesbians living in a homophobic world may share certain experiences, problems, and dilemmas, they argue that this does not necessarily "create a descriptive or ontological category" (ibid.).

O'Connor and Ryan discuss the concept of identification in the context of sexuality and desire. Identification is said to be the process by which one develops into "what one would like to *be*" (i.e. one identifies with persons of the same sex) and it is counterposed to the question of "what one would like to *have*" (i.e. one's sexual object choice, namely, persons of the other sex) (ibid.: 239). They point out that while this could led the way to recognizing that "masculinity and femininity are not present from birth" but must be constructed (ibid.: 242), psychoanalysis has continued to link these concepts to biological sex and thus to infer gender as a given. From there we are led in a straight line (so to speak) through a series of steps: Since there are only two sexes, every person must belong to one of those sexes. Since the two sexes are complementary, homosexuality must be the result of an identification gone "wrong" and of "a failed or deviant development" (ibid.: 237, 245). Thus have gender and sexual desire become inextricably linked in psychoanalytic (and other) theorizing, often causing many to feel self-hate, shame, self-doubt, etc.

O'Connor and Ryan conclude their book with a brief postscript in which they point out the challenges awaiting psychoanalysis if it is to find some way of conceptualizing lesbianism non-pathologically: the many points of theory that would need to be unraveled, the various assumptions about gender that would need to be relinquished, the cherished notions that would need to be rethought, the language and terms that would need to be revised, the developmental schemas that would need to be retooled. They are left wondering what will become of ideas like:

> the classical Oedipus conflict as the required passport to sexual maturity, the breaking of the maternal dyad by the intervention of a paternal figure, and the gendered split that is supposed to be achieved between who is identified with (same-sex) and who is desired (different sex)?
>
> (ibid.: 268)

116

These are hard-hitting questions which make clear what is at stake. In order to accommodate a meaningful theory of lesbianism, psychoanalysis would have to change, and change drastically, because its very foundational concepts would be undermined and exposed as inadequate. Although the particular concerns expressed by O'Connor and Ryan are specific to psychoanalysis, the kind of theoretical problems they raise might just as well be addressed to Jungian theorists. Jungian theory, too, would have to be examined, dismantled, and overhauled, its reliance on contrasexuality as an explanatory principle would have to be abandoned, its sacred notions would have to be scrutinized, and its obsession with various "opposites" would have to be re-imagined. O'Connor and Ryan wonder whether psychoanalysis is up to such a task, whether it is ready to adopt the pluralistic view that would be demanded. They close their book with an ambiguous remark: "Our hope is that such a strategy will avoid the splitting off of lesbians from psychoanalysis, and will hold the tension of complexity and ambiguity in order to enhance the lives of people who seek to engage in psychoanalytic psychotherapy" (ibid.: 274). Are they optimistic or is this a caveat? And what would we say about analytical psychology? Is it willing and ready to reconsider itself?

Lesbians and psychoanalysis

Glassgold and Iasenza organize the essays in their book into three major sections: theoretical issues, clinical concerns, and future implications. The essays in the first section treat psychoanalytic theory more generally than O'Connor and Ryan's detailed analysis. The authors of these essays take psychoanalysis to task for imposing its prejudices on lesbian clients under the guise of theory, for continuing to insist that homosexuality is abnormal and pathological, for retaining questionable and reductive assumptions about the development and meaning of homosexuality, and for failing to get beyond the limitations imposed by modernity. Alternative viewpoints are presented, most of which are cogent condensations or elaborations of many of the points made by O'Connor and Ryan. In addition, an alternative account of lesbian development is included which challenges many of psychoanalysis' assumptions by incorporating a feminist analysis of various relational, social, and cultural factors which play a part in lesbian development.

The second set of essays is focused on clinical issues and on those aspects of psychoanalytic theory which significantly limit psycho-analysis' relevance to members of non-dominant groups. There is an attempt here to incorporate "queer theory" into a discussion of lesbian development, to identify the factors which distinguish the psychological challenges lesbians are likely to experience by virtue of their being lesbian, to elaborate on the social, historical, and cultural contexts which produce particular intrapsychic conflicts, and to propose ways of rectifying psychoanalysis' racist, sexist, and heterosexist assumptions.

The last series of essays is directed toward developing new ideas in relation to lesbian theorizing. There are efforts here to con-ceptualize the marginalized experience of being lesbian, to offer more empowering and less reductive and devaluing accounts of lesbian development and sexuality, to address and/or deconstruct psychoanalytic notions of self, gender, identity, and the hetero-sexual imperative, to propose alternative guidelines for conceptual-izing the therapeutic frame, and to introduce feminist revisionings into psychoanalytic theorizing. Included in this last section is a chapter by Downing in which she again facilitates a discussion between Jungian and Freudian theory and crafts "An Archetypal View of Lesbian Identity" which is very engaging.

Some of the essays in this book attempt to break new ground, while others seem to reflect a conservative penchant as they try to rescue the concepts of gender, "masculinity," and "femininity," in order to use them to provide new explanations and descriptions of lesbian experience. Yet, I would say that Glassgold and Iasenza have fulfilled their primary goal – "to liberate psychoanalysis from its colonial legacy by integrating the truths of lesbian lives with psychoanalysis to develop new frames of vision for psychoanalytic theory and practice" (1995: xxiv) – by providing an open forum for new ideas.

8

"SANDRA"

PROFILE

Sandra is a 44-year-old white woman who was born in Canada of a Canadian mother and American father, but has lived in the United States for most of her adult life. She was married to a man for eighteen years, but is now divorced and shares joint custody of two pre-adolescent daughters. Although Sandra had had a physical relationship with her roommate at boarding school, she does not consider that to have been a lesbian relationship. Sandra got involved in her first lesbian relationship about three months before this interview.

INTERVIEW SETTING/PROCESS

I knew Sandra for several years prior to this interview, but we had become close friends only in the year or two before the interview. We had spent many hours talking about deeply personal matters and she had allowed me to observe her in her individuation process, a process in which she has been engaged diligently, long, and consciously. In addition, Sandra brought to this discussion her profoundly psychological outlook on life. I believe that all of this contributed to the highly personal level at which Sandra explored my question with me.

THE INTERVIEW

Since Sandra's experience of coming out is quite recent, the focus of her response was on that experience: how she has negotiated it and what it has meant to her so far. Sandra is rigorously

119

self-examining. She has watched herself, observed the process, and thought a lot about how it has impacted her life. One of the things she has noticed is how very hard it has been "to find language" for this experience because "it has been such a feeling experience and not an intellectual one – though there are parts that are that, too." And because it is all so new, she is particularly aware of the ways it has required her to change.

The decision to come out was a process for Sandra that involved a struggle to get to a place from which she could allow herself "to let go of things that I thought kept me safe – restrictions, perspectives, views." For Sandra, to be safe has meant to feel "in control" and to avoid situations where she would not know the outcome. To get involved with a woman she had to let go of these things "in favor of following something far less understood within myself" and "without knowing where it would go." This "something" she could describe only as "a feeling or a wanting – an experience of energy." The process of letting go did not happen smoothly or all at once. It "kept starting and stopping" as she kept "trying to do it right." What she has learned from this is that by letting go of the need to control the outcome, she has "opened up to this incredibly rich part of my life that I would not have had access to otherwise."

When Sandra first allowed herself to realize that she was feeling strongly attracted to a woman, she was afraid. For two weeks, she experienced a time of "terror." It was a feeling of "Oh, no, I don't want this to be happening" and a fear that if she did not do something to stop it, she "was going to be entering into the realm of being out of control." Sandra associates much of this reaction to her concerns with how this would affect her kids and her fear of making a mistake that would hurt the other person if things did not work out. This was a moral decision: could she proceed without knowing the outcome if it might hurt others?

Sandra's concern for her children has been one aspect of her resistance to coming out and a major factor in her current decision making: what will "coming out" mean to them, how will it affect their lives, will they be able to handle it, how it will be for them to go to school the day after she tells them "that their Mom's a dyke" (knowing they will take with them this "incomplete version" of what it means to love a woman)? How will it be for them if they feel they need to keep it secret? More than anything, Sandra fears that her own experience of having been emotionally abandoned by her parents will become their experience when she comes out to them. She fears that she has mothered them in a way that will not prepare them for dealing with this. But she is committed to telling them, knowing she cannot live feeling as split as she does at the moment.

When Sandra thinks about all that has happened over the past few months, she can see that, in the end, her decision to proceed was made really within the larger context of her past experiences and history. She can look back at certain past experiences "that now look much more like an attraction to women or at least a woman-based way of looking at the world that I've had for a long time." She remembers telling a friend three years ago: "I don't want to be gay." It is obvious to her that her feelings for women did not spring up suddenly in the past few months. This is a part of her that has "always been there" though it was not accessible to her. Whenever these feelings had come up in the past, she had had no framework within which to look at them, no way to make them "tolerable," so she would discount them.

Sandra had spent a good part of her life "trying to fit into a heterosexual world" where she thought she was "supposed" to find a partner. This had involved a life-long struggle "of not fitting in," of trying not to take that on as a failing, of "trying to interpret how I could be seen in that world and get what I wanted from that world," of needing to believe "that things might change," of feeling overall a lot of sadness, aloneness, and anger. There were men out there who had what she wanted ("the other side of a relationship"), but she could not understand how to get access to them in a way that would be acceptable to her. She never felt acceptable "in a heterosexual gender-conscious world," so she would find herself "trying to stretch what was acceptable" to her. But this would only leave her feeling inadequate because she was unwilling to present herself to the heterosexual world in ways that were acceptable to it. Her lesbian friends, on the other hand, would tell her – even before she came out – that she was attractive. This gave Sandra a "sense of being appreciated" among women for how she presented herself as a woman in that world.

Sandra spoke of the heterosexual world as if it were "out there somewhere" and she were somewhere on the outside – which is how she has always felt. "How that's changed is that it just doesn't matter anymore." She is clear now, both intellectually and emotion-ally, that her inability to fit in was "not about me" and that she no longer needs anything from that world. She does not feel hostile or "anymore disconnected than I did before, but there isn't that struggle." Her relationships with the men she has known from before have not changed, but she no longer needs to ask herself the old questions in relation to any new men she meets. In most ways, however, her life has not changed much: "What my world looks like now is it's expanded to include one person – mostly that's the change." She also has the option now "of being part of another community" if she wants to. She will explore this over time with her lover, but Sandra does not feel a "need to belong to the lesbian world" just because she has always wanted "a world." At 44, she already has a life and a community of friends.

Once Sandra was able to allow herself to let go of trying to fit into the heterosexual world, she felt "a lot of relief." Coming out gave her "permission to stop" struggling, to recognize that trying to be heterosexual "wasn't necessarily the right thing for me to be doing – struggling in that way to get a whole life." Overall, Sandra's experience of loving a woman has not been comparable to her experience of loving men. It has not been an experience of "the same thing pointed in some different direction." Rather, it has been "almost not of the same universe" (although "the physical/sexual part . . . started off to seem similar because it was my body in both situations"). Sandra is constantly being made aware that this is an experience with aspects that "I haven't even conceived of yet."

> "I keep finding ways in which I experience myself in loving a woman that are so core to my sense of self and missing previously. There is a sense of being worthy and therefore of being able to take in what I so badly want."

What Sandra has wanted so badly is "not easily" expressed, but it includes wanting to feel loved and wanting to experience herself as worthy.

Sandra believes that a prerequisite to her coming out was her long struggle to claim an identity as a woman. She needed this before she could face the challenge of her sexual orientation: she needed to feel secure enough in her identity as a woman.

> "Part of my self-assessment in the heterosexual world has always been: 'Maybe the problem is that I'm not enough of

a woman – that I don't have these attributes that sell in that world enough.' So, if I'm not enough of a woman, what am I?"

Perhaps she was "too butch," she thought, remembering how she had been a tomboy as a little girl – how it had confused her: she was not allowed to just be herself. She needed to be "a little girl" as everyone expected. Today, she can see how all of this gave her an experience of feeling "less than." Sandra's experience of coming out has been "exactly the opposite: I am even enough of a woman to be in a loving relationship with a woman." She has come to see herself as having "enough" of the characteristics that are important to her and she refuses to let them go. Instead, she has "officially let go" of a definition of "woman" that was not hers to begin with, though she "bought into it enough" that it took her the better part of 40 years to get to a point where she felt able "to claim being a woman" as a part of her identity.

Sandra feels she is too new at loving another woman to claim lesbianism as a sense of identity. It will take time for her to sort this out – although she acknowledges that her sense of "gayness" cannot be dated simply in terms of the few months that have passed since she decided to act on her feelings. That act of coming out was, in fact, "a quantum leap" for her. At this point, Sandra feels comfortable internally saying something like "I'm a dyke" because it evokes the renegade part of her that she has always liked. But she also is "conscious of the value in the terms 'lesbian' and 'dyke' and, in my mind, of the respect they deserve." She is not sure that she has "a right to call herself a dyke after 44 years of heterosexual life" and only three months in this relationship with another woman. "People say that's what I am now and I don't have a problem with the label, but I'm not sure I can use it for myself without thinking I haven't earned it yet." In addition, she wonders at the implications of claiming to be a lesbian, as if "one day I wasn't a lesbian and the next day I am." She believes that time will change things; she can see that she feels differently now than she did even a month ago. She has noticed that as she does "more walking in the world knowing I'm in a relationship with a woman." She is looking at the world "with a new consciousness."

While Sandra acknowledges that the lesbian "piece" of her identity "has been out there" really since her adolescent experiences at boarding school, she also realizes that, for many years she "would not hold and bring in and look at" this aspect of herself. In effect, "at some level at varying points in my life. . . it has been a possibility [but] one that I chose not to think about."

Sandra sees a role for the lesbian community in this process of incorporating her gayness: if she were to claim lesbianism as an identity now, "it really becomes about describing behavior" and about whatever understanding she has taken from her lover. "Whereas if I have experiences in the community, then it becomes a much wider sense of identity." She is beginning to get some of this from lesbian friends who now consider her to be a part of their world. This "may be my first experience of being part of the community all on my own." She is not sure how large a part the lesbian community may play in her life. She already has "a sense of community as a part of my world that is very much woman-based – my friendships are my community and they are all women virtually." Hers is very much "a self-constructed community." She does not find much appeal in the idea of entering into an already-existing culture "because I know there are going to be parts that don't work for me." She is not sure that she wants to be seen as a member of any pre-established community. However, she loves the company of women and "if that's what that community has to offer, then I will like it."

Sandra feels that she has "always strongly identified with women" and seen them as "great people to be around." She has loved her women friends and even had wondered at times: "If I get along so well with women, what was I doing with my life?" But she had not felt a strong desire for a particular woman. It was only when she experienced such an attraction that she felt compelled to look at her feelings. Now she can say that the love she is experiencing in this relationship with another woman is "vastly different" from how she has loved women before. In some ways the "same stuff is there" that she has found with friends – this relationship, in fact, "came out of that." However, this love for this particular other woman

> "went into a much deeper and more complex and many-faceted experience because of the commitment that the sexual piece brought with it, the greater vulnerability, and the potential for so much more going back and forth between the two of us."

The sexual element of this relationship is a part of what makes it so different from Sandra's other intimate relationships with women. It is an aspect that she finds "so enormous." It seems to take her closer to wanting and needing "to risk knowing that about myself and engaging in experiencing that with someone else." For Sandra, "trying out something in the face of a need" is very different from just trying it out consciously. She feels that her decision to be with a woman was "a conscious choice" but that it "came out of hitting bottom." She had to allow herself to think "that there was maybe another way." As a result, the sexual piece of her relationship is

"very deep – it has its fingers in every part of my life and experience of the relationship and the way I experience myself and the other person, the way it shifts me in my day . . . and interacts with daring to want and need. To be alive in that way is not my common experience, but I find myself that way now in loving a woman."

Sandra entertains the possibility that she and this other woman are "just sexually compatible." But it seems more likely to her "that in loving a woman there is just this infinite stuff that's available to me now that wasn't before":

the capacity to feel connected, the capacity to feel pleasure, the need, the role that talking plays in it all, all the different levels on which communication takes place and how it's processed and what I do with it, how that feeds back into who I am to myself.

A lot of the feedback is at an intellectual level, because of all the talking that occurs between her and her lover. "But there seems to be an awful lot that goes on at an absolutely core level of being" which she relates to "all the ways in which I get to feel held and to hold, to feel who I am if I can hold."

I felt compelled by this second spontaneous reference to the word "core" to ask Sandra to say more about what "core" means to her.

"I think of what it isn't, which is intellect and maybe understanding. I think it's hard to have words for it. I think it's beyond or outside of words. It's more than just feeling. It's tone and body stuff and sense and energy."

125

Sandra struggled again to find language, starting and stopping several times as she attempted to give verbal expression to such a feeling experience. Finally, she said "maybe" it has to do with soul.

> "I don't know what soul is. . . . when I think of soul I think of something very uniquely mine and I certainly mean that by 'core' – sort of stamped with my identification, with all the potentials that I have. And I guess it does mean it's the part of me that's not restricted, not afraid, because I can't bring my intellect to bear on it, to fuck it up."

Sandra recognizes that this relationship with a woman has a "magical part" that is hard to talk about, but that feels like "a big component." By "magical" she means parts she does not understand but which feel very powerful because they "have energy that's unique to me. I don't even know how to think about them let alone talk about them. I just know they are there and I feel them." She has wondered whether or how much of her experience in this relationship is related specifically to loving someone who is a woman. It has seemed to her so far that loving another woman has not been problematic as such. Where the experience has been difficult is where it has led her "to come up against my own stuff." This has been an experience which has involved "lots of self-discovery" and "new experiences of parts of my personality that I wasn't able to be with before," especially her capacity to want and need. In this relationship, she has found herself inexplicably "open to the possibility that someone could care enough that I could therefore want enough and share my want." This had never seemed to be an option before: "I don't think I've ever trusted enough before to do that."

How she has come to trust so much is "sort of a mystery" to Sandra. She wonders whether this has to do with the individual person or with this being another woman. It is "certainly possible" that her sense of trust is related to gender, especially since the level at which she and her lover relate seems based to some extent "in the physical connection." It is there that Sandra comes to feel "it could be true that someone would care, that it could be true that I'm worth it." This is a new belief for Sandra "and trying on that belief based on trust is, at least in part, about it being a woman." She bases this both on her past experiences with men (where the quality of connection was different and she had less trust in those connections) and on her past experiences with women friends

("How is it that I have that kind of powerful relationship with ten
women in my world and none with men?"). Sandra has come to
the conclusion that many women in heterosexual relationships "let
go of the need for that connection because it isn't available." They
simply "don't expect to get what they need." In Sandra's experience, this has seemed like "an unspoken part of the deal" with
men. To return to relationships with men, she would have to accept
"the reality":

> "I'm not going to get this kind of communication, I'm not
> going to get this kind of holding, I'm not going to get this
> kind of understanding, I'm not going to get this kind of
> energy, I shouldn't expect to be responded to in this way, I
> shouldn't expect these needs to be met."

One aspect of coming out that has been especially meaningful to
Sandra has been the experience of coming out to friends, most of
whom were straight. She knew there was a risk that they might not
understand, but the overall accepting, even supportive, responses
she has received have made this experience "a time to really
reaffirm my value to them." Part of what grounded her through
this experience was that she had "an image of coming out" as a
positive experience. This was a choice she was making. "What kind
of a woman in middle age would make this choice?" she asked
herself. Her answer: "A woman I would like."

MY EXPERIENCE OF THE INTERVIEW

In the kind of methodology I am using, my previous relationship
with Sandra was not a concern in and of itself. In fact, in the end,
I came to believe that it enhanced my ability both to be present for
this interview and to hear more deeply than I might otherwise have
been able to.

This interview was unique in that I had thought originally that I
would interview only women who had been "out" for some
substantial amount of time and who felt "committed" to a lesbian
lifestyle. I reasoned that this would "ensure" my obtaining a truer
picture of what it means to live as a lesbian. Why would I interview
someone who was just newly out? What would she know? How could

she talk of her love for women without framing it only in opposition to her experience of men? All of that has turned out to be a simplistic view. Though Sandra has been out for a relatively short time, her capacity to engage life from within a lesbian relationship touched and amazed me.

It was Sandra, really, who made me understand that the question of loving another woman, while framable in contrast to men, is also a question of world. For someone who was so newly out, who had never had this experience before, who was most likely to compare this experience against her experiences with men, she spent very little time talking about men or how her experience of loving a woman was different. It was more like a whole world opened up to her, as if through this fusion of horizons with a "same" Other something entirely new had emerged.

And Sandra's use of the word "core" was entirely spontaneous. I had been very careful not to mention it to her beforehand. Frankly, I found it almost eerie that this word emerged once again in dialogue. I gave up on seeing it as a coincidence and wondered, with a great sense of caution, whether it really did represent something "essential" or archetypal. Perhaps this was something that all lesbians could come to some consensus on. Perhaps this was an expression of some form of *consensus gentium.*

9

WEAVING A RESEARCH DESIGN

Feminism, Gadamerian hermeneutics, and Jungian practice

The difficulty involved in weaving together these three traditions has something to do with the complexities of each, but more to do with the fact that each stands in isolation from the others. Only a few feminists, unless they have been steeped in a philosophical discipline, know anything about hermeneutics and even fewer have admitted to any interest in Jung. And few philosophers, unless they are already feminists, have taken seriously the need to make philosophy relevant to women, and even fewer have attested to any awareness of Jung. Very few Jungians, unless they have been exposed inadvertently to philosophy, have indicated any interest in investigating the hermeneutical underpinnings or philosophical implications of Jung's ideas, and even fewer have professed any familiarity with feminist theorizing. As a result, each of these traditions knows little about the others. This leaves me with a problem of huge proportions: how to structure a conversation among them. My solution is to give each a chance to be heard separately while keeping the conversation open so each can add to the conversation when there is something to be said.

WHAT DISTINGUISHES FEMINIST RESEARCH?

Feminist researchers do not agree on much, except perhaps on the belief that conventional research has "consistently given priority to the values of the white, middle-class men who have been its main practitioners" (Peplau and Conrad 1989: 383). Feminist critiques of traditional "objective" research usually stress the fact that the knowledge produced by these procedures is hardly "objective" or value-neutral because the researcher's personal and cultural biases are subtly but systematically imbedded in every aspect of a research effort and thus often allow prejudice and stereotypical thinking to be lifted to the status of "objective facts and findings." As a result, such research often has yielded not more knowledge about women, for example, but only a view of women as "other," as "an alien object that does not reflect back on the knower" (Westkott 1979/1990: 61).

Many feminist voices from various disciplines have been involved in ongoing conversations aimed at attempting to identify criteria which might define and distinguish feminist research in a way that could explain its "distinctive power" (S. Harding 1987a: 6). No definite consensus has yet emerged from these efforts, partly because there are so many different feminisms and partly because many have come to realize that "any research method can be misused in sexist ways, and . . . no method comes with a feminist guarantee" (Peplau and Conrad 1989: 379). That is, the feminist agenda can be accomplished in a variety of ways; for example, by making visible something which previously had been invisible or had gone unnamed, by giving voice to those who often have been silenced or suppressed, by forcing us to recognize that much of our knowledge about "human beings" is often actually knowledge about men, by analyzing gender and its effects, and by penetrating and reconceptualizing "official interpretations of reality" (Cook and Fonow 1986/1990: 74).

I will attempt here to sketch out my own version of a feminist approach to research based on and distilled from various feminist theorists and interwoven with my own thinking. I am convinced that feminist inquiry qualifies "as a paradigm shift in the Kuhnian sense" since it offers a world view by which one can "see things one did not see before" (Nielsen 1990: 19, 20). This in turn yields the anomalies which allow, even force, alternative accounts to be developed.

Sandra Harding, a highly respected feminist philosopher of science, has suggested that one of the problems involved in identifying a distinctive feminist approach to research has been the tendency of researchers to intertwine the three essential aspects of research: epistemology, method, and methodology. She suggests that feminist researchers apply a feminist consciousness to each of these areas separately. Harding also identifies three specific charac-teristics which distinguish feminist scholarship: (1) the willingness to generate research problematics and frame questions "from the perspective of women's experiences" (1987a: 7); (2) the selection of subject matter according to women's actual concerns; and (3) the use of strategies which place the researcher "in the same critical plane as the overt subject matter" (ibid.: 8). In keeping with this framework, I will address each of these areas/features separately, although I expect that it will soon become clear to the reader that these various elements are not entirely independent of each other.

EPISTEMOLOGY: FEMINIST AND TRANSITIONAL

> I do not need epistemology to justify my desire, my life, my love. I need politics; I need to build a world that does not require such justifications.
>
> (Phelan 1993: 777)

Epistemology is that branch of philosophy which addresses questions such as: How do we know what we think we know? Who can be a knower? What are the limits of and criteria for knowledge? In spite of feeling sympathetic toward Phelan's position, I must admit that I do not believe that we can really escape such questions – although I do think we can and must challenge the answers usually provided by traditional epistemologies. There are lively debates in many fields of study, feminist and otherwise, over what constitutes a reliable epistemology or even over whether epistemology is necessary. Probably most feminists would concur with Hekman that while feminists generally "agree on the nature of the problem" – namely, the "masculinity" and androcentricity of western science – "they cannot agree on an alternative" (Hekman 1990: 122).

However, despite this lack of consensus on a solution, most feminist researchers are likely to concede that what is really unique about feminist research is the way in which the researcher looks "through a lens shaped by the epistemological assumptions" of feminism (Cook and Fonow 1986/1990: 80). What precisely these epistemological assumptions are, however, is certainly not a settled matter in spite of numerous attempts to formulate a set of feminist epistemological principles.[1] My aim here is not to identify the essential criteria of a "correct" feminist epistemology. I do not believe that there is such a thing. Rather, my objective is simply to locate myself along the feminist continuum by explicating the major features of my particular feminist lens, in keeping with the urging of McKenna and Kessler who insist that it is the duty of researchers "to enumerate the features of their own lens and tell why it is a better lens through which to view the world than the others currently available" (1985: 244, quoted in Kitzinger 1987: 190).

A framework for a feminist epistemology

Harding has suggested that there are at present three major groups of feminist epistemologies: feminist empiricism, feminist standpoint theories, and the transitional epistemologies. She argues that the aim of both the feminist empiricists and the standpoint theorists is to produce a "successor science" that will correct the inadequacies and deficiencies of Western science and thus be more objective and "better" than the traditional models. The transitional discourses, on the other hand, are inclined to challenge the very notion of a better science, arguing that the basic tenets of the traditional epistemologies are irretrievably mired in Enlightenment thinking and in the assumptions of "modernity." These transitional epistemologies, which are still in the process of emerging, are generally "deeply skeptical of universalizing claims" or of any attempts to construct "a" feminist perspective (1987b: 188).

Harding cites two groups of these skeptical or postmodern epistemologies: a group of "otherwise disparate discourses" (semiotics, deconstruction, and psychoanalysis) and the writings of women of color. All of these transitional approaches, according to Harding, remind us that there are always "many 'subjugated knowledges' that conflict with, and are never reflected in, the dominant stories a culture tells about social life" (ibid.). Harding celebrates the tensions among all of these discourses, but advises caution. Noting that it is too early to assess the long-term impact of the transitional epistemologies, she advises that it may not yet be time for women to "give up what they have never had" – namely, an opportunity "to know and understand the world from the standpoint of their experiences" (ibid.: 189).

Although Joyce Nielsen does not directly link her discussion of feminist research methods to Harding's outline, she too discusses each of these categories, referring to the transitional epistemologies as "postempirical" and noting two traditions within these approaches: "the interpretive and the critical" (1990: 7). She considers the standpoint epistemologies to be among the critical approaches and she discusses the interpretive approaches first as "the hermeneutic tradition" (ibid.) and later as the "dialectical processes" which characterize recent feminist inquiry and which can be grounded using Gadamer's idea of "the fusion of horizons" (ibid.: 26). In the end, however, because Nielsen is concerned with issues of validity and reliability, she proposes that feminist inquiry should reflect a blending of "empirical, interpretive, and critical" (ibid.). This is a subtle privileging of the empirical in that it treats empirical observations as if they exist prior to interpretation. She explains her strong stand in favor of empiricism as a way "to help protect and guard against the use of superstition and personal bias" – even though she then goes on to acknowledge that empiricism "does not guarantee much" (ibid.: 31).

Westkott, on the other hand, criticizes the tendency of empirical researchers "to assume a fit between consciousness and activity," thus ignoring the many known discontinuties between the two (1979/1990: 64). She believes this assumption reflects male experience in patriarchal society, where males generally are given the freedom to act on their conscious ideas, though the extent of this freedom can vary enormously depending on factors such as race and class. Westkott argues that women as a whole have been denied this kind of freedom; that, for women any sense of freedom exists alongside cultural requirements of "unfree, conforming behavior" (ibid.: 64). In other words, "the assumption of a convenient parallel between consciousness and activity" simply does not hold true for most women and, therefore, to consider only reported or observed behavior "is insufficient" when trying to understand women's experiences (ibid.: 64, 65). I would add to this two related points: that all of what she says is doubly true for lesbians and that this "convenient parallel" entirely omits considerations of unconscious factors. That is, there simply is "no one-to-one relation" between what a human being expresses and what was consciously intended, or between something we see and its possible meanings (Brooke 1991: 129). For Brooke, as for me, one important implication of this is that "existence is lived as a metaphorical reality" (ibid.: 129–130). Empiricism, therefore, cannot hold the key to psychological understanding.

I am not taking an absolutist stand against "the scientific method," nor am I entirely dismissing traditional approaches to research. I concede that these methodologies have a place in feminist research even though I have not found them to be relevant when attempting to understand complex human phenomena. However, I would argue that the underlying assumptions of these mainstream methodologies must be seriously examined and challenged and that their pervasive influence must be relativized in order to make room for non-traditional approaches. In refusing to accept the scientific method, I have rejected all of its basic concepts and assumptions: objectivity and neutrality; empiricism, the search for universal laws which operate on the basis of cause and effect; and the belief that the "best" way to legitimate knowledge is to render a "true" representation of what "really" happened.

An epistemology without a name

I have adopted an epistemology which is both transitional and interpretive. I do not have a name for this epistemology, though I am inclined to describe it generically as postempirical and to locate it at the confluence of several streams of thought: postmodernism (including aspects of deconstructionism and poststructuralism),[2] social constructionism, and the modified standpoint theories. I must stress that this is not an eclectic epistemology but a pluralistic one in that it attempts to hold the tension among all the participant discourses in a relatively coherent if unstable framework.

Although I do not necessarily endorse the entire postmodern project (even if it could be defined and agreed upon), I do resonate with many of its recognized features and with its desire to unsettle the foundations of modernity. I especially appreciate its intention to undermine "the grand 'normalizing' discourses" (Flax 1990b: 39), its mission to "decenter the world" (Flax 1990a: 56), its challenges to notions such as a unified self, unitary truth, or privileged knowledge, its deconstruction of language, and its deep skepticism toward any essentialist/dualistic/hierarchical categories. Yet there are aspects of postmodernism that I, like many other feminists, find troubling or wanting.[3] I am uncomfortable with the possible consequences of a strictly postmodern approach and, so, I find myself feeling ambivalent, valuing the power of the postmodern view while feeling apprehensive that its "critical and deconstructive spirit" could lead us into "an increasingly decentered, unstable, disorderly and uncivilized world" in which "raw power" will rule and the "most vulnerable . . . would be the first to suffer" (Cole 1993: 96).

What I take from poststructuralism specifically is the willingness of many of its adherents to maintain a place for some kind of subject and subjectivity. Butler, for example, explains that: "The critique of the subject is not a negation of the subject, but, rather, a way of interrogating its construction as a pregiven or foundationalist premise" (1992: 9). As I understand it, poststructuralism posits an individual who is "collectively and discursively constituted" and is assigned a subject status that is opposite to liberal humanist ideas of the subject (Davies 1990: 62). Poststructuralism replaces the idea of an essentialist self with a constructed self, one which is continuously (re)defined by "the various discourses in which one participates" (ibid.: 64). Individuals thus are products of a process rather than being the essential constructors of their "selves." In addition, poststructuralism holds that categories are defined discursively and not reductively. So, for example, the category "women" is *not* defined to be "all people who happen to have female genitals," but rather as "the discursive category of female/woman and the experience of being discursively constituted as one who belongs in that category" (ibid.: 54). In keeping with this, subjectivity then conveys the sense that one is "discursively, interactively, and structurally *positioned*" in multiple and sometimes contradictory ways (ibid.). Poststructuralism thus allows for a "self" which is "continually constituted through" these various discourses but which maintains the status of "a *speaking subject*" (ibid.: 57). My major objection to poststructuralism is that although I concede that subjectivity is in part discursively produced, I am not convinced that it is *only* that. I do not believe that we yet know enough to take such a definitive stand.

My use of social constructionism is restricted to a certain emphasis that I find useful, namely, its premise that all knowledge is "socially and historically constituted" (Westkott 1979/1990: 61). That is, knowledge always "results from the conditions of its production, is contextually located, and irrevocably bears the marks of its origins in the minds and intellectual practices of those . . . who give voice to it" (Stanley and Wise 1990: 39). In other words, knowledge does not exist in a vacuum. It is always constructed and understood from a particular standpoint and from within a particular context, and it cannot be separated from the observer's "location" (historical, social, class, race, gender, etc.). As a result, social constructionism also insists that various "taken-for-granted" categories (e.g. sexual orientation, gender, the individual, the self, science) be vigorously challenged and redefined in ways that will "startle, shock, anger or surprise the reader" (Kitzinger 1987: 190).

On the other hand, my reservation with social constructionism is that while I am ready to see all human knowledge as constructed, I am not entirely ready either to abandon all attempts to find "truth" nor am I prepared to accept that all constructions of knowledge are equally legitimate. In addition, while I concede that identity is in part "socially constituted and historically determined" (ibid.: 187), I am not convinced that it is *only* that. This seems to me to be another premature conclusion. In any case, like Stanley and Wise I would argue that, for now at least, we must keep certain categories (like race and gender) since they are not likely to disappear in the foreseeable future and are still needed in order to "construct the discourses of oppression" (1993: 220).

My identification with standpoint theories comes solely from my belief that every position is in effect a standpoint position since *no* position can really be neutral or impartial. In that sense, I claim several standpoints: a feminist standpoint from which I define my epistemology, a lesbian standpoint from which I experience a sad but empowering awareness of being marginalized, outside-ed, silenced, and ignored, and a Jungian standpoint from which I am committed to rescuing the unconscious and some version of subjectivity.

Having so painstakingly outlined my epistemology, I should now acknowledge my belief that any "search for epistemological security" is bound to fail (Packer and Addison 1989: 291). While I can assert that I have been guided by the structure I have outlined here, I must admit that my laying claim to an epistemology is still no guarantee either that I have followed it successfully or that it really does justify my claims to knowledge. I can only say I did my best.

SUBJECT MATTER: LESBIAN EXPERIENCE

Another important feature of feminist research according to Harding is that it attempts to examine phenomena that are relevant to women and about which women themselves "want and need" to know, rather than to answer questions which "men have wanted answered" (1987a: 8). Nielsen maintains that such a focus on women's distinctive experiences is, in fact, the "irreducible element" of feminist research (1990: 19). Reinharz calls it a "shared radical tenet underlying feminist research," one that starts from the premise that "women's lives are important" and "worth examining" (1992: 241). Westkott suggests that the goal here is to redress "the distortion and misinterpretation of women's experience" that has prevailed in conventional social science research (1979/1990: 59). I believe that all of these points are particularly relevant to the subject of lesbian experience which historically has been distorted or made invisible by mainstream researchers.

In addition, the unassuming phrase, "subject matter", has particular power in Gadamer's dialectically based hermeneutics. Gadamer's investigator is an "inquiring subject" who "encounters" the subject matter "through a questioning responsiveness" (Palmer 1969: 165). In hermeneutical inquiry, there is no separation between subject and object. Nor is it the task of the questioner "to construct 'methods' to bring the object within his grasp." Instead, the questioner must stay open to the subject matter and thus allow her/himself to be "interrogated by the 'subject matter'" itself (ibid.) The questioner, in other words, is placed under the microscope alongside the subject matter. This gives the subject matter the power to propel the questioner into self-questioning. This was certainly my experience throughout this project.

According to Gadamer, another distinguishing feature of contemporary hermeneutics is that it is more concerned with questions than with answers. Therefore, before we can even begin looking for answers to questions, we must first try to understand what motivated the question itself. In other words, how do we come to choose a particular "text" (or topic) for interpretation. "Do we have a free choice about these things?" (Gadamer 1981: 106). Can we approach a topic with "neutral, completely objective concern"? Gadamer's answer is a resounding "no." We cannot escape the various motivations, prejudices, and presuppositions, conscious and unconscious, which are "at play determining us." These factors lead us to select topics which affect us "in a personal way" and they are implicit in the questions we ask (ibid.). While Gadamer admits that the task of fully illuminating our motives and preunderstanding is nearly impossible even to imagine, he insists that we must make the attempt to do so since these presuppositions shape both our questions and the statements we receive in response. These presuppositions, conscious and unconscious, "hidden" or "vague," must be elucidated (that is, foregrounded) any time a question comes to us (ibid.: 108). The investigator must always and continually examine how her/his attention has been pulled toward this particular text. "The answer," Gadamer asserts, "will never be that it communicates some neutral fact to us" (ibid.: 107).

And so it is with the topic I have come to select: the experience of one woman loving another woman. As I have tried to make clear in previous chapters, this subject matter holds a very personal and even passionate interest for me. From the beginning, I felt certain that there could be no such thing as *the* lesbian experience. There might be some commonalities, perhaps even some patterns, but I expected that there would also be unique elements in the experiences of each individual lesbian.

I realize that it is not popular among many feminist and/or lesbian theorists to focus either on individual or subjective experience. To do so will be seen by some as lacking in political analysis. Others, however, have defended the concept of subjectivity. Flax, for example, asserts that she feels compelled by her own experiences "to stress the subjective and intersubjective aspects of 'conversation' or its absence" as a way of recovering what many postmodernists "ignore or obscure," namely, "our non-linguistic aspects" (1990b: 12). Cook and Fonow (1986/1990) discuss women's subjective experiences in the context of attending to the significance of gender in women's lives and argue that feminist investigations often focus on the personal sphere and on subjectivity as a way of validating a woman's interior world. Stanley and Wise make the point that feminism is "deeply and irrevocably connected to a re-evaluation of 'the personal', and a consequent refusal to see it as inferior to, or even very different from, 'science'" (1993: 21). Cole adds to this that she has found "a strong theme" in much lesbian theorizing: "the importance of *personal epistemic responsibility* or *authenticity*" (1993: 39; emphasis in original). This, she notes, has led "individual lesbians to take up the project of generating their knowledge claims out of their own experience and from their own standpoints" (ibid.).

In spite of all of this, I am sensitive to the various criticisms of individual or subjective experience, not so much because I agree with them, but because I believe we must hold the tension between personal/individual/subjective/inner experience and the impersonal/collective/objective/outer world without privileging either. In point of fact, I do not consider these two areas of human life to be so distinct or separate from each other – nor do I posit them as sets of "opposites" framed in the language of dualistic extremes. To speak of individual experience is not to promote "individualism" (that theory which proposes and valorizes a totally independent and autonomous human being). To speak of individual experience is merely to express the belief that each person is in some ways distinguishable from all others, endowed with a set of traits, shaped by his or her environment, and capable of expressing something about her or his experiences. I would argue that each of my interviewees of necessity presents her individual story within a context larger than her own individual life and that every story thus makes a contribution toward illuminating the various contexts of lesbian life itself.

Similarly, to speak of subjectivity is not to deny the constructed and historical nature of subjectivity nor to present the human subject as "the ultimate reference point for the status of all that is seen" (Palmer 1969: 144). Such an understanding of subjectivity, also called subjectivism, creates a subject–object split and results in a world which is "subject-centered" and in which there is no meaning except "with respect to man, whose task is to master the world" (ibid.). Subjectivity, as I am using it, is a "phenomenological experience of 'what it's like to be' a certain conscious being" (Honderich 1995: 857). It thus refers to the realm of personal experience, including inner experience, and simply implies that each person sees from some unique perspective (whether constructed or otherwise).

FRAMING THE PROBLEMATIC: MY QUESTION

Sandra Harding argues that one of the goals characteristic of feminist research is that of generating research problems which begin in women's experiences and which are framed from the perspective of women, especially from the perspective of "women's experiences in political struggles" (1987a: 8). She elaborates on this by explaining that an oppressed group is not usually interested in the pursuit of "so-called pure truth" but would rather know "how to change its conditions" or "how to win over, defeat, or neutralize those forces arrayed against" it (ibid.).

The initial question that I posed to each participant – "What is it like for you to love another woman?" – was certainly framed from the perspective of women. Though men perhaps have been curious about why one woman would love another woman rather than a man, this is a question about women's experiences which is addressed to women for the benefit of women. In the current political atmosphere, any question which allows a lesbian to articulate her experience (rather than explain or justify it) is potentially a political question since it can shed light both on her personal experience as well as on her "political" experience as a member of a doubly oppressed group (being female and lesbian). But lesbians are not just an oppressed group. Until very recently, we also have been a truly invisible group (except for isolated portrayals in films, on TV, or in books, most of which have been orchestrated to serve the fantasies of men). Phelan makes a similar point when she argues that "lesbians engage in politics whenever they become visible as lesbians, as they challenge assumptions about heterosexuality" (1993: 785). I would propose, therefore, that any study which makes lesbians more visible *on our own terms* meets Harding's criteria of posing questions which help us take meaningful steps toward changing our conditions.

LOCATING THE RESEARCHER: HORIZONS AND PREJUDICES

Most feminist researchers acknowledge that the researcher is, in fact, an involved person rather than a neutral observer. As a result, they insist on "locating the researcher in the same critical plane as the overt subject matter" (S. Harding 1987a: 8). This requires that the researcher be explicit in informing the reader about any background factors as well as any "class, race, culture, and gender assumptions, beliefs, and behaviors" which may have influenced the design of a research project (ibid.: 9). By placing these factors "within the frame of the picture that she/he attempts to paint," the researcher is no longer portrayed as "an invisible, anonymous voice of authority," but becomes instead "a real, historical individual with concrete, specific desires and interests" (ibid.). Harding is careful to distinguish this from engaging in "soul searching" (although, she remarks parenthetically, that perhaps "a little soul searching by researchers now and then" can't be all bad) (ibid.). Harding goes on to explain that:

> We need to avoid the "objectivist" stance that attempts to make the researcher's cultural beliefs and practices invisible while simultaneously skewering the research object's beliefs and practices to the display board. . . . Introducing this

"subjective" element into the analysis in fact increases the objectivity of the research and decreases the "objectivism" which hides this kind of evidence from the public.

(ibid.)

Reinharz argues that whereas conventional researchers typically consider personal experience to be "irrelevant" and likely "to contaminate a project's objectivity," many feminist researchers consider it to be "a valuable asset for feminist research" and essential to countering "pseudo-objectivity" (Reinharz 1992: 258). She notes how these efforts to include the personal also effectively "reintroduce passion" into research, resulting in "a disruption of conventional research etiquette" (ibid.: 259). This "strategy of 'starting with one's own experience'" (ibid.) draws on what Reinharz has called "a new 'epistemology of insiderness' that sees life and work as intertwined" (ibid.: 260). Reinharz notes that although some of this kind of writing might appear to be confessional, it is really an admission and explication of the researcher's standpoint. In keeping with this point of view, many feminist researchers write about their research in the first person and using an informal style (as I generally have chosen to do in this book) and they tend to discuss how their lives provide a context for their work (as I also have attempted to do).

Some feminist researchers also have indirectly addressed the issue of prejudice. In a move which parallels Gadamer's efforts to "rehabilitate" the concept of prejudice, Cook and Fonow point out that a researcher's feminist values and consciousness are actually an important "source of knowledge and insight" (1986/1990: 75) and play a constructive part in shaping all aspects of the research including its goals, topics, and procedures. Stanley and Wise make the related point that we "cannot have 'empty heads'" and that theory cannot be "untainted" by our experiences (1990: 22). Their solution to this dilemma relies on their idea of a "feminist consciousness," that is, on what they see as "women's unique view of social reality" (1993: 120). Although I share the intent of these calls for a feminist consciousness, I would argue that this, in and of itself, does not solve the problem. If anything, feminist consciousness is itself a "prejudice." Only by foregrounding this prejudice, along with all others, can we hope to allow any kind of 'truth' to emerge.

I have foregrounded my horizons and prejudices both in the

141

chapters specifically dedicated to that (namely, Chapters 1 and 3) and in other places where this seemed appropriate and relevant.

METHOD: INTERVIEWS

The hermeneutic method is not hard to understand, but it is damnably difficult to practice. The method is dialogue. Questions are answered through the give and take of discussion, through the dialectics of exchange between two subjects. What makes interpretation hard is granting the other the status of subject, seeing that the . . . other person is a carrier of meaning, and letting their meanings question our own understandings.

(Steele 1982: 3)

Sandra Harding has defined methods as "techniques for gathering evidence" or data (1987a: 2). The method I have used is a fairly standard one: the interview. The origins of a feminist focus on dialogue can be traced to the work of early researchers who came to realize that the textbook advice they had been given about interviewing did not work and who thus learned "to allow the respondent to 'talk back'" to them (Cook and Fonow 1986/1990: 76). That is, keeping a distance between themselves and their respondents only served to limit communication and to hinder the process of trying to gather "worthwhile and meaningful information" (Nielsen 1990: 6). In a move that echoes Gadamer (as we will soon see), Kitzinger takes this a step further in a way by declaring that the interviewer is not "the expert" in determining what is "true" about the interviewee's account (1987: 68). In any case, as a result, many feminist researchers have come to reject the notion that there must be "a strict separation between the researcher and the research subject" in order to produce "a more valid, objective account" of reality (Cook and Fonow 1986/1990: 76).

It has been primarily through Gadamer that I have come to understand that the task of interviewing is ultimately a matter of *being* rather than of *doing*, and that it relies more on what he calls a "partnership of conversation" than on methods or techniques (1989e: 21). This partnership of conversation involves an unstructured interaction and exchange between co-participants. This is a conversation in which each participant is trying to reach a genuine understanding about something. The investigator does not attempt to arrive at absolute or final or certain "results," but focuses instead on maximizing understanding of the phenomenon under study.

Considered phenomenologically, the interview situation actually involves two interrelated phenomena: (a) the phenomenon of the subject matter which is being explored; and (b) the phenomenon of the interview itself. In the interview, the focus is on what occurs between the two participants. Both are led by the subject matter itself. The interviewer's role is to facilitate a revelation of the subject matter that is as complete as possible. The interviewee is, in a sense, the channel of such revelation. The interview proceeds on the basis of, and in fact relies upon, a continuous series of mutual acts and moments of interpretation between the participants. The conversation between the interviewer and the respondent results in a "text" about the phenomenon being explored and becomes an "object" of further interpretation, reflection, and analysis – a task I have undertaken in Chapter 13.

Using language borrowed from Brooke's explication of Heidegger, I have come to conceptualize the interview situation as a phenomenon of "being-in-the-world" that occurs "in" consciousness. Consciousness is "that irreducible, non-optional occurrence within which the world comes into being" and "the open clearing that gathers the world together" (Brooke 1991: 43). Although this latter phrase is awkwardly phenomenological (since it attributes the act of gathering to an inanimate object), it seems to offer an apt and suggestive image of what can occur in "the open clearing" of an interview: it can become a space which, like a vacuum, draws to itself all that comes within reach. I see this as an image of containment, something akin to what occurs in the alchemical retort.

Brooke (citing the work of Merleau-Ponty, Jung, and Romanyshyn) also places much emphasis on "the bodiliness of psychic complexity" (ibid.: 128) in conjunction with the workings of the unconscious. His concern is with what happens in therapy, but his description is applicable to any exchange between participants in any conversation, including an interview:

> What is manifest may be perceived and responded to by the
> therapist without having been held and known in the light of
> reflection. That is why access to "the patient's unconscious"
> is found, as often as not, while reflecting on one's own bodily

presence and responsiveness. . . . An implication of this point is that interpretation is not inference, a leap into the patient's mind, but the hermeneutic articulation of latencies that are immediately present, however subtly.

(ibid.: 129)

Selection of participants

I had only two criteria for selecting participants for this study: (1) that a woman self-identify either as "a lesbian" or as currently in a lesbian relationship; and (2) that she be sufficiently articulate verbally that she would be capable of describing her experiences and of engaging in an in-depth conversation with me. Given that my objective was not to prove a hypothesis, but rather to use the material gathered in order to demonstrate a methodology and to illustrate a constructive use of some theoretical points, I decided on a relatively small number of participants, namely, six. All of them were located informally, that is, they were women whom I either knew personally or whom I found through a mutual acquaintance. In some methodologies, this might be considered questionable. In the case of hermeneutical research, however, the primary aim of research is to achieve a deeper understanding of one's subject matter. Therefore, anyone who has had experiences relevant to the subject matter is a legitimate resource. In this context, the fact of any prior relationship between the interviewer and the interviewee becomes either irrelevant or potentially helpful (for example, in facilitating a more immediate sense of trust). In all cases, once I had identified a potential participant, I contacted her, explained the nature of my project, and requested her participation.

The question of diversity was by far the most perplexing issue that I faced in locating potential interviewees. Feminist researchers typically seek to recognize the diversity of women's experiences in some way and to discuss diversity in terms of factors such as race, age, class, economic status, educational background, etc. There have been basically two avenues of response to this issue: (1) an insistence on avoiding universalized conclusions about "all" women's experiences; and (2) attempts to make study samples better reflect the demographics of the group being studied. In terms of the first type of response, Sandra Harding, for example, emphasizes that we must speak of "'women's experiences' *in the plural*" in order to acknowledge that the experiences of women vary across many categories, e.g. class, race, and culture (1987a: 7). Others have called upon researchers to avoid trying to establish "*universal* facts or laws about human behavior" (Peplau and Conrad 1989: 385). Gerda Lerner has suggested that instead of attempting to prove universal claims feminist researchers should consider highlighting the "intersections" where diverse experiences meet or overlap (1977: xxii, cited in Reinharz 1992: 253). O'Connor and Ryan recommend that researchers try to find "a way of understanding lesbian diversity and difference" that does not try "to homogenise the category," but that helps us focus on "the structuring of lesbian oppression, rather than in anything supposedly inherent in lesbians" (1993: 22). I have tried – though not always successfully – to keep in mind all of these ways of seeing as I have constructed this work.

The second context for diversity is much more difficult to address and revolves around two series of important questions: (1) What actually constitutes diversity? Can or should the researcher attempt to achieve diversity across all categories of "difference?" In a small sample such as mine, would this be meaningful?; and (2) Is the call for diversity sometimes just another "form of colonialism, manipulation, or exploitation" (Reinharz 1992: 257)? Are efforts to diversify research samples, no matter how sincerely intended, driven by questionable motives? Some women of color, for example, have asked "why white women should study black women in the first place" (ibid.). Are they really interested in black women or are they trying to exploit a market and/or appear to be "politically correct?" Is an attempt to "balance" a sample in some way simply a form of tokenism? Should a researcher avoid any attempt at diversity by only interviewing women like her/himself?

These are extremely difficult questions. I certainly do not have answers – only more questions. I regret to admit that I did not resolve this issue in any way that feels satisfactory. I did make some attempt to locate women who were "different" from me and from each other in some way, but my sample is not really diverse. For example, I have only one non-white interviewee and the ages of my interviewees fall within a range of only eleven years (33 to 44). In the end, I simply settled for trying to be aware of and sensitive to all of these issues wherever I could and within the confines of my own horizons. This was definitely not a solution; it was simply a way to proceed. I can only hope to find a better way in the future.

145

Interview process

The actual interviews were conducted informally. I attempted to set each interviewee at ease by explaining to her that I was not trying to "prove" any hypothesis and, therefore, that I was not seeking a "correct" response or any particular "answers." I explained that I was interested only in what my question would evoke for her and how she would respond to it. I entered each interview with only the one question: "What is it like for you to love another woman?" I did not draw up a list of "focus" or "guiding" questions because I felt that these would serve to bias the direction the interview might take since it would have structured the interview in accordance with my preunderstanding. I opted instead to allow, as much as possible, for a free exchange of questions and answers, for a "play" of conversation. In all cases, the conversation was allowed to follow its own course, coming to an end when I, as the interviewer, had no more questions to put to the interviewee and when the interviewee expressed a sense of having nothing more to add. It was made clear to each interviewee that she could contact me at any point to amend or add to what she had said.

My question was a fairly simple one intended to evoke a subjective response. It was deliberately informal, open-ended, and non-directive, a question that could be interpreted, meaningfully and differently, by each respondent. Embedded in this one question there were, of course, other questions: What does it mean to this woman that she loves this particular other woman – or women in general? How does it affect her sense of herself and how she sees the world? How does she come to make sense of her own individual life in this context? In what larger contexts does she frame this aspect of herself? However, any and all follow-up questions that were actually asked emerged from the dialectical process itself though always, of course, from within the horizons of both participants or as a result of the fusion of these horizons.

I encouraged each interviewee to see the initial part of the interview as a kind of monologue and to let herself be led by her initial response to the question. I intervened in this process only when it seemed to me that the interviewee was stuck and looking to me for some assistance. During this part of the interview, I did not want to interrupt the interviewee's momentum, so I took only sparse notes, for example, if I felt moved or puzzled by something she had said. Once the interviewee seemed to have exhausted her initial response, I allowed myself to interact more freely, that is, more in the style of the "to-and-fro" of conversation (a phrase often used by Gadamer). I asked questions as they presented themselves to me, but I also tried to keep the conversation somewhat focused on those comments which seemed especially relevant to my original question – even though I believe that every comment, even one which seemed tangential – could not be irrelevant since it had emerged as a result of the question and our dialogue. Borrowing (entirely out of context) from Palmer, I would say that I was guided most in these interviews by a desire to allow the interviewee to "exist as a meaningful oral happening in time, a being whose true nature and integrity can shine forth" (1969: 18).

Process used in writing narratives

The process of creating the narratives was in some ways similar to the process of conducting the interviews in that it, too, involved a to-and-fro movement, this time between me and the various versions of the "text" (that is, the audio tape of the interview, the draft of my transcription, the interactions with the interviewees to clarify any revisions to the draft, and the final text). I listened to each tape several times and transcribed those portions of the interview which seemed to capture some essential element of that interviewee's story. Then I read and re-read and worked the material, attempting to create a certain amount of coherence by pulling together related comments. Finally, guided by a commitment to maintaining the spirit and voice of each participant, I produced a working draft of each narrative. A copy of the draft was given to each participant with a request that she review it to verify that it correctly represented what she had intended to convey, that I had not misrepresented or misinterpreted her in any way, and that the narrative portrayed her sense of what it has been like for her to love other women. This was a point at which I was concerned with accuracy. The narratives were revised to incorporate any and all comments received from each participant.

It was not until I was near the end of this project that I came to appreciate how very difficult it is to write an account of an interview. Genuine conversation, like life, is simply not linear. I went into every interview with the desire to try to amplify whatever would be said. That worked to some extent. But, on the whole, conversation often has the characteristics of free association (as Freud knew and Jung often resisted). So, it was a challenge for me to create narratives which would be readable *and* would provide a site of intersection between theory and experience.

My decision to present the narratives chronologically was based on my realization that each interview was inevitably the product of, or at least affected by, the preceding interview. That is, my horizons and my understanding had been irrevocably altered by each previous interview. Therefore, it seemed only fitting for me to present them in the order in which they had occurred. It was only when I came to write my reflections that I consciously allowed myself to include ideas "tainted" by previous interviews. I was, at this point, less concerned about accuracy than about allowing something to emerge through my interplay with the text, something that I hoped would contribute toward a better understanding of my subject matter.

A note about the interviewee as "text"

As already noted, hermeneutics is a tradition rooted in text interpretation. Gadamer recognizes "a profound difference" between how words function in conversation versus how they are used in literature (1989e: 43). However, he argues that "the extension of the concept of the text to include oral discourse is hermeneutically well grounded" since both situations rely on "communicative conditions that, as such, reach beyond the merely codified meaning-content of what is said" (ibid.: 33).

The idea of reading a person "as if" she or he were a text to be interpreted and understood is an integral aspect of Jungian practice where "text" is a metaphor for psyche and psyche can be "read" *as if* it were a text. It is extremely important here to emphasize the metaphorical nature of this "as if." After all, a person is not really an "object" or an impersonal, disembodied text. This distinction between the methods of literary criticism and those of human research is a critical one and raises concerns about the interviewer's ethical responsibilities. An interviewer, like an analyst, "must be responsible to others in her work in ways that the literary critic is not" (Flax 1990b: 131). When we are dealing with human subjects, theories and interpretations matter in ways they would not in the context of literary criticism. In human science research the idea of reading a human being as if she or he were a text must not be understood literally or reductively, as if the human subject were "nothing but" (to use one of Jung's favorite phrases) an object to be studied "objectively." The hermeneutic stance is, in fact, an attempt to resist the enticements of such an approach.

METHODOLOGY: GADAMERIAN HERMENEUTICS AND JUNGIAN PRACTICE

Sandra Harding defines methodology as "a theory and analysis of how research does or should proceed" (1987a: 3). Stanley and Wise regard methodology as "a 'perspective' or very broad theoretically informed framework" (1990: 26). The methodology I have chosen, hermeneutics, is an interpretive methodology, that is, a methodology which expects knowledge to emerge from dialogue and in the form of "an unpredictable discovery rather than a controlled outcome" (Westkott 1979/1990: 62). The researcher is not the controlling agent either of the process or of the results and the inquiry is grounded "in concrete experience rather than in abstract categories" (ibid.). The particular version of hermeneutics that I am drawn to use as a methodology is a branch of hermeneutics which culminates in, and is most profoundly expressed by, the thinking and writing of Hans-Georg Gadamer, although it is also theoretically informed by Jungian and post-Jungian theory and practice. Since my discussion of hermeneutics will be somewhat lengthy and involved, it will occupy a separate chapter.

10

"JOAN"

PROFILE

Joan is a 43-year-old African-American woman who has known since she was 5 years old that she was attracted to women. Her first sexual experience with a woman occurred when she was about 14 or 15 (while she was dating the one and only man she was ever involved with). Since then, she has been in two long-term relationships (of five years and thirteen years) and is currently involved with a woman she has been seeing for three years. Although Joan is not "out" in her workplace, she has been politically active in the gay community for many years. Joan prefers the term "gay" to "lesbian."

INTERVIEW SETTING/PROCESS

I have known of Joan for many years, having met her briefly probably fifteen years before the interview. We have never moved in the same circles as such, but we do seem to have shared some mutual acquaintances. Joan is a storyteller and responded to many of my questions by telling stories of situations which seemed to her to illustrate her thoughts and feelings.

THE INTERVIEW

Joan has been aware of her attraction to women "since I was a little kid." Perhaps because of this, parts of our conversation lingered over those early years. Joan remembers as a small child having a doll which was as big as she was and on which she would practice kissing. However, by the time she was 9 or 10, loving other girls "did not seem like a good possibility" given the negative attitudes she had noted from others. But Joan was still very curious. So, by the age of 12, she had seen the film *The Children's Hour* and was reading whatever she could find about homosexuality, including novels about lesbian relationships/sex. By age 14 or 15, she had had her first kiss and sexual experience with another woman. Joan believes that her family knew about her feelings, since she made no effort to hide the books she was reading, but this was a subject that was never talked about. Everyone was too busy trying to care for the nine children in the family, of which Joan was the youngest. Even in later years, when her mother became aware of her political activities in the gay community, her sexual orientation was never talked about directly.

Joan was very involved in dance as an adolescent and had many occasions to go to New York City during some of her teen years. There she had the opportunity to meet many gay people and to be "exposed to the possibility of a gay life style." It was then that she started dating women, typically women who were much older than she. Joan's first long-term relationship began when she was about 18 years old. It lasted for five years, ending when the other woman was killed in an auto accident. Joan was devastated and felt suicidal, but had no one to talk to since her relationship with this other woman had been intense but isolated.

Like most of the women I interviewed, Joan's initial response to my question was to note how hard it was to put words to this experience. She found it "just unbelievably hard to explain" her love for other women "because it's just something I've always felt all of my life." She once was involved with a man for two or three years, at the tail end of high school, but for Joan "women have always been it." For her, "there's just nothing like sleeping with a woman." Loving another woman is simply "very exciting. There's just nothing on earth like it." She theorizes that one element of the excitement might be related to the fact that it is "considered taboo" in our culture; perhaps that "makes it even more exciting." She takes great pleasure in "knowing" that others "are missing a lot." Over the course of our conversation, Joan was able to identify the characteristics she values the most in a relationship with another woman: warmth, companionship, sex, and understanding. For Joan, having a relationship with another woman is "like a special friendship" in which she can be understood. "I don't think anybody else understands me but another woman."

"JOAN"

For Joan, warmth means things like coming home after a bad day and having someone there that she can talk to and who will listen to what she has to say. "And what we might do is just go lay in bed and hug or just like hug up and read a book together or something like that." Warmth is a kind of tranquil feeling Joan gets just because that someone is in the room with her.

> "Warmth is knowing that they're there . . . when you come back home. And when it's time to go to bed at night, you guys are going to hug up together, or even just be in the same bed. . . . there's the warmth of just being together in the same area."

Warmth is about knowing someone will be there for you whether "you're sad . . . or happy." Joan's desire for companionship seems quite related to all of this. When she talks about what companionship means to her she thinks of having someone in her life with whom she can go bowling, play in the snow, take the dog out, sit and look at the fire; and someone she could count on in times of crisis – for example, if something happened and she were hospitalized.

When Joan talks of warmth, she remembers especially her second long-term relationship with S. It lasted thirteen years and came to an amicable end about three years ago. They are still good friends. To this day, Joan feels that it is S. who really knows her. "She knows what moves me." Joan is still somewhat nostalgic about that relationship, noting that she cannot get that same sense of warmth from anyone else today, not even from the woman she is seeing currently. She wonders if this is because she is "not really trying" at this point, but believes that it really just takes time to gain that kind of warmth. "I guess that comes with the years. . . . I've been seeing D. for three years, but it's not the same. But that's going to be true of any relationship. None are the same."

Until she was about 35, Joan found sex to be the focus of her relationships with other women. She grins: "When you're younger, sex does seem to sweep your life a little more." But as she got older, Joan began "looking for a little more than that also." Today, she can describe exactly what that was:

> "a woman who was very independent, a woman who could think and really do on her own, who could probably build half a house if she really wanted to, if she was determined enough, who had knowledge about everything and anything."

Joan has always valued relationships where she could learn something from the other person. Sometimes these have been simple things (for example, S. taught her to love fresh flowers and Joan regularly insists on having arrangements of them around her apartment). Sometimes this has involved learning more practical things (for example, learning how to do household repairs). For Joan, this focus on the exchange of learning between lovers is an essential element of relationships between women, and a feature that distinguishes them from the heterosexual relationships she has observed around her. It seems to her that in straight relationships "the man wants to say 'I'm doing all of these things, you're not doing them, I'm not even going to teach you how to do them. You just do this and that.'" Conversation between men and women, in Joan's experience, "goes to everything else but how you do this." Men are more inclined to say "'I'll take care of it, honey,'" than to teach a woman how to do things so that she can be independent.

To be independent is clearly important to Joan. She realizes she may be stereotyping "the male creature" (even says she knows one man who is different from this), but it appears to her that a man is typically afraid that a woman will come to know more than he does. "The male wants to be the stronger. You can't be equal." She believes this is often the result of peer pressure and his fear of being called a "wimp." Joan does not feel hostile toward men, but she does notice that she has "more patience with women than I have with men." From the stories she tells, it is clear that Joan treats women differently from men, with more concern for their feelings and perhaps a greater sense of compassion.

An extension of Joan's emphasis on independence seems to be her strong opinions about having a separate living space even if she spends a great deal of her time with her lover. "One of the reasons that I wanted to maintain a separate house is because I wanted my separate identity along with that together identity." Joan is convinced that living together eventually creates some kind of "turmoil." When lovers live separately, "You're only a phone call away." Having separate spaces is beneficial to the relationship. There are times when she comes home from work and she just wants to be alone, when she needs "quiet time" to think and totally relax. This has nothing to do with not loving the other person. "It's a matter of it's your own space and it's your own time. I've always been like that. . . . I need to breathe." For Joan, it is also important to have separate friends even though she and her lover may spend time with them.

Joan explains that her sense of a "together identity" does not mean that she is a different person when she is with her lover. The only thing that is different is her experience of a sense of togetherness, when there is "a certain aura that covers both of you." This is a feeling that "never leaves you if you've been together a long time." It is an experience that requires two people and is not something that can be experienced alone. "It makes you feel good that there's somebody out there that knows you, that really knows you." This feeling of being known and understood is very important to Joan.

> "It means a lot to be understood, it really does. The lover I'm going with now is just starting to understand me. I honestly think it does come with time. My previous lover (S.) understands me to this day, knows what I'll do, knows what I won't do."

Joan feels that the woman she is seeing now "doesn't know me as well yet." Joan believes that the mutual understanding she longs for will come eventually, but only with hard work, especially a willingness to comfort each other and thus bring more feelings into the relationship.

Another thing Joan looks for in a woman is that she must be a feminist. In fact, she must be, or have been, "involved in something political. . . . She can't be a talker and not a doer." Joan herself spent a number of years being very active politically. Eventually, she noted, "there had to be a wake up call." She was getting older and realized that she had neglected the personal dimensions of her life. It was then that she started thinking about what she wanted out of life: being political would not feed or house her, and she "needed to start thinking about having a long-term relationship."

Joan "hates" the terms "bulldagger" and "dyke" "because they present a stereotype." They remind her of terms like "nigger." Joan much prefers the term "gay" if she has to use a label at all, but she would really prefer to avoid such categories altogether. (She tells a story of being called a "nigger" as a little girl by another little girl with whom she was sharing a hospital room. This other little girl did not understand "the content" of this stereotypical word, having probably overheard it from her parents, and was intending to convey a compliment as she was telling her parents that she and Joan, that "nigger girl" in the other bed, had become friends. "It was just a word to her." She did not understand how much she had hurt Joan with this stereotypical word.)

For Joan, even "gay" is used by the outside world to imply that she is "different" from them, which she does not really believe. Joan attributes the need for and use of such labels to "politics" and to the need to be somehow visible. It is not that she rejects the concept of identity as such, but that such words contain derogatory stereotypes. She would rather be called by her name than be described by a particular word because she feels that she simply does not fit any of the stereotypes that are "out there" in reference to these labels. Joan thinks that "too many people let words guide their life." A word like "lesbian" is just "a mold." She notes, for example, how it is now "in" for a lesbian to shave her legs in public at the annual Women's Music Festival in Michigan, as if there were never before any lesbians who shaved their legs; they were doing it all along, she jokes, but in the privacy of their campsites. So, even though people are trying to break this mold now, there is still a mold out there that Joan would prefer to resist.

In terms of identity, Joan sees herself as "a gay black woman." Her "first number one issue is the color of my skin. . . . Second of all is that I'm a woman. Third is that I'm gay." It is not that Joan believes she really is different from others, it is others who use her skin color (through stereotyping) to create a sense of difference. Therefore, it is her skin color that Joan is most immediately aware of in the world and which makes her notice herself as "different." Since she has no control over her skin color, she cannot "decide to tell" that she is black (or that she is a woman). But she can choose whether or not to disclose that she is gay. Joan is known as a strong feminist at work and is outspoken about her views, but she has chosen to not be "out" at work. "My personal life is my personal life, but I'll defend anybody else." Joan is very aware of the experience of feeling oppressed and discriminated against on the basis of both her skin color and her sex. To come out as gay brings up for her the slogan: "Three strikes and you're out."

In spite of being reluctant to use categorizing words, Joan is very direct and quick to affirm that loving other women is something that will always be a part of her life. She sees her involvement with women as lifelong, as something that "always will be for me." Nothing, she says, will ever change that. To love another woman is "a high."

"There's no feeling greater on this earth than loving a woman. . . . It's just a good feeling, a truly good feeling, from the sex, to holding, to being together, to thinking together, all of it. And I wouldn't trade it for the world. . . . It's the feeling that all your mental and physical needs are being met. . . . And that accounts for a lot of how you go out there and see the rest of the world."

MY EXPERIENCE OF THE INTERVIEW

Joan was the only woman I interviewed who had been consciously aware of her feelings for other women from such an early age. She was also the one who had had the least amount of experience in relationships with men. As a result, it seems to me, Joan was, on the one hand, at a disadvantage in trying to describe her experiences with women, having very little context or horizon within which to formulate her ideas except from within what she admitted were her own stereotypes of men. On the other hand, however, this minimal experience with men seemed to allow her to simply focus more directly on women. However, in the end, interestingly enough, some of her conclusions were very similar to the conclusions of others. For example, her emphasis on wanting to be independent seems directly related to the issue of being free of gender roles and refusing to be inhibited by the stereotypical notions that the culture might like to impose.

On the whole, I cannot help but wonder how much of Joan's experience of relationships is derived from having been the youngest of nine children, an experience that I, as an only child, can only marvel and cringe at. During our conversation, Joan made a reference, almost in passing, that she is drawn to older women, especially "women who are mothers" (literally speaking) and spoke proudly of how she had formed relationships with some of the children of her lovers.

While we were talking, I noticed how Joan regularly made use of the pronoun "them" in referring to a woman lover. I could hear in this the long years of practice at hiding. I am a realist. I respect the choices Joan has made in deciding to restrict the places in the world where she is "out" (and her reasons for so doing). But I must admit that listening to her on this issue stirred up some very sad and angry feelings for me, none of which, certainly, had anything directly to do with Joan at all. It just reminded me of the fact that lesbians and gay men live in an unsafe world, a world in which it is sometimes dangerous to be perceived as significantly "different" from what is considered "normal." It also makes me feel incredibly privileged in having been led to find a segment of the world where I can live and work on a daily basis without giving much thought to all of this. I wish I could say it makes me want to go out and try to change the world by becoming more active politically. But it does not. On a good day, it just makes me shrug my shoulders. But on a bad day, to be really honest about it, it makes me feel like giving up on humanity as a whole.

As explained in Chapter 9, I had some misgivings about my contrived attempt to make my sample look more diverse by actively seeking a woman of color whom I could interview. I am no less conflicted about this today than I was before. The experience of being a lesbian of color has dimensions of oppression that I have never experienced for myself and thus can only imagine or theorize about. As a result, though I have tried to convey some of Joan's views on these matters, I am very aware that I cannot write about them with the same sense of empathy that I bring to the 'generic' experience of loving another woman. Therefore, although I feel privileged to be able to present some of Joan's story, I am only too aware of the huge amounts of her experience that I must be missing and that I can only hope others will explore.

11

HERMENEUTICS AS METHODOLOGY

This chapter has four interrelated objectives: (1) to provide a context for Gadamer's hermeneutics, (2) to argue the case for hermeneutics as a methodology of choice in Jungian investigations, (3) to support my claim that Gadamer's hermeneutics offers a philosophical foundation for Jungian practice, and (4) to outline the operating principles of such a methodology.

LOCATING GADAMER AMONG THE MAJOR STRANDS OF CONTEMPORARY HERMENEUTICS

There are a variety of ways by which one might attempt to contextualize the major strands of contemporary hermeneutics. I will discuss only three of these since my primary objective is simply to provide a frame of reference for Gadamer's hermeneutics as the basis for my methodology. I make no claim to being a Gadamer scholar, although it is a fantasy of mine to someday be one.

The first context for locating Gadamer comes from Palmer (1969) who discusses six definitions of hermeneutics:

1 "as theory of biblical exegesis" (ibid.: 34), a mainly German tradition with its roots in the Reformation;
2 "as philological methodology" (ibid.: 38);
3 "as the science of linguistic understanding" envisioned by Schleiermacher (ibid.: 40);
4 "as the methodological foundation for the *Geisteswissenschaften*" (i.e. the human sciences) (ibid.: 41) proposed by Dilthey and represented currently by Betti;

5 "as the phenomenology of *Dasein* and of existential understanding" (ibid.) which may be traced in a line from Husserl
through his student Heidegger to his student Gadamer; and

6 "as a system of interpretation" (ibid.: 43) identified with the
phenomenological hermeneutics of Paul Ricoeur.

In this framework, Gadamer is presented as Heidegger's successor
and as the one who provides "the philosophical foundation for a
radical critique" of modernist ideas of interpretation (ibid.: 217).

Bleicher, who focuses strictly on contemporary hermeneutics,
provides a second context for locating Gadamer. He organizes
his overview by identifying the three conflicting responses to
"the problem of hermeneutics" (1980: 1): (1) the "hermeneutical
theory" of those like Betti who, in the tradition of Schleiermacher
and Dilthey, are concerned with developing a methodology aimed
at acquiring knowledge which is "relatively objective"; (2) the
"hermeneutic philosophy" of Gadamer who, building on Heidegger, reformulated the problem as one of coming to a common
understanding of a shared world (via his concept of the fusion
of horizons), and (3) the "critical hermeneutics" of those who,
like Habermas and Apel, try to combine "a methodical and
objective approach with the striving for practically relevant
knowledge" that will challenge reality, not just interpret it (ibid.:
4). While Bleicher also refers to Ricoeur's phenomenological
hermeneutics, he concludes that it is not a distinctive strand of
hermeneutics although it does bring the other approaches "into
sharp relief" as it attempts to integrate them (ibid.). In this
framework, Gadamer is again portrayed as the successor to Heidegger, but he is also distinguished from the "modern" Betti to his
right and the critical theorists to his left, and positioned thus as
someone who cannot be understood through either of those
categories.

Neither Palmer nor Bleicher make any reference to postmodernism. However, this is the backdrop against which I will offer a third
context for Gadamer. As we have already seen, postmodernism is
not easily defined, nor are its origins indisputable. Most scholars
trace its beginnings to the work of Nietzsche, but some point to
Husserl. In any case, probably the most provocative and influential
branch of contemporary postmodernism is Derrida's deconstructionism. Although Derrida and Gadamer are linked by their
respective positions as interpreters of Heidegger, and although

there is arguably some common ground between them, each develops Heidegger in a radically different direction and, as Madison notes, "they are not out to do the same kind of thing" (1991: 124).[1] Flax argues that deconstruction is, in some ways, "a radical form of hermeneutics" (1990b: 38). Hekman refers to Gadamer, along with Derrida and Foucault, as "influential postmodern thinkers" and argues that Gadamer is "an ally of postmodern feminism" (1990: 8, 13). Zuckert includes both Gadamer and Derrida in her book entitled *Postmodern Platos* (1996). Grondin maintains that French deconstruction (represented by Derrida) and German hermeneutics (represented by Gadamer) are "the two streams of thought defining Continental philosophy" currently (1994: 135) while Michelfelder and Palmer describe them as the "two powerful currents of contemporary European thought" (1989: 1). All of this allows us to position Gadamer at the very least in the gap between modernity and postmodernity. Although I am not aware that Gadamer has ever claimed to be "a postmodern philosopher" as such, his opposition to modernity is beyond dispute and attested to by his many critiques of its most basic premises.

I should note that there are certainly other contemporary hermeneutical thinkers who have taken hermeneutics into other, more overtly psychological directions. Arguably, the most notable of these is Ricoeur whose work might seem to be a more obvious and relevant choice for a hermeneutical analytical psychology. Although I do find a number of intersections between the thinking of Jung and Ricoeur, I also find some significant differences between them – not unlike the differences I experience between Ricoeur and Gadamer who represent "distinctive paradigms for contemporary hermeneutics" (Aylesworth 1991: 63). Ricoeur, for example, maintains a "reflective distance" from the text and treats it as "a linguistic object" while Gadamer engages the text in conversation as a "thou" and thus resists "the methodological alienation" of the text/subject matter/other (ibid.). In addition, Ricoeur's heart seems rooted primarily in phenomenology, as when he proposes that hermeneutics be grounded by being grafted onto phenomenology (Ricoeur 1980: 238). While I find phenomenology to be very compatible with Jungian practice, I find Gadamer's hermeneutics to be far more compatible with my Jungian soul.[2]

GADAMER'S HERMENEUTICS AND JUNG'S PRAXIS

Gadamer on methodology and truth

To speak of Gadamer's hermeneutics as a methodology is somewhat problematic. Gadamer is rather suspicious of method, seeing it as a kind of substitute for understanding. Palmer even describes Gadamer's hermeneutics as "the antithesis of method," explaining that it is "closer to the dialectic of Socrates than to modern manipulative and technological thinking" (1969: 165). Gadamer takes the position that hermeneutics "precedes the idea of methodical science developed by modernity" (1981: 113) and that, unlike science, it is not concerned with "amassing verified knowledge" (1960/1993: xxi) or with arriving at "teachable and controllable ways of proceeding" (1976: 27). He argues that the application of scientific methods to the field of human understanding is, at best, inappropriate and he believes that it is the responsibility of philosophy to lead the way in overcoming "the one-sided orientation toward the scientific fact" in "an age credulous about science to the point of superstition" (1960/1993: 552). Gadamer does not dispute "the necessity of methodical work within the human sciences" (ibid.: xxix), but he believes that the essence of research is really to be found in "the creative imagination" of the researcher and in the "inescapable" realization that there is always a "tension between truth and method" (ibid: 552). What is needed, he insists, is not a procedure, nor a system of rules and techniques, but rather some way of addressing the most fundamental question: "how is understanding possible?" (ibid.: xxx). In other words, Gadamer's basic concern is philosophical – "not what we do or what we ought to do, but what happens to us over and above our wanting and doing" (ibid.: xxviii).

Gadamer's concept of "truth" is complex. For him, truth is never final, but always "becoming." It is multiple, but not "relative." It is elusive. It can be revealed or disclosed, but never "proved." It cannot exist separate from the horizons and perspective of the knower. It cannot be measured or validated as "correct" on the basis of its correspondence to some "fact." So while Gadamer refuses to abandon the concept of truth, he insists on a view of it which makes it forever barely graspable.

Jung on methodology and truth

Jung also is extremely skeptical about the use of methods, theories, and techniques for trying to understand the psyche. As a result, there are only a few entries in the General Index of the *Collected Works* under "methods" and only one under "methodology." Jung admits to having a "methodological standpoint," but it is "exclusively phenomenological" (CW11: 4). He claims that this "is the same [viewpoint] as that of natural science": that is, it is "not Platonic philosophy but empirical psychology" (ibid.: 5). However, in spite of his frequent claims to being a scientist and an empiricist, and his repeated disclaimers of being a philosopher, Jung has very little patience with the methods and concepts he associated with conventional science (the scientific method, the experimental method, statistics, the reductive interpretations of "facts," and causal explanations). He repeatedly criticizes all such methods, especially for their emphasis on "explanatory principles" – which, he insists, are "only points of view" (CW8: 5) – and for their focus on identifying the commonalities rather than the anomalies of psychic life, thus leading them to miss the enormous variation that occurs among individuals. Jung believes that psychic reality can never be conveyed through "a conceptual average" (CW10: 499) or "the unreal ideal or 'normal' man" of scientific study because the "true and authentic carrier of reality" is the individual or "*concrete* man" (ibid.: 498). For Jung, what is really distinctive about facts "is their individuality"; reality, in effect, "consists of nothing but exceptions to the rule" and is always characterized by "*irregularity*" (ibid.: 494). When "averages" and "norms" are used, every individual is made to "suffer a levelling down" and psychological reality is lost in a sea of meaningless "facts" (ibid.: 499).[3]

Jung's approach to truth is about as complex as Gadamer's. Although he often slips into the language of "eternal" truths and appears to entertain the idea that there are some "absolute" truths, Jung operates strictly within the realm of psychological truth and so there is never a question for him of whether a psychological fact is accurate. Psychological facts can never be measured, but are always true. Any other attitude (e.g. applying the scientific method to "prove" psychological facts) only impedes psychological understanding. "In order to escape the ill consequences" that result from "an overvaluation of the scientific method," Jung argues, we need instead to combine "well-defined concepts" (CW6: 674) with the "extensive use of an indirect method," namely a method which relies on observation and description (ibid.: 672). This is about as close to a formal methodology as Jung ever gets.

Jung and Jungians on hermeneutics

Although I feel convinced that Jung's methodology (to the extent that he can be said to have had one) was fundamentally hermeneutic, I have also come to realize that any attempt to reconstruct "a" method from Jung's writings would be to miss Jeremy Carrette's admonition that Jung cannot be placed in a "methodological straitjacket" (1992: 204). Jung, in fact, used a multiplicity of languages: "the language of the natural scientist, the empiricist, the religious mystic, the post-psychoanalyst or the phenomenologist." Carrette points out that attempts have been made to reduce Jung's method to "one easily defined and self-contained [methodological] category" in order to make it less confusing (ibid.). He criticizes those who claim to present "a definitive or standard reading" of Jung because Jung makes use of so many languages that "any of these could determine our reading of the text" (ibid.: 205, 209). He commends instead those who, like Brooke, simply acknowledge that Jung cannot be limited to one particular language (in Brooke's case, phenomenology) and who get on with the task of showing only that a "particular method is central to the spirit of [Jung's] work" (ibid.: 205). So, while I am convinced that hermeneutics is central to the spirit of Jung's work, I am not concerned with proving that hermeneutics was Jung's only methodology or even that Jung was essentially and only "a" hermeneut. Rather, paraphrasing Carrette's comment about Brooke's project in relation to phenomenology, I am only interested in rescuing Jung for hermeneutics by presenting a view of him "as an inarticulate" hermeneut (1992: 208).

Jung, in fact, never discussed hermeneutics as such at any length in his writings and there are only a few references to hermeneutics in the *Collected Works*, although from their tone one can gather that Jung saw his own method as hermeneutical. For example, he footnotes a reference to his "synthetic" or "constructive" method as follows: "Elsewhere I have called this procedure the 'hermeneutic' method" (CW7: 131fn6). In another footnote, he refers to "the importance of hermeneutics" in helping the psyche make conscious links between the past ("the ancestral heritage which is still alive in the unconscious") and the present, thus creating a vital link between consciousness "and the historical psyche which extends over infinitely long periods of time" (CW14: 474fn297). In another passage, Jung specifically links his use of amplification to hermeneutics: "The essence of hermeneutics," like the essence of amplification, "consists in adding further analogies to the one already supplied by the symbol" (CW7: 493). Then, in a letter written to Henry Corbin in 1953, Jung claims Schleiermacher as one of his "spiritual ancestors," explaining that: "The vast, eso-teric, and individual spirit of Schleiermacher was a part of the intellectual atmosphere of my father's family . . . unconsciously he was for me a *spiritus rector*" (Jung 1973 [May 4, 1953], quoted in Nagy 1991: 2).

Roger Brooke, in his rather remarkable book *Jung and Phenomenology* (1991) has accomplished the task of demonstrating rather convincingly that Jung employed a hermeneutic method in his investigations into psychic life. Brooke starts by referring to Steele's successful efforts "to identify Jung as a fairly consistent hermeneut" and then cites a remark of Hillman's that Jung's particular focus on understanding clearly places him within a stream of thinkers which includes Dilthey and Nietzsche (1991: 29). In the end, Brooke concludes for himself that Jung's method was "essentially hermeneutic" (ibid.: 49) and points to an assortment of evidence: Jung's valuing of purpose and meaning above "objectivity," his awareness that truth is shaped in the context of history, his great interest in reading and interpreting ancient and classical texts, his focus on trying to understand rather than explain psychological phenomena, his recognition that understanding is inseparable from interpretation, his way of "reading" and interpreting the various expressions of psychological life (for example, dreams, drawings and paintings, physical symptoms, and behaviors), and his sensitivity to the "constituting power" of language in under-standing (ibid.: 49).

Only a handful of other writers have shown any interest in acknowledging or exploring Jung's connections to hermeneutics. Hillman makes reference to Dilthey, Heidegger, and Husserl in his writings and acknowledges "the fundamental debt that archetypal psychology owes" to Jung, our "immediate ancestor in a long line that stretches back through" Dilthey and others (1975: xi). Steele's book on Freud and Jung is still "to date, the only extensive hermeneutic critique of Jung's work (at least in English)" (Brooke

1991: 141). Steele makes the case that both "analytical psychology and psychoanalysis are hermeneutic disciplines" (1982: 344) and that the analytic dialogue, in its ideal form, is "a model for hermeneutic inquiry" (ibid.: 4). He is convinced that the "core" of the theoretical disagreements between Jung and Freud was "hermeneutic, not scientific" (ibid.: 230).

Karin Barnaby and Pellegrino D'Acierno edited a collection of interdisciplinary papers entitled *C.G. Jung and the Humanities: Toward a Hermeneutics of Culture.* Despite its subtitle, this volume contains papers which are not concerned with hermeneutics as such. It focuses instead on generating "a 'post-Jungian' reading of Jung" (1990: xv) and on demonstrating how Jung's work has contributed "to the interpretative methodologies of the humanities and social sciences" (ibid.: xv). There is one very short essay by Edward S. Casey, Professor of Philosophy, which has some bearing on Jung and hermeneutics in that Casey briefly discusses Jung's attitude toward language and image, and points out intersections between Jung's thinking and the ideas of various thinkers including Heidegger.

Renos K. Papadopoulos and Graham S. Saayman edited a collection of essays called *Jung in Modern Perspective* (1991). Three of these essays have some relevance to the discussion of Jung as hermeneut: psychologist Joseph F. Rychlak points out the link between dialectics and teleology, theologian Morton T. Kelsey argues that Jung's thinking offers a base from which to consider questions of meaning and transcendence, and philosopher Lauri Rauhala discusses some methodological connections between hermeneutics and psychology and some interesting ideas about how Jung's work intersects with Husserl's and Heidegger's.

David Holt, an English analyst, has included a piece entitled "Jung and Hermeneutics: The Hidden Reality" in his book of essays (1992). It is an interesting meditation on hermeneutics, but it does not address Jung's connection to hermeneutics or the place of hermeneutics in Jungian practice. There are brief discussions of Gadamer and Ricoeur, but no reference to any connections between either of them and Jung. Holt's intent in this essay is to give the reader an idea of what hermeneutics has meant to him and to demonstrate how Ricoeur's hermeneutics can be of help in reading Jung.

The opening line of a paper by James L. Jarrett entitled "Jung and Hermeneutics" reads: "Jung is a Hermeneut, something which he himself fully acknowledged" (1992: 66). Jarrett, like Steele, believes that Jung broke from Freud "over a hermeneutic matter" (ibid.: 74) and he is convinced that although Jung "never had a kind word" for Heidegger, these two men "had far more in common than either would have admitted" (ibid.: 81–82). Jarrett also believes that Jung shares "much common ground with Gadamer and Ricoeur," even though Jung probably would have been disappointed by their being "so thoroughly unpsychological" as to insist that a writer's intentions are irrelevant to text interpretation (ibid.: 82).

More recently, D. S. Hewison, in an article entitled "Case History, Case Story: An Enquiry into the Hermeneutics of C. G. Jung," claims that Jung makes "frequent references to his method as being that of hermeneutics" (1995: 384), although he cites only one of these. Hewison is interested specifically in showing how Jung's use of case histories evolved as Jung matured and moved from psychiatry to psychoanalysis and then to analytical psychology. Hewison argues that there was a corresponding evolution along the way in Jung's methods from his early use of methods based in the natural sciences toward a method that was increasingly hermeneutic.

SOME COMMON GROUND BETWEEN GADAMER AND JUNG

The task of identifying some common ground between these two thinkers is not a very difficult one since their work is at the very least exceedingly compatible. Both are engaged in a remarkably similar project: a quest to understand whatever phenomenon lay before them by accepting it on its own terms, and both are possessed of a remarkably similar attitude of openness toward their subject matter. Despite their differing emphases, their attempts at understanding rely essentially on the same principles for "coming into the circle the right way." I will identify and discuss these interrelated, even intertwined, principles mostly as they are applicable to oral discourse (i.e. the interview setting). I have chosen to structure this section using the concepts and language of Gadamer because my intent is to demonstrate how Gadamer's thinking can be seen to provide a philosophical grounding for what Jung did in practice.

1 The dialectical character of understanding

For Gadamer, understanding (if it is possible at all) is achievable only through dialogue. He looks to Plato's dialogues as examples of the "ceaseless dialectical and dialogical labors" which produce a conversation that "not only transforms us but always throws us back on ourselves and joins us to each other" (1989c: 101). These dialogues, according to Gadamer, hold "the great secret of conversation" (ibid.). Gadamer refers repeatedly to the idea that conversation is a partnership and that a conversation is genuine only when it is not exactly the conversation that the partners had set out to have. That is, genuine conversation is not "conducted" by either partner. It "occurs" between them. Neither partner knows in advance where the conversation will take them or what its outcome will be because both are led by the subject matter. Therefore, something can emerge from this conversation which had not existed previously and which is different from what either partner could have arrived at individually. This is a truth "which is neither mine nor yours" (Gadamer 1960/1993: 368).

Gadamer employs the metaphor of "play" to explain the ontological nature of conversation: the partners in a conversation engage in a "to-and-fro movement" much like the "to-and-fro movement" of a game (ibid.: 103). As the players become totally absorbed in the spontaneous movement of the game, the play asserts its "*primacy . . . over the consciousness of the player*" (ibid.: 104, emphasis in original). That is, the play takes on a life of its own and "the player experiences the game as a reality that surpasses him" (ibid.: 109). Subjectivity, in a sense, "forgets itself" as the players surrender themselves to the play of the game (Ricoeur 1981: 186). The partners in conversation also lose themselves in the "to-and-fro" movement of conversation, in the give and take of asking and listening. This movement transcends the subjectivity of both partners who have, through this process, become a "we" rather than an "I and Thou."

It is in this movement that truth "happens." That is, for Gadamer, understanding is always an event, an experience, and its purpose is always to come to an understanding of the subject matter. To have an experience we must be prepared to allow something unexpected to happen, to notice when "something is not what we supposed it to be" (1960/1993: 354), and to admit that what we already "know" about the subject matter may be incorrect or insufficient. Gadamer exhorts us to use "an inner ear" (1989b: 124) and to transpose ourselves "into the other," not in order to understand that particular individual, but in order to understand what is being said about the subject matter (1960/1993: 385). If we focus on the other person rather than on what that person is trying to communicate to us about the subject matter, Linge explains, "the dialogical character of interpretation is subverted" (1976: xx).

Gadamer also insists that "understanding is always interpretation" because interpretation is simply the act of making explicit whatever one has understood (1960/1993: 307). Interpretation does not lead us to understanding; it only shows us what understanding really is: an interpretation or approximation of what one has heard of what was said and from within the context of the interpreter's tradition, prejudices, and presuppositions. Therefore, interpretation can never be more than an attempt to understand which is plausible but never definitive. In addition, interpretation "is always on the way" – that is, it is continually in a process of (re)formation (1981: 105). Therefore, there can never be a single "right" or "final" interpretation. In fact, Gadamer declares, "there is something absurd about the whole idea of a unique, correct interpretation" (1960/1993: 120).

Gadamer acknowledges that the process of achieving understanding does not always proceed smoothly. We often "speak past each other" and sometimes we even are "at cross-purposes with ourselves" (1989d: 57). This does not mean that understanding is impossible, only that it has limits. This is not a problem since all human experience is limited, especially in the context of the various limits imposed on us by language. Limitations, disruptions, and breaches of understanding all simply force us to refer again to the text in order to ask more questions about what was written or said, and attempt again to translate the meaning of the text. In an interview situation, these moments become opportunities to ask more questions in order to rectify or verify one's interpretation or understanding.

Jung on the dialectical character of understanding

Jung reiterates, time and again, that his therapeutic method is dialectical. It involves "a dialogue or discussion between two persons" (CW16: 1). The analyst is a "fellow participant" with the analysand (ibid.: 7) and must treat the analysand as an equal partner having "the same rights as" the analyst (CW18: 1172). Jung sees this kind of partnership "in a common process" to be a fundamental requirement of dialogue (ibid.). Of course, Jung's approach to understanding is psychological and his focus is therefore on the other person's experience rather than on the subject matter as such. However, I believe it is arguable that Jung's focus on the individual is really a focus on the psyche which, ultimately, *is* his subject matter. In addition, Jung, like Gadamer, realizes the limits of understanding, noting for example that "perfect understanding of another individuality is totally impossible" (CW7: 461).

Although Jung argues in some places that "understanding is not an exclusively intellectual process" (CW8: 468), he often associates it with the intellect and with the function of directed thinking that belongs to consciousness. He acknowledges, however, that intellectual understanding cannot, by itself, accomplish very much. It can produce interpretations, but interpretations and understanding are meaningful only to the extent that they further the goal of having an experience of the psyche (that is, in Gadamer's terms, of experiencing understanding as an event).

Jung's descriptions of the workings of the transcendent function often reverberate with Gadamer's ideas of play. For example, in an essay on the transcendent function, Jung argues that consciousness cannot be in control of this process, that "the lead must be left as far as possible to the chance ideas and associations thrown up by the unconscious" (CW8: 178). This allows a dialogue to occur between consciousness and the unconscious, a "shuttling to and fro of arguments and affects," which if successful "generates a tension charged with energy and creates a living, third thing," the transcendent function (ibid.: 189). Paraphrasing Gadamer, we might say that this third factor belongs to neither consciousness nor the unconscious (that is, it is "neither mine nor yours"); rather, it transcends both "partners."

2 Linguisticality

Language for Gadamer has a "fundamental priority" in our lives in that it forms our thinking and our world view, and thus it shapes our experience of the world as a whole (1960/1993: 401). In fact, our world is world only to the extent that "it comes into language" (ibid.: 443) since it is language which makes the disclosure of being possible. Language is not a barrier to understanding, nor does it limit our capacity to reach an understanding; rather, it is the medium through which we can hope to reach understanding with others about something. That is, language mediates between us and the world. Our choice of words is a deliberate though not always conscious attempt to convey meaning. Every word carries with it not only its consciously intended meaning ("the said"), but also "the unsaid" – that which cannot be conveyed because it is never possible to convey all of the meaning (1960/1993: 458) and because the mind of the interpreter is not "in control of what words of tradition reach him" (ibid.: 461). In addition, language is possessed of a "multivocity"; that is, words and concepts contain a wealth of history and may have many shades of meaning, some of which are unconscious and "go on speaking together in the background" (Gadamer 1989b: 121).

Gadamer argues, therefore, that language is fundamentally metaphorical and that it works symbolically. Gadamer discusses "symbol" in the context of differentiating it from "sign." A symbol, unlike a sign, "can be interpreted inexhaustibly" because it represents the "unrepresentable" (1960/1993: 74, 154). It must be "lingered over" to get at its meanings (ibid.: 152). Gadamer is not concerned with ascertaining the "correct" meaning of a word, as if a word could have a fixed meaning or reflect some "pregiven order of being" (ibid.: 457). By treating language as symbolic, particular words can be made to come alive with meaning, to speak more deeply than mere surface appearances would suggest. In this context, amplification might consist, for example, in offering a substitute word or a metaphorical interpretation of a word, always looking for what Jung called "a click," that is, for some resonance on the part of the other. In this way, amplification becomes an act both of interpretation and of translation.

Jung on language

Jung's interest in language can be traced back to an early period in his career when he conducted what have come to be called "the association experiments." In these experiments, Jung explored the role language plays in communication between consciousness and the unconscious. Jung came to recognize that there are two languages: one used by consciousness, which requires the use of speech and language, and one used by the unconscious, which requires images (dreams, fantasies, drawings, etc.). Interaction between these two languages is achieved through "the magic of the symbol" which bridges the gap between them (CW13: 44).

Like Gadamer, Jung is careful to distinguish "symbol" from "sign." A sign represents something known while a symbol is "the best possible formulation of a relatively *unknown* thing" (CW6: 815). A symbol is "a living thing" which emerges spontaneously as a "mediatory product" of the tension between consciousness and the unconscious (ibid.: 816, 825). A symbol must be interpreted in order to understand a situation, even though this can never be done fully or definitively since the symbol always points beyond itself to some meaning which is difficult to express in language since it represents either something unknown or something which is in the process of "becoming" (as Gadamer might say). According to Jung, the "hermeneutic significance" of a symbol is served when we do not try to reduce it to something we *already* know (CW7: 492). Jung's primary method for working with symbols is amplification, a procedure which operates on the principle that in order to understand the meaning of a symbol one must "stick with" (or "linger over") the image and bring to it all possible associations, whether personal or cultural, whether provided by the analyst or the analysand.

While Jung tends to privilege image in the way that Gadamer privileges language,[4] he is fully aware of the symbolic capacity of language, noting that language is "a system of signs and symbols that denote real occurrences or their echo in the human soul" (CW5: 13). In other words, language, like image, carries meaning and can be understood symbolically. Jung also has a great appreciation for the ways in which language shapes our experiences and the meanings we take from them.[5] He also acknowledges connections between language and tradition, noting that words acquire their meaning through social as well as personal influences and that "*thinking in words* is manifestly an instrument of culture" (ibid.: 17). In another essay, he acknowledges that we are constantly "confronted with the history of language" since the linguistic categories by which we assign meaning "are historical categories that reach back into the mists of time" (CW9i: 67).

3 Self-understanding

For Gadamer, "the being of the interpreter" is crucial to, and ever present in, every interpretation since this is what the interpreter "brings along" in anticipation of wanting to understand something (1981: 136). Therefore, all understanding involves self-understanding. Decisive to the process of self-understanding is the ability to experience a "Thou," that is, to fully recognize the otherness of the text which stands before us asserting "its own rights" and requiring "absolute recognition" (1960/1993: xxxv). Self-understanding, in effect, is "the light that one can bring to another and which constitutes . . . 'the authenticity of Being-with'" the other (1989c: 95). Self-understanding is possessed of some continuity, but it is lacking in "unshakable certainty" (ibid.: 97) because the continuity of self-understanding "consists in constantly putting oneself into question" (1989b: 119). For example, one must lose oneself in the process of entering a text "in order to find oneself" – even while not knowing "in advance what one will find oneself to be" (1989d: 57).

There are factors which limit our capacity for self-understanding: We are historical beings who can never stand outside our tradition or outside the accumulation of our own historical experiences and we have a "dimension of unilluminated unconscious" which can never be totally illuminated (Gadamer 1981: 103). Yet, self-understanding proceeds not in linear fashion, but "from a relentless inner tension between illumination and concealment" (ibid.: 104). As a result, it is continually changing, "always on-the-way" (ibid.: 103), and never complete.

Gadamer had expressed some hopefulness in *Truth and Method* that "a hermeneutical consciousness" was "gradually growing" in the human sciences and "infusing research with a spirit of self-reflection" (1960/1993: 285). Twenty years later, however, he declared with a sense of "intense urgency" that we are still badly in need of self-understanding today "for we live in a condition of ever-increasing self-estrangement" (1981: 149).

Jung on self-understanding

Jung believes that the work of psychotherapy is dependent upon the being of the analyst since "all psycho-therapeutic methods are, by and large, useless" (CW7: 342). It was Jung who convinced Freud that every analyst-in-training must undergo the same rigorous process of self-examination as the analysand so as to minimize the impact of unanalyzed prejudices on the analysand. "Personal and theoretical prejudices," according to Jung, "are the most serious obstacles in the way of psychological judgment" (CW16: 237). He believes they can be overcome "with a little good will and insight" and "adequate self-criticism" (ibid.). Yet he also realizes that "no analysis is capable of banishing all unconsciousness for ever" since every new situation will evoke new unconscious contents (ibid.: 239). Therefore, we must expect that this is a process that goes on "endlessly" (ibid.).

Jung, like Gadamer, also notes the tragedy of our "progressive alienation" from ourselves. He phrases this as an alienation from our "instinctual foundation" and attributes it to our preoccupation "with consciousness at the expense of the unconscious" (CW10: 557). He believes that through a process of widening consciousness, we can counteract this and establish "a function of relationship to the world of objects, bringing the individual into absolute, binding, and indissoluble communion with the world at large" (CW7: 275) – thus achieving, in Gadamer's language, the capacity to form a "we" from the "I and Thou." Jung is aware, much like Gadamer, that this is critical to communal life. Without it, we are likely to project our own shadows onto our neighbors with catastrophic results.

4 Tradition, historicity, and subjectivity

As was already discussed in Chapter 3, Gadamer argues that even before we begin to interpret anything at a conscious level, we already have brought to the task a perspective or way of thinking that is informed by the way something is already understood within our tradition. That is, understanding is always historically situated. To see tradition only as an obstacle to be transcended or set aside only alienates us from our own historicity. Our situatedness does not necessarily prevent or hinder understanding. Rather, it can be the horizon or condition through which understanding even becomes possible. Self-knowledge, while helpful to understanding, cannot dissolve these forces of "effective history" since no amount of self-reflection will allow us to step outside of our horizon. Gadamer is emphatic on this point: "The consciousness of being conditioned does not supersede our conditionedness" (1960/1993: 448). That is, being aware of our conditionedness does not mean that we can act as if we had not been conditioned.

In a related move, Gadamer disputes the concept of subjectivity arguing, in effect, that there is no such thing as subjectivity because none of us is that independent of our tradition. That is, we are so conditioned and shaped by our tradition that very little can be purely "subjective" and our prejudices cannot be "our personal property alone" (Warnke 1987: 78). Therefore, understanding, which results from an interplay between tradition and the interpreter's anticipation of meaning, cannot be reduced to "an act of subjectivity" (Gadamer 1960/1993: 293). Gadamer has been accused both of abandoning subjectivity and of arguing in favor of it. But I believe Madison's assessment is the most accurate: Gadamer's purpose "is not to abandon subjectivity, as if it were some dreadful metaphysical construct which gets in the way of the advent of Being (*Ereignis*), but to arrive at a less 'subjectivistic,' less Cartesian conception of it" (1991: 134).

Jung on tradition, history, and subjectivity

Although Jung considers history to be outside his usual purview, he has written a number of essays dealing with the relationship between history and psychology, and he makes occasional references to the role of history and tradition in human life. For example, he recognizes that every idea has "historical antecedents" (CW9i: 69), that the past is "just as important" as the future because we cannot imagine the future without a sense of "the continuity of history" (CW17: 250), and that the continuing differentiation of consciousness is dependent upon our linking ourselves to the past through new interpretations of our tradition – otherwise, we are doomed to a "a kind of rootless consciousness" (CW9i: 267). This is not to say that Jung thinks history itself is all that important. He does not. In the end, he dismisses events of history as "profoundly unimportant" (CW10: 315). What is important for Jung, as always, is how history affects the individual. For Jung, history is merely one of the layers of collective life.

Jung's method of amplification provides another example of Jung's respect for the stream of tradition. Through amplification, the individual's images, symbols, and metaphors are placed within and linked to the larger context of cultural myths, stories, history, etc., the point being to further the individual's relationship with the unconscious layers of the psyche. It is a procedure which leads us to discover "lines of psychological development . . . that are at once individual and collective" (CW7: 493). That is, through amplification we are moved beyond what is literally said to a larger context.

174

For Jung, psychic existence embraces both the objective and subjective levels of experience. It is "subjective in so far as an idea occurs in only one individual. But it is objective in so far as that idea is shared by a society" (CW11: 4). Jung is fully aware that there are historical and cultural forces which contribute to an individual's historicity and to the formation of prejudices. An individual's subjective prejudices are not really so subjective. They are "carefully constructed" over a lifetime of "colliding with the environment" (CW16: 236). In most cases, a subjective prejudice is really a "variant of a universal human experience" (ibid.) and is received by the individual "from the stream of tradition and from environmental influences" (ibid.: 241). Only a very small portion of prejudices are consciously chosen. Rather, we and they are forged "by external and objective social influences" and "by internal and unconscious forces" (ibid.). Like Gadamer and Heidegger, Jung makes a distinction between subjectivity and "*subjectivism*" (CW11: 777). He rejects the latter, but expresses some concern at the tendency of some "scientifically-minded" people to dismiss the subjective side of psychic reality in favor of "*facts*" (ibid.: 767). What Jung insists upon, however, is that we always see subjectivity within a larger context – that is, as Jarrett notes, Jung "always wants to check the subjective to make sure it is not purely idiosyncratic" (1992: 79).

5 An attitude of openness and good will

Even if we accept Gadamer's efforts at rehabilitating the concept of prejudice, we are still left with another difficult question: since we cannot avoid our preconceptions, how can we "distinguish the true prejudices, by which we *understand*, from the *false* ones, by which we *misunderstand*" (1960/1993: 298–299)? According to Gadamer, the preconditions to a partnership of conversation are that the partners share a desire both to understand and to be understood, that they are willing "to recognize the full value" of the other's view while at the same time holding on to their own arguments (ibid.: 387), and that they accept that the text/other has something to tell them. "One must seek to understand the other, and that means that one has to believe that one could be in the wrong" (1989b: 119). Gadamer's term for this readiness to be so open to the other is "good will."

Good will is demonstrated through our willingness to ask

questions to which we do *not* know the answer (rather than questions intended to prove ourselves right). It is marked by a willingness to put ourselves, our ideas, and our prejudices at risk by giving them "full play" (1960/1993: 299). In this paradoxical move, we are truly opened up to the possibility of experiencing "the other's claim to truth" (ibid.) and we can truly respond to the text instead of feeling compelled to defend our preconceptions. We can feel free to revise our previous understanding, "not because we are prepared to believe anything" but because we are really interested in learning about the subject matter (Weinsheimer 1985: 167). As Warnke (1987: 86) puts it, we must accept that the text "is a better authority on the subject matter" than we are; otherwise, we will only be able to confirm our original opinion.

Thus dialectics is really the "art of testing" one's own beliefs rather than those of the other person; it is "the art of thinking" not "the art of arguing" (Gadamer 1960/1993: 367). The purpose of conversation is not to find the blind spot of the other or to hold the other "to something he or she said," but to hear what the other has really wanted to say and even "to strengthen the other's viewpoint so that what the other person has to say becomes illuminating" (1989d: 118, 55). Gadamer tells us, in fact, that we cannot really defend any evidence we have gathered until "all efforts to doubt it have failed" (1989b: 120). This is "part of the moral aspect of the so-called objectivity of research .... a nonnegotiable moral achievement" that far surpasses any attempt to ensure objectivity through the use of some method (ibid.).

Jung on openness and good will

According to Hillman, Jung's method requires "that one go to the phenomenon itself, judgment suspended" in order to reach the place "where the soul clamours for understanding" (1981: 290). This attitude of openness, which has been described by Brooke as "an attitude of respectful receptivity toward psychic phenomena" (1991: 90), is often associated with Jung's willingness to dispense with theoretical knowledge in order to approach "the task of *understanding* with a free and open mind" (CW10: 495). Jung is very aware that there is no way that even the most experienced therapist can "know the psyche of another individual" (CW17: 181). Instead, in most cases, the therapist must rely on "goodwill," that is, on establishing "human contact" with the other. This means that the therapist must not enter the therapeutic process with "a fixed belief in some theory." That could undermine the partnership by putting the therapist in the position possibly "of riding roughshod over" the analysand's "real psychology." Instead, human contact can be achieved only if both partners are unfettered by "prejudice" and are willing to put their respective points of view at risk by comparing them (ibid.). In another passage, Jung also cautions that in every deep encounter with an analysand, the analyst's "philosophy of life" and convictions are put in jeopardy and may be "shattered" by repeated collisions "with the truth of the patient" (CW16: 180). The therapist must be prepared for this and "must abandon all preconceived notions and, for better or worse, go with [the patient] in search of" whatever will be healing for that patient (ibid.: 184). In other words, both therapist and patient must allow themselves to be led by the subject matter (i.e. the psyche).

Jung understands that "the purpose of research is not to imagine that one possesses the theory which alone is right, but, doubting all theories, to approach gradually nearer to the truth" (CW8: 569). Jung constantly tries out new ideas and methods because he is convinced that no insight can ever be the final or only word. The issue is never to prove that one is "right," but to help people "get hold on their own lives" (CW7: 493). We do this by accepting the other just as he or she is (as a Thou, we might say) and by maintaining a "deep respect" for the individual "and for the riddle of" his or her life (CW11: 519). To attain such an "unprejudiced" attitude "is a moral achievement on the part of the doctor" (ibid.).

Finally, we might consider how Jung, in the course of his famous "confrontation with the unconscious" (1913–1917), made a deliberate decision, as Humbert describes it, "to allow the unconscious to speak" and "to remain open to what might happen" (1988: 9). Humbert analyzes three German words or phrases that Jung used in describing this encounter: "*geschehenlassen* (to let happen)" which he describes as an "attitude of openness" (ibid.); "*betrachten* (to consider, to impregnate)" which he translates as "to realize" (ibid.: 10, 11); and "*sich auseinandersetzen* (to confront oneself with)" which he relates to the moment of consciousness (ibid.: 12). As Humbert's discussion makes clear, this experience of Jung's became foundational to his method and its underlying attitude of openness toward the unknown and the other.

6 The priority of the question

For Gadamer, questioning is essential to dialogue and to enticing a thing encountered into disclosing itself. It is questioning that "places hermeneutical work on a firm basis" because only one "who has questions can have knowledge" (1960/1993: 269, 365). It is the question which "breaks through into the open" that "makes an answer possible" (ibid.: 366). Referring to Plato, Gadamer argues that asking questions is more difficult than answering them and that the ability to ask questions is "a critical distinction between authentic and inauthentic dialogue" (1960/1993: 363). Asking questions is easy only if someone is trying "to prove himself right" rather than trying to gain insight since there is no risk involved (or point) in asking a question to which one already knows the answer. If one wants to ask a meaningful or "true" question, that is, a question "that is intended to reveal something," then "one must want to know" – and, in order to do that, one must acknowledge that one does not already know something (ibid.). Only when we can admit that we do not know something will we be led to ask "a particular question" (ibid.: 366). Therefore, the art of questioning, like the art of conversation, has nothing to do with winning arguments, but is the art "of conducting real dialogue" (ibid.: 367).

Gadamer argues that once one accepts the priority of the question over the answer, it becomes clear that there is no "method of learning to ask questions, of learning to see what is questionable" (ibid.: 365). The art of questioning is neither "a craft that can be taught" nor a technique intended to help us "master the discovery of truth" (ibid.: 366). Rather, since the art of questioning is the art of seeking truth, it is also "the art of questioning even further" because someone who really wants to know something will continue to ask questions "until the truth of what is under discussion finally emerges" (ibid.: 367, 368). This is another unending task, of course, since everything said as an answer to a question "gives rise always to a new question" (1989c: 95)

Jung on questions and not knowing

Although Jung, to my knowledge, never discusses "questioning" as such, he was certainly driven by a voracious curiosity. In reflections written toward the end of his life, he declares that:

In my case, it must have been primarily a passionate urge toward understanding which brought about my birth. For that is the strongest element in my nature. This insatiable drive toward understanding has, as it were, created a consciousness in order to know what is and what happens, and in order to piece together mythic conceptions from the slender hints of the unknowable.

(1961: 322)

On the whole, Jung's work is permeated with a willingness to admit that there is so much he does not know. The unknowable is simply a fact for him: "Since we do not know everything," he writes, "practically every experience, fact, or object contains something unknown" (CW11: 68). In the context of working with the unconscious, "we simply do not know what we are dealing with" (CW10: 312). Even the "self" is "essentially unknown" (CW11: 956). And his "constructive method" works on the principle of building "towards an unknown goal" (CW3: 423).[6]

Jung's way of approaching the unknown is probably no more obvious than in his writings about working with dreams. For example, Jung advises that we "treat every dream as though it were a totally unknown object" and thus allow it to "lead us closer to its meaning" (CW10: 320). When working with a dream, he assumes that every dream is like "a text which I do not understand properly" because it contains certain unknown words or because "the text is fragmentary" (CW18: 172). In these situations, Jung applies "the ordinary method any philologist would apply in reading such a text." Jung does this because he believes that the dream has something to say even though its language is difficult for us to understand. So, he simply starts by admitting to himself that he does not understand anything about the dream. "I always welcome that feeling of incompetence because then I know I shall put some good work into my attempt to understand the dream" (ibid.: 173).

7 Agreement and 'the fusion of horizons'

It is basic to Gadamer's hermeneutics that the partners in a genuine conversation are dedicated to achieving some kind of agreement about their subject matter.[7] Only then can they "part from one another as changed beings" whose "individual perspectives" have been transformed (1981: 110). In line with this, the "first

179

condition" of dialogue for Gadamer is that we try to be sure "that the other person is with us" (1960/1993: 367) by making every effort "to eliminate false agreements, misunderstandings, and misinterpretations" (1989d: 56). Gadamer is fully aware that agreement is "shaped and reshaped" over the course of dialogue and that it may be impossible to achieve complete agreement since even between only two participants "this would require a never-ending dialogue" (ibid.: 56, 57).

Reaching agreement is not about accommodating the other, or giving in to the other's opinion, or creating a synthesis of views. Rather, as Warnke explains, reaching an agreement involves "integrating the tradition or opinions" of the other into our "search for the 'truth'" and attempting "to come to some kind of position that both they and we can support" (1987: 102). But how does such agreement occur? To answer this, Gadamer introduces the concept of "the fusion of horizons." To understand this rather complex idea, we will need to build on Gadamer's concept of horizon as it was discussed in Chapter 3.

Gadamer acknowledges that in order to understand what a text is trying to tell us, we must transpose ourselves into the historical horizon of that text. However, this in itself is not sufficient. We will keep our own standpoint "safe" this way and we may come to understand the other's horizon, but we will not come to any agreement about anything or arrive at any meaningful or intelligible truth for ourselves. We merely will have treated the other as "the object of objective knowledge" who has no claim to truth (1960/1993: 304) *and* we will have disregarded the perspective of our own horizon. We must not (and really cannot) disregard ourselves this way. Rather "into this other situation we must bring, precisely, ourselves" (ibid.: 305). Our own horizon is decisive in "re-awakening the text's meaning" and must be brought into play (i.e. put at risk) in order to keep open every possibility of understanding (ibid.: 388). The problem is how to find some way of acquiring a "higher" point of view that will enable us to apprehend "not only our own particularity but also that of the other" (ibid.: 305). Gadamer points out that there are always tensions between the interpreter and the text/other. The task of hermeneutics is not to cover up these tensions by trying to synthesize the two horizons into one, but rather to bring out the tensions consciously (i.e. through foregrounding). If we can hold that tension while we also leave ourselves open to the other, a "fusion of horizons" will result and the tension will be dissolved, thus allowing the partners to come to an agreement about their subject matter that goes beyond the initial position of either participant. Whether the participants change their positions or not, the understanding that results from this fusion is deeper than what each began with because the views of each partner are now informed by the position of the other.

Jung on agreement and horizons

Jung consciously (though not always successfully) resists making authoritative statements. He believes that claims by the analyst to "superior knowledge" are pretentious and that the analyst, in order to treat someone psychologically, must give up "all authority and desire to influence" (CW16: 2). Instead, the analyst must adopt "a dialectical procedure consisting in a comparison of our mutual findings." Jung declares that this is "possible only if I give the other person a chance to play his hand to the full, unhampered by my assumptions." Here Jung clearly treats the idea of "mutual findings" as a step in the process of reaching understanding (ibid.). Like Gadamer, Jung is intent on reaching some agreement with the other. He knows that it does not really matter "whether the doctor understands or not, but it makes all the difference whether the patient understands" (ibid.: 314). That is, if only the doctor understands then there is a danger that this understanding is "from the standpoint of a preconceived opinion." But if only the patient understands, then there is a loss of contact between the patient and the doctor, and any "understanding" will reach only the patient's intellect and, therefore, will not be fully experienced. Therefore, meaningful understanding must be "an agreement which is the fruit of joint reflection" (ibid.). In addition, both partners must be totally engaged in this dialectical process so that each will enter into a "reciprocal reaction with [the] psychic system" of the other (ibid.: 1). This is "like mixing two different chemical substances: if there is any combination at all, both are transformed" (ibid.: 163) and can part as Gadamer's "changed beings." This requires that the analyst put her/himself at risk by becoming "susceptible to influence" by the analysand so that something can happen or emerge between them that could not otherwise have occurred (ibid.). Implied in all of this is a tension between the doctor and the patient which, via the transcendent function, will constellate the symbolic material necessary for individuation. I believe it is arguable that Jung's concept of the transcendent function in fact operates much like Gadamer's idea of the fusion of horizons.

Jung believes that understanding, as it deepens, "becomes increasingly subjectivized" (CW10: 532) and thus threatens to create a barrier between the partners in conversation. That is, "sooner or later" things reach a point "where one partner feels he is being forced to sacrifice his own individuality." Jung's advice is "to carry understanding only to the point where the balance between understanding and knowledge is reached" since "understanding at all costs is injurious to both partners" (ibid.). In other words, understanding is not about accommodating or giving in to the other.

In a couple of passages that bring to mind Gadamer's discussion of transposing ourselves into the horizon of the other, Jung cautions that if the analyst only "moves within a psychological sphere that is similar in kind to the patient's" (that is, within the horizon of the other), then "nothing of fundamental therapeutic importance has happened" (CW16: 544). At best, the analyst may lay the foundations for understanding (the horizon) of that person and may gain "some inkling" of the otherness of another person, "to respect it, and to guard against the outrageous stupidity of wishing to interpret it" (CW7: 363). This may be useful, but it will not help in coming to terms with what is disturbing the patient. To do that, Jung says, requires "an encounter between my premises and the patient's" (CW16: 544).

POSTSCRIPT: FEMINIST CRITIQUES OF GADAMER

Feminist critiques of Gadamer are relatively rare (at least in English). In one almost hostile critique, Robin Schott accuses Gadamer, rightly to some extent, of ignoring cultural and other power differentials. She seems however to ignore the fact that Gadamer's position is, in effect, an appeal. That is, he is arguing for the ideal, for a way to establish conditions of genuine dialogue by employing good will, engaging in a partnership of conversation, recognizing the role of prejudice and historicity. Schott accuses Gadamer of "bracketing" various power differentials (1991: 205). Perhaps he is guilty of that. Perhaps he is not able to foreground these factors as he would have us do. Perhaps this is his "flaw." In any case, the problem I have with Schott's critique is that it lacks imagination and does not suggest any "program of renewal." Her points are legitimate, but not very helpful.

On the other hand, other feminists thinkers have turned to Gadamer's ideas and seen them as compatible with a feminist perspective. Nielsen, for example, argues that feminist inquiry is characterized by a move toward and reliance upon dialectical processes and she refers to dialectics and Gadamer's fusion of horizons as a "next step in knowledge generation," a kind of "post-feminism" (1990: 29). Nielsen acknowledges that a fusion of horizons is most constructive when all of the participants "are free to engage in unlimited dialogue," that is, when there is "a context of equality" (ibid.: 29, 30). So, she concludes that feminist re-searchers should address themselves to finding ways of "removing the structural features and barriers that distort or limit open, free dialogue" (ibid.: 30). In this way, she argues, feminst research will come "closer to realizing, or at least better exemplifying" Gad-amer's idea of the fusion of horizons (ibid.: 31) – which, clearly, she thinks would be a good move. Her suggestion, I believe, qualifies as "a program of renewal."

Hekman argues for a feminist postmodernism that would further the agendas of both movements. She restricts her discussion of postmodernism to Foucault, Derrida, and Gadamer because she sees their work as "particularly germane to feminist issues" (1990: 8). She admits that it is easier to present a case for Gadamer as a postmodernist, than to establish his "relevance for contemporary feminism" (ibid.: 15). She identifies two problems she sees in relation to Gadamer and feminism: (1) How can Gadamer's reliance on tradition and prejudice be relevant to an anti-traditional move-ment like feminism? Hekman discusses this question and concludes that Gadamer's views simply "do not amount to an advocacy of bias" (ibid.); and (2) How can Gadamer's embracing of values that are typically seen as "feminine" be helpful since that merely substitutes a "feminist epistemology" for a "masculinist" one (ibid.: 16)? Hekman discusses this issue and resolves it by concluding that Gadamer's position actually provides "material for an attack on the gendered connotations of ways of knowing" (ibid.: 17).

I propose that Gadamer's hermeneutics is entirely compatible with a feminist perspective. In spite of some problematic areas, there are innumerable links and a huge territory of common ground between them. I believe that the following quote supports my claim. It is from Judith Butler, a leading feminist philosopher –

who, to my knowledge, never discusses hermeneutics or acknowledges Gadamer. In the context of noting "the ambivalent implications of the decentering of the subject," Butler alludes to the difficulties involved in "owning" what one has written once it has been taken up and inevitably changed by others (1993: 242). Butler goes on to say:

> This not owning of one's words is there from the start, however, since speaking is always in some ways the speaking of a stranger through and as oneself, the melancholic reiteration of a language that one never chose, that one does not find an instrument to be used, but that one is, as it were, used by, expropriated in, as the unstable and continuing condition of the "one" and the "we," the ambivalent condition of the power that binds.

> (ibid.)

I cannot be sure that Gadamer would have written such a statement, but I believe he would find it to be entirely compatible with his own thinking.

CONTEMPORARY THINKING ON HERMENEUTICS AS A RESEARCH METHODOLOGY

Since there are so many versions of hermeneutics, it is not surprising that there is as yet no consensus about the fundamentals involved in what might be called a hermeneutic methodology. In the last chapter of his classic text on hermeneutics, Palmer suggested and summarized his "Thirty Theses on Interpretation" (1969: 242). He had hoped these would serve as guidelines for literary interpretation. However, even he has come to the conclusion, regretfully and many years later, that he "was never able to carry through the manifesto" that appears at the end of his book and by which he had hoped to delineate "an alternative method of interpreting literary texts."[8]

Discussions about the nature of a hermeneutic methodology and how it may be applied in a research setting have just begun and very little has been written in the context of psychological research. The most ambitious effort to date has been Packer and Addison's *Entering the Circle: Hermeneutic Investigation in Psychology* (1989). This book contains a collection of diverse studies, all of which are examples of interpretive research, and it includes comprehensive introductory and closing chapters.

Packer and Addison characterize hermeneutical research as "exploratory, discovery-oriented" and aimed at generating theory rather than at testing hypotheses (1989: 7). They believe that a hermeneutical approach to research offers "a *better* perspective on the world than the traditional twins" of rationalism and empiricism (ibid.: 14) and they argue that, in the human sciences, research methodologies must not and cannot be reduced to a set of procedures. They identify four major points of comparison that differentiate hermeneutics from traditional approaches (points not very different from those made by many feminist researchers and discussed in Chapter 9). A hermeneutic methodology:

1 refuses to accept notions such as the neutrality of the observer and the subject/object split;
2 asserts the belief that all knowledge is the result of interpretation and therefore can never be "certain" or "value-free";
3 is committed to producing narrative accounts which attempt "to keep discussion open and alive, to keep inquiry under way" rather than searching for causal explanations or "regularities and predictive laws" which can be tested and validated (ibid.: 35, 25); and
4 rejects the concept of "objectivity" and the correspondence theory of truth.

Packer and Addison also make the point that a hermeneutical methodology in contrast to most traditional methodologies does not seek to avoid making interpretations. In fact, hermeneutic investigation assumes the inevitability of interpretation and looks to the hermeneutic circle as a guiding principle. They describe the hermeneutic circle as being made up of two arcs: a "forward arc" through which the investigator approaches the subject matter from a particular perspective and a "reverse arc" through which the investigator makes sense of, evaluates, and interprets what has been understood (ibid.: 33). While the forward arc of projection requires that the researcher consciously recognize (foreground) what is involved in his or her point of view, it also encourages the researcher to adopt a stance that is "engaged and concerned" rather than "detached and neutral" (ibid.: 34). The return arc of interpretation is framed as a movement which allows something to show itself to us. The aim is not to uncover some universal or timeless truth, but to understand our subject matter better. It should be noted that both arcs are formed within the context of the researcher's "tradition" and "prejudices" and that they are not as distinct as Packer and Addison imply. That is, projection is already a form of interpretation and interpretation is already rooted in projection. In any case, this brings us to the question of how we can evaluate or "test" our interpretations.

Interpretive inquiry and the question of reliability and validity

The narratives which I constructed from the interviews and my reflections on them involve interpretations of what was reported to me since both are based on my understanding of what I heard. There is no doubt in my mind that this does not make my account any more or less "true" than any other accounts which might be constructed either by the interviewees themselves or by any other interpreter. Understanding is never merely a reproductive act; that is, it is "always a productive activity as well" (Gadamer 1960/1993: 296). One understanding, therefore, is not necessarily "better" than another, and there are likely to be any number of different understandings.

Ricoeur makes a similar point when he argues that, in the realm of human action, there will be always a variety of interpretations. For this reason, to validate an interpretation is not the equivalent of verifying an interpretation. Validation is appropriate for argumentation (for example, in "juridical procedures"), but not for the interpretation of human activities (1973: 32, 33, quoted in Brooke 1991: 42). In another passage, Ricoeur makes a different but related point: something happens when we write down what we have heard or thought; "writing renders the text autonomous with respect to the intention of the author" (1981: 139). In other words, the meaning of the written text is no longer limited to, or by, the author's intentions. The written text, in a sense, "transcends" the psychology of the author and the "psycho-sociological conditions" which produced it. The text "thereby opens itself to an unlimited series of readings" according to the various "socio-cultural conditions" of its readers. Thus, the text "decontextualizes" itself in such a way that it can be "recontextualised" – for example, "in the act of reading" (ibid.). I would qualify Ricoeur's view by arguing that it is not the text which transcends its conditions, but the reader who, bringing different horizons to the reading of the text, may transcend the conditions of the text through a fusion of horizons with the text.

Packer and Addison (like Gadamer and Heidegger) remind us that, in order to "insure" that interpretations do not consist of conjecture, speculations, or "undisciplined guesses," we must recognize our "responsibility to prepare" ourselves to "enter the circle" appropriately, that is, guided by a desire for "reciprocity" and by "a sense of the complexity of the human relationship" between ourselves and our research participants (1989: 277). This focus on "coming into the circle in the right way" is hermeneutics' response to the concepts of reliability and validity as they exist in conventional scientific research where the emphasis is on developing techniques, strategies, and procedures that will minimize bias. *Reliability* is usually associated with dependability and consistency, and it generally requires some probability that results be duplicated by other neutral observers under similar conditions. *Validity* usually refers to a correspondence between "data" and "fact" and typically involves linking "observation-statements" to "theoretical-statements" in order to produce hypotheses which can be "tested" according to their ability to identify the "causes" of things and to predict future outcomes (ibid.: 24). These two concepts, of course, rest on a number of questionable assumptions, for example that "objective" facts are superior to "subjective" facts, that there is a one-to-one relationship between perception and fact, that "facts" are neutral and measurable, that there is a "neutral" observer who is in a position to determine what is "fact," that human beings operate in a predictable manner, that prediction is an indicator of understanding, etc.

The evaluation of interpretive accounts

It has been argued by many that traditional science's concepts of reliability and validity are simply not relevant or appropriate to qualitative research. Kitzinger counters traditional methodologies by repudiating the idea that only the researcher is "the expert" who "can distinguish truth from falsehood" (1987: 68) and by refusing to engage in a search for "facts" which would support a particular version of the "truth." She is convinced, for example, that lesbians construct a variety of accounts about lesbianism by which they negotiate and interpret their own experiences. Therefore, she conducted her interviews "without any checks for reliability or validity as these are usually understood" because, as she explains, her aim was "not to obtain 'the truth' about lesbianism but to collect and explore the variety of accounts people construct about lesbianism" (ibid.: 71).

Moustakas takes the position that reliability in qualitative research is not dependent upon replication or the ability to produce "consistent accounts" (1994: 143). Rather, it is about being able to interpret the "data" from a variety of standpoints or to explore "the same issues in different contexts." And he argues that validity in qualitative research should not be considered in relation to objective "facts" but rather in relation to the researcher's ability "to understand and represent people's meanings" (ibid.).

Banister *et al.*, take a similar stand and argue, in effect, that all components of an interpretive account "are treated as valued resources rather than factors that must be screened out" (1994: 14). They propose that qualitative research is characterized by three features:

(1) *Indexicality* The objective of qualitative research is not to produce findings which can be replicated, but to render visible the factors (horizons, prejudices, language) which shaped the research and to ensure "the rights of the informant to speak" (ibid.: 11).

(2) *Inconcludability* Interpretive researchers accept that a totally controlled research setting is impossible and undesirable, and that there will be a "gap" between the meaning of what was reported/observed and what appears in the researcher's account (ibid.: 12). This is seen as an opportunity or "space for a reader to bring their own understanding of the issue to bear on the text" and thus "to supplement" the researcher's account (ibid.).

(3) *Reflexivity* Attempts to "erase" subjectivity do not lead to objectivity. Subjectivity, in fact, is "a resource, not a problem" (ibid.: 13). To pretend neutrality is often "disingenuous" since even "a position of distance is still a position." Thus, an "objective" account is really a subjective account and any account which refuses to acknowledge this may actually be dangerous (ibid.).

Packer and Addison reiterate Ricoeur's warning that, when dealing with interpretive accounts, "evaluation is not simply validation" (1989: 282). They discuss four alternative criteria:

(1) *Coherence* (that is, intelligibility). Since coherence is "not inevitable," a conscientious interpretive researcher will need to verify an interpretation "by searching out and focusing on material that doesn't make sense" (ibid.: 281).

(2) *External evidence* (that is, asking respondents to verify the accuracy of interpretations). There are several problems associated with this: First, it does not lead to recovering the individual's original intent, but requires that the respondent recall (i.e. reinterpret) what s/he meant. Second, respondents can "misunderstand their own activity" (ibid.: 284) – which is not to imply that the researcher "knows better" than the respondent, but to make the point that even the respondent's view "cannot provide an objective standard" for evaluating interpretations (ibid.). Third, the researcher's theoretical frame of reference and resulting interpretations might not be accessible to the respondent.

(3) *Consensus* (that is, attempting to produce an account which is accurate and makes sense to others). But who will be asked to make sense of our interpretation? And does agreement guarantee correctness? A better solution might be to "promote reasoned disagreement with our peers" (ibid.: 286), but even there peers "may fail to reach consensus not because their interpretations are flawed but because incommensurable perspectives prevent reasoned disagreement, and people talk past each other" (ibid.).

(4) *Practical implications* Since interpretive accounts do not usually yield "testable predictions," Packer and Addison discuss other ways of considering the implications of an interpretive account (ibid.: 287). For example, they cite Fischer's suggestion that we look to see if our interpretations "prove useful for understanding . . . and for maneuvering in the everyday world" (1987: 8; quoted ibid.). Or, acknowledging the "emancipatory interest" of interpretive inquiry, they cite Lather's suggestion that we look to see if our interpretations make us more aware "of the contradictions hidden or distorted by everyday understandings" and thus help direct our attention "to the possibilities for social transformation" (1986: 259; quoted ibid.).

In the end, Packer and Addison conclude that while these are sound criteria, they do not ensure the kind of validity and reliability that traditional methods attempt to achieve. In fact, they insist, the search for such security is like a quest for the Grail and should be abandoned. Instead, these criteria should be used, but only to help us evaluate whether our account "answers the practical, concernful question that directed [our] inquiry" and whether it has "the power to change practice" (ibid.: 289).

In the context of my own efforts, I would say that I take something from all of these positions. Like Kitzinger, I am not searching for "truth." In keeping with Moustakas' recommendations, I have chosen to interpret my findings from several standpoints (Jungian theory, lesbian studies, a feminist perspective) and to validate people's meanings by having the interviewees verify the accuracy of my narrative accounts of the interviews (rather than my interpretations of them). In line with the criteria suggested by Banister *et al.*, I believe that I have met the spirit of these by foregrounding my theoretical horizons, by refusing to present a definitive account of lesbian experience or to control the interview setting, by making visible the elements of my theoretical framework, and by addressing the issue of subjectivity.

I also believe that I have incorporated Packer and Addison's four criteria. In terms of coherence, I have scrutinized every interpretation and involved others in helping me test their intelligibility. In terms of external evidence, I have involved my interviewees by asking them to read and "validate" my narrative accounts of their interviews. In terms of consensus, I have sought the input and feedback of others and look forward to the "reasoned disagreement" of my peers. In terms of practical implications, I have focused my efforts on the Jungian community and have dedicated myself to confronting its heterosexist, sexist, and racist foundations.

Of course, all of these efforts to meet some criteria for evaluating interpretations are probably still not a perfect solution – but neither, I would argue, is the quest for objectivity, etc. In the end, those of us engaged with interpretive methods must admit that the evaluation of interpretive inquiry will never be accomplished through techniques and procedures and that interpretations will always "be risky and sometimes incorrect" (Packer and Addison 1989: 289). We will never produce "a universally acceptable account" or an account that will "remain true for all time" (ibid.: 290, 289). However, this does not excuse us from trying to find guidelines that will serve the aim of achieving some "true" understanding of our subject matter and that will help us monitor our efforts to produce "better" accounts. In the end, however, we can never be sure, absolutely sure, that we have succeeded in our attempts at understanding. Even hermeneutics "has no magical recipe for evading dogmatism" or avoiding "opinions and pronouncements" (ibid.: 291, 292). Instead, we must acknowledge that psychology "will never be paradigmatic" quite in the same way as the physical sciences and reject attempts to ensure "validity" since these "only exacerbate" the problem of dogmatism (ibid.: 291, 292). Packer and Addison call instead for an attitude of self-critique that would leave us, as interpretive researchers, free "to ferret out anomalies rather than try to prove ourselves correct" (ibid.: 291).

In conclusion, I do not claim to have successfully overcome all of the problems and difficulties associated with interpretive inquiry, but I am willing to let my methodology stand on its own terms without claiming that it is the only way to proceed. In other words, in the same way that I do not expect those who take the path of science to acknowledge, incorporate, or argue in terms put forward by the various interpretive and qualitative methods, I have not attempted to justify my own way of proceeding by recourse to the terms and methods of science.

Hermeneutics is as much a guiding philosophical attitude as a methodology. However, when joined together with Jungian practice, it does meet the criterion that Sandra Harding has described for a methodology in that it provides me with a theory and set of principles that tell me how I should proceed. That the "how" is very fluid and relies to a great extent on my willingness both to be acted upon and to respond in the moment certainly makes it a non-conventional methodology, but this also imbues it with a potential for discovery that I, like Gadamer, have found exciting:

> Understanding is an adventure and, like any other adventure, is dangerous. Just because it is not satisfied with simply wanting to register what is there or said there but goes back to our guiding interests and questions, one has to concede that the hermeneutical experience has a far less degree of certainty than that attained by the methods of the natural sciences. But when one realizes that understanding is an adventure, this implies that it affords unique opportunities as well. It is capable of contributing in a special way to the broadening of our human experiences, our self-knowledge, and our horizon, for everything understanding mediates is mediated along with ourselves.
>
> (Gadamer 1981: 109–110)

12

"NANCY"

PROFILE

Nancy is a 33-year-old white woman. Right after college, Nancy joined the Navy. This was a very happy time for her until she was "outed" and discharged in a traumatizing "witch hunt." Currently, Nancy is employed and in her third year of law school. She had been in a committed relationship, but it ended last year. Nancy is active in sports and takes great pleasure in her athletic interests and abilities.

INTERVIEW SETTING/PROCESS

This interview was conducted long after the others because one of my original interviewees had declined to be included in this book. I did not know Nancy before the interview. Some of her friends were very surprised that she had agreed to be interviewed since she is such a very private person who does not often share much of her internal world with others. Although Nancy did seem somewhat guarded and hesitant at first, it was obvious that she wanted very much to tell her story and to convey to me both the pain and the joy that being a lesbian has brought her.

THE INTERVIEW

Nancy had been thinking about my question since we had talked on the phone. The "first thing" she wanted me to know was: "I can't think of how it's different from loving anybody." Nancy dated men in the past and even "came very close to getting married on a couple of occasions" – but "the physical thing wasn't there."

Nancy cannot see any real difference between straight and gay relationships, and she feels strongly that the quality of her love for another woman is not essentially different from what a man and woman feel toward each other. "If you really love somebody, I don't think that the gender really makes that much of a difference."

Nancy cannot remember exactly when she became aware of her attraction to women, but she also cannot remember "ever really being attracted to men." She had some vague awareness in high school, but did not give it much thought until she was in college. She is not sure how she came to believe that it was "wrong" to be a lesbian since her parents are "very open minded and very liberal in a lot of respects." But there was "a lot of turmoil" at home. Her mother had suffered a major disability when Nancy was young and Nancy "didn't want to rock the boat" or add to any problems. Everyone "had very high expectations" of her and she was deter-mined not to disappoint them. Today Nancy's family is very supportive, but at the time she was afraid to take the chance of telling them.

It was only when Nancy got to college that "the awareness really started hitting" her and she began "subconsciously . . . to face reality." It was her first exposure to anyone who was "out." She began to think: "Well, maybe it isn't wrong because they don't seem so unhappy." But by that point she was very involved in her sorority:

> "and they were like family and I did not want to hurt them or do anything that would cast a bad reputation upon them, so I bottled up even more. . . . By that time the lie was just too big. If I had come out it would have hurt a lot of other people. I wasn't willing to do that. So, I probably did what a lot of young lesbians did – I drank a lot and just tried to kill everything that I felt."

This was like "living two lives": "knowing" she was attracted to women, but feeling she had to date men in order to keep her secret. She did not want to be different. There was "a lot of peer pressure." There was also a lot of internal pressure and hurt from being conscious that she was "playing a part." Nancy is aware that she has paid a price to hide so much from others. She tends to be "very protective" of her feelings and "to put up a wall" with others. As a result, she has been "probably a lot more lonely than I had to be." She does not regret this altogether. She had some good times and some wonderful friends. "It was worth it."

Nancy always knew she was "different" and she thought that being a lesbian "was wrong, but I really didn't dwell on it." She feared "the consequences" of being discovered. Even when she eventually came to realize that society often judges something to be wrong when it is not, there was "still that fear of repercussion, of what society will do to you" – or to the ones you love. And there was an additional factor: Nancy knew that she "wanted to work for the government" and that any hint of being a lesbian would be problematic.

For two years, Nancy loved her life in the Navy. "I felt like I belonged somewhere." She knew that she was making a choice: either she could "go with" her feelings toward women or she could have her career. "At that point, I wanted my career." Nancy loved her very demanding job and did very well at her various assignments. She was told that she was "a natural-born leader." She traveled a lot and even lived overseas. It was all "exciting" and "a lot of fun." So it felt worth it to put her feelings aside. She did not think about it much. She was very busy.

The problem started when a new commanding officer was assigned to her station. He was "very conservative" – and out "to get rid of potential lesbians." He had done it before "and was very proud of it – and he was going to do it again – and he did." The whole thing started for Nancy when she broke up a fight between a woman and a man who wanted the same job. Nancy told both of them that they were acting "stupid." The woman was crying and Nancy "made the mistake of putting my arm around her." She would have done the same thing for a man. "It was just one of those instincts." The man accused Nancy of taking the woman's side. Later on, when Nancy heard that this woman was being investigated, she "didn't take it seriously." She thought it was "ridiculous" – "until they came after me." People were being questioned on the basis of rumors. Suddenly Nancy was dragged into the investigation. They thought she knew more than she did. Eventually, Nancy was threatened with a court martial and pressured into admitting that she was a lesbian (even though she had never been with a woman at that point). She insisted that she did not know anything about anybody else, but felt "put in a position where it was either save my skin or hurt somebody else . . . I would have done *anything* to have kept my job – but I would not destroy other people."

"You go into a situation thinking well, yeah, I'm wrong because society perceives this as wrong. And then you go into an institution where it's a crime. I had never been in trouble in my life and the day they arrested me and charged me with sodomy I could have died. But . . . instead of crumbling, I got very belligerent to the point that I think if I had let them see me cry, they might have been easier on me."

Nancy's last six months in the Navy were a nightmare. The Navy hid the fact that she was being discharged. She was even promoted and given her next set of orders *after* she had already resigned her commission. They told her to keep quiet "and life would be a lot easier" for her, so she did. By the time she realized that she was being used "it was too late." They had promised her an honorable discharge, implying that it would be a medical discharge, but it was not: "When I actually had my paper stamped and it said 'homosexuality' all over the bottom of it, I wanted to crawl under a rock and die – because now that's a public record."

Nancy will never "know the truth of how they came after" her, though she does not believe that anyone was out to get her personally. She "was probably in the wrong place at the wrong time." She believes that what happened "wasn't as much of a gay issue" as a sexist one. If the military wants "to get rid of women all they do is say you're a lesbian and you're *gone.*" Nancy is able to separate her feelings about the Navy itself from her feelings toward the individuals who were responsible for what happened. She still takes pride in the Navy, but she is angry about "the hypocrisy" that allows women to be so badly treated while some married men have "sexual relationships with every woman" in their command.

Throughout this ordeal, Nancy had absolutely no support in her immediate environment. Everyone who cared about her was afraid to get close to her because she "was under such scrutiny and they didn't want to be implicated." Nancy understood: "You have no constitutional rights in the military, so you're always walking a thin line." There is an assumption that "if one of you is a lesbian, then all of you are – you must be if you all get along." Nancy does not know whether the Navy conducted a full investigation of her, but everyone she had used as a reference to enter the Navy has never answered any of her calls since she returned from the Navy. And, to this day, she has had no contact with any of her Navy friends for fear of putting them at risk. Nancy did get some support from her family. She told her sister first because she "was scared to death" to tell her parents, though no one was surprised or disturbed by her coming out. Her father was very supportive throughout, but her mother was very upset at first that Nancy was "giving up" her career. Nancy feels like she has lost a part of her past. "I had life before the Navy and then I had life after the Navy."

Nancy had always been "an overachiever." She links this to being a lesbian and to thinking she "had to be better than everybody else – because I had this 'difference.'" But "the Navy literally beat the ambition out of me." Her discharge "destroyed" her. She got through it by "numbing out the world." There were times in the beginning when she got so tired of everything that she did think about taking "the easy way out." She was "tired of fighting society" and she felt "like a loser." She just wanted to be left alone. She went "into hibernation" for a while, working jobs "where no one would ask me questions." After about a year of this, however, she realized that she could not give up everything she loved to do just because others might try to put her down.

By the time Nancy left the Navy, she felt that she had nothing more to lose. Everybody was accusing her of being a lesbian, so she thought she "might as well go for it." She "just didn't care" anymore. So, when Nancy met a "wonderful" woman, she "just wasn't going to let the opportunity slip away this time." She will never forget the sense of relief in that first experience. "We were together and I thought: 'Everybody thinks this is so wrong and if it's so wrong how come it feels so wonderful?'" After that, "there was no turning back"; she finally felt "free." Unfortunately, by the time Nancy left the Navy her self-esteem was "at rock bottom," so she ended up in a number of relationships she "shouldn't have gotten into" – some of them abusive. "It just took a while to get back on the right road" and to rebuild her self-esteem. She had to do "a lot of healing" before she could make any relationship work. It took time and a support system of friends who challenged her to get on with her life and who gave her the "good swift kick" she needed to get her life back on track.

As for the Navy, "They haven't heard the last of me." Nancy has a plan – and law school is a part of it.

This experience with the Navy "was definitely a turning point" in Nancy's life. She no longer feels bitter about it, but she will never forget it. It has taken Nancy over seven years to get over what happened. In spite of this, she counts herself as "lucky – at least I'm alive." She has known people who were not so fortunate. She tries now to use what she has learned from this experience, to see "how it's made me a stronger person." Nancy has been able to make some meaning out of this traumatic event, possibly because of her religious upbringing. Although she is not involved in any organized religion, Nancy feels that she is in some respects "deeply religious." When she looks back on her life, she sees "a purpose for everything that happened – because as bad as it has been sometimes, usually something good has come out of it." Even on bad days, she is able to think that she has been through all of this "for some reason – and it's not over yet. . . . Something very positive is going to come out of it." It was meant "to get me on my path, whatever it is." So, she has no regrets about what happened.

> "I did what I had to do. I can sleep with it. I'm not always happy and it will still make me cry on some days, but I probably know myself better than a lot of people ever have the opportunity to know themselves . . . I'm very sure of who I am. I know what I want and I know the prices that have to be paid sometimes. . . . Part of me says, well I wish I would have realized and been a stronger person and come out before I'd gotten mixed up with the sorority, but I had one heck of a good time and I made a lot of very good friends. And in some respects I look back on my life and say, well, despite it all I've had the best of two worlds."

In spite of her "generic outlook" on love and relationships, Nancy knows that her actual experiences of being with men were very different from her experiences with women. When she talks about loving a woman, her face lights up: "There's a great deal of joy there. We're very much alike – somedays so much that it's frightening!" Nancy feels a certain "closeness and an intimacy" with women that she never had in her relationships with men and which she sees as somehow self-evident in relationships between women because women are more intuitive and lean more toward "the emotional side." She also feels "a link" or "bond" with women

197

that is "hard to put into words." Loving another woman is "just one heck of a nice feeling" and Nancy tries "never to take it for granted." She knows, from experience, that "you never know what tomorrow is going to bring."

For Nancy, intimacy with women is reflected in her ability to let down the wall of her defense system, though she does protect herself "to a point" because she does not want to get hurt. But this is still different from her relationships with men where "there was definitely some artificiality" and a sense that "this doesn't feel right" and that she "couldn't get as close." The wall was "just there" and would not come down. Nancy notes, however, that this wall is there only with men who seem to have a sexual interest in her. Otherwise, with male friends, "the walls are down."

Today Nancy wonders whether she would ever have come out if the Navy had not forced her out. Would she have gotten married just to do what society expected of her? She believes that things "would have come to a head eventually one way or another" – maybe when she got tired of being "lonely" and "miserable" – though not while she was in the Navy because "it was against the rules – and I wasn't going to break them."

Nancy is now out in most areas of her life. She does not "go out of her way" to tell others that she is a lesbian, but if people ask, she is "honest about it." The people at work "know"; they have "put 2 and 2 together" since Nancy takes a woman with her to company picnics and functions. It is the same at school. When her relationship ended last year, a number of school friends were getting divorced at the same time and "so we'd sit around and tell horror stories and it really wasn't that different for any of us – it didn't matter the gender of the relationship, the problems were all the same."

Law school has been significant in Nancy's life. She knows she is not the same person now that she was when she started and she gives much of the credit for this to one of her professors who allowed her, as a class assignment, to write a paper:

"She gave me the chance to say what really happened to me. I'd never had that chance. Nobody'd ever listened without passing some kind of judgment and it was just sort of like this rock was lifted. . . . It was such a relief. . . . She said it was a good paper and I began to realize that there was nothing wrong with me. I just had to decide to stop being a victim."

Nancy started to regain her old assertiveness and ambition after this, but, sadly, she also grew out of her relationship. Her lover had "liked the beaten, downtrodden, not so strong me."

Nancy no longer feels so wrong about being a lesbian and she no longer feels a need to put parts of herself aside: "I am what I am and if people don't like it that's their loss because I have a lot to offer people. It's not that it doesn't hurt, but life goes on." What helped Nancy overcome these feelings of being wrong was being around other lesbians in the community and coming to realize she is not so different. Nancy says that she is "learning to fight back." She is not very "political," but she will stand up for herself and others. The fear is still there, but she knows how to deal with it now. "I know if they knock me down, it's going to hurt, but I can get back up and I can swing just as hard back." Having a lot of friends has helped. She has people she can talk to at work and at school.

Nancy blames herself to some extent for the things that happened to her. She was living a lie and she "was the one who made the lie bigger." There were things she wanted out of life and she was willing to pay the price to get them. "I had a double life, and I knew it." Nancy came to the conclusion that though the Navy had knocked her down, she was the one keeping herself down. "I had kept myself down all these years – because it was easier to stay down than to get up and get punched again." She knows there are "negative forces" in society working to keep her down, but she realizes she does not have to let them succeed. She took a good look at herself and decided that she was "a strong enough person to stand up" for herself. She always had been "and it was just time to start doing it again."

"I'm aware of all the negative forces, but sometimes I think you have to shove back, and you might shove them all the way back but that pendulum swings a little differently each time and it never gets as bad as it was."

Nancy considers her lesbianism to be part of her identity.

> "It's not a lifestyle for me, it's life. The fact that I'm attracted
> to women is who I am. It wasn't a *choice* – which always makes
> me laugh because who would choose a lifestyle where you
> have to be so closeted and lonely half the time and secretive.
> It's definitely who I am – it *wasn't* a choice."

If she had had a choice, Nancy might have married a man – "but
it wouldn't have been right. That's just not me." It would have been
like telling her she had to switch to being left handed. She could
do it, but it "doesn't come naturally and it's no fun." She has
"always" had an orientation toward women – "that's really all I
know." She could only play the part of being straight. Today, most
of Nancy's friends are gay, "so I don't *have* to play the part – I don't
have to put up the front – I don't have to put wasted energy into it
– and I really don't have that much of a double life anymore." As
a result, life is "a lot more satisfying."

MY EXPERIENCE OF THE INTERVIEW

The long gap between all of the other interviews and this one had
both an upside (I felt like I knew more) and a downside (I felt out
of practice). It helped that Nancy had such an interesting and
intricate story to tell, one appropriately full of the ups and downs
of lesbian life. I found myself at several points during her story
shaking my head in disbelief at the way she was treated by the Navy
and the suffering she had endured when her life was torn apart. I
wanted more people to hear about this outrage. I felt like I
wanted to become more politically active. Maybe I will in time.

Nancy's very guarded style sometimes made it difficult for me to
maintain the ideal "to-and-fro movement" of conversation. There
were many long pauses as she searched for the right word to use or
for some way to help me understand something or for some way to
discreetly and carefully describe a situation so as not to incriminate
someone who might still be at risk. Yet Nancy's sincere desire to
convey her story was palpably clear throughout the interview.

One of the things that struck me most powerfully was Nancy's
repeated reference to the image of a wall. There were moments
when I felt like she was still behind one as she tried to talk to me.
That, more than anything else, made me realize how much we all
struggle, more or less, behind some kind of wall in fear of the

consequences of being discovered. Certainly Nancy's wall is thinner and lower than she has had to make it in the past, but I find myself wondering whether, or at least how, any of us gets over our respective defenses or recovers from our experiences of hiding or rallies from the traumas of discovery. Can we ever be who we could have been without these obstacles? Would we want to be?

13

"FINDINGS" AND REFLECTIONS

Imagine how many Lesbians there would be in the world if we got the kind of airtime and publicity that heterosexuality gets.

(Penelope 1992: 40)

I have tried in this book to weave together a number of narratives. Some were mine, some not. Some were theoretical, some philosophical, some very personal. Some were lesbian, some feminist, some Jungian, some Gadamerian. My intention has been to create a kind of lesbian fabric woven from the warp of lesbian experience and interlaced with the woof of theory. I will not try to review or summarize all that has been discussed in this process. Nor will I attempt to present any definitive conclusions, as if this combination of threads could produce only one type of fabric. Much of what I have come to understand about lesbianism has already been said along the way. So, as a way of bringing all the strands together, I will reflect on my "findings" in the spirit of musings and impressions, of wonderings and questions, of thoughts and feelings.

REFLECTIONS ON INTERVIEW THEMES

There were a number of themes which repeated themselves in one form or another as these six women described their experiences of loving another woman. I do not know whether any of these themes is "essential" to lesbian experience as such, but I was struck by the consistency with which these themes appeared and reappeared in some way in all of the interviews. This is not an exhaustive list. It merely represents a set of themes which were identifiable by me, given my horizons and these particular participants.

1 Desire to provide a context

Each of these women pondered my question, wondering where and how to start. They did not all speak from the same location or in the same language, but there was clearly a desire to go back to the beginning, to explain how their love for women came about, to make sense of their experience against the backdrop of their own histories. Embedded in this desire to convey context, it seems to me, is another element: a desire to acknowledge the enormous change in world view that either is the product of, or produces, a lesbian consciousness.

For Paula, the focus was on a particular relationship as the context that would explain and make sense of the present. It was this relationship which tipped the scale in her long struggle with her sexuality. For Eileen and Sandra, it seemed more important to interpret current experience in a way that would shed light on the past and cast the present as an outgrowth of the past. For them, the transition from heterosexuality to lesbianism, while not simple, did not involve a long drawn-out struggle, but was rather something like opening the door into a world they had not imagined previously. In Ann's case, on the other hand, there is a dramatic break between the past and the present, a moment of rupture during which she made a deliberate shift in behavior. Her context was as much intellectual and political as emotional. Nancy, too, experienced a rupture between past and present, but hers was traumatic and devastating. She did not choose to be "outed," but she also does not regret it since it freed her to live fully in the present and to be more open about her life-long attraction to women. For Joan, loving other women has been the context for her entire life. She could not imagine telling her story without telling me about the very beginning, when she was a very small child. But she, too, had a painful story to tell. The sudden and tragic loss of her first love has had an indelible effect on the present context of her life.

This theme of providing context is somewhat mythological, like cultural stories of creation or legends of how things were before some great event. Such stories are generally intended to present a structure within which a people might come to understand their origins. In a sense, such explanatory myths serve the purpose of epistemology helping us to justify ourselves, our beliefs, our world view, our history, our holy texts. Typically, these are sacred stories that tell us how we came to "be" who we are and that connect us to our community. All of this is reflected in these stories.

2 View of lesbian experience as a series of choices

Each of my participants seemed to see her lesbianism as resulting, in some way, from one or more choices she had made – although their reasons for making these choices and the types of choices involved varied greatly. Ultimately, each has had in a sense to invent her own choices. Ann, for example, made an intellectual and conscious decision to be with women. This was a decision that grew out of her politics and was motivated by a desire to be free from stereotypical gender role expectations, but it was also a personal decision in that she wanted more intimacy in her life. She felt she could not get either of these needs met with men. Sandra, too, made a decision that had an intellectual component. Coming out threw her into a conscious struggle between her desire for intimacy and her need to feel safe and in control. Initially, this resulted in attempts to rationalize her way out of her feelings, but eventually she was able to convince herself, intellectually, that she would survive the consequences, whatever they were, of following through on what she was feeling. For Paula and Eileen the choice to be with women was driven mainly by emotional considerations, but re- quired a deliberate recognition and acceptance of how this de- cision was going to change their world views and their relationships with others. The choice to live as a lesbian was not without risks. Joan, though she could not remember a time when she was not attracted to women, has likewise had to face and make many choices relative to how she can safely live a gay life. Ironically, even Nancy – who feels strongly that her lesbianism is *not* a choice – tells a story about choices. She was not given much of a choice about coming out, but she has had to make many conscious choices related to her sexuality. For many years she had chosen not to acknowledge her feelings to herself or to anyone else. When confronted by Navy investigators, she chose not to sacrifice a comrade in order to protect herself. Only now is she slowly making different choices and gathering the determination to create choices where she can.

This element of choice, variously expressed, highlights the complexities involved in living as a lesbian and is even a source of pride for some. Each has confronted and made conscious choices to act on her sexuality without benefit of cultural support or images and often in spite of hostility and obstacles. While heterosexual women also face many choices in their lives – and also from a position of subordination – they are rarely called on to make a choice relative to their sexuality that will have the consequences of a "coming out" (either to self or others). Heterosexual women do not typically have to choose between involvement in a fulfilling relationship on the one hand or social support on the other. Whatever choices they do make are made within the context of the dominant heterosexual culture they share. Even a choice to get involved in an unsanctioned relationship (e.g. an interracial relationship) does not carry with it the stigma attached to being seen as a lesbian. The choices a woman makes in order to act on lesbian feelings automatically take her into the margin: if she "chooses" to "be" a lesbian, there must be something wrong with her; if she was "born that way," she needs to be "cured." I do not make this comparison between lesbians and heterosexual women in order to diminish the difficult decisions heterosexual women face every day. Their choices, while safer in some ways because they reside within heterosexual culture, can also be more difficult because their lives intersect more intimately with the world of men. I make this comparison only to differentiate the disparate decisions and choices that women (and men to some extent) confront daily in a heterosexist culture. Whether the choice to live as a lesbian is truly a "choice," I do not know. Certainly, for some of us, being in the margin has some appeal. (For example, Sandra is attracted to being a "renegade" and Ann and Paula see it as a way to be free of gender role expectations.) What I do know is that the choice to live as a lesbian, while often compelling, is not uncomplicated.

3 Contrasting the experience of loving women to the experience of loving men

Each interviewee considered whether (or how not) to place this experience in contrast to men, the world of men, or the heterosexual world. I believe that there were two factors at work here. The first is the already discussed desire to provide a context in order to have one's experience understood by someone else. The second is the tendency, when trying to describe an experience, to do so, at least in part, by contrasting it to other experiences which seemed "different" so as to create a framework within which to identify the meaningful components of the new experience. This is related to, though not identical with, Jung's idea of "the pull of opposites." That is, experiences can be contrasted with each other or seen against different horizons – without being "opposites."

Joan was the only interviewee who spoke with little recourse to her experiences of men, although she did feel moved to offer her own view of men. She could concede that probably her view was stereotypical, but it was against the horizon of that stereotype that she placed and made some sense of her experience of women, of what she looks for and of what she finds. She told stories that would illustrate the ways she treats women and how this is different from how she perceives men treating women. All of the other interviewees seemed to feel unable to tell their stories meaningfully without making comparisons to their experiences of men. This seemed to help them make sense out of their choices. None of them hated or even disliked men. Their various decisions to choose to be with women seemed to reflect their sense of what was missing for them with men.

4 Impact on sense of self

Every interviewee struggled to find words to describe the uniqueness of her experience of her self in relation to women. Paula spoke of the "fit" she feels with her partner and how this lesbian relationship touches her "at a very core level." Ann identified some of the "core issues" involved in the evolution of her sense of self and spoke of the "fullness" she feels in the company of women. Eileen used words like "central" and "fundamental" when describing how she has been affected by loving women. Sandra recognized that in loving another woman she has experienced herself in ways that are "core to my sense of self" and she referred to "this infinite stuff that's available to me now that wasn't before." Although Joan insisted that she is not a different person when she is with a woman than when she is alone, she did become eloquent in describing the "aura" of a "together identity" that she experiences when she is with a woman whom she loves. Nancy is aware that she had been living a double life before she came out, which meant hiding a large part of her self from others and from herself. This, along with her traumatic separation from the Navy, drastically affected her ability to maintain a sense of self-esteem. Now, with women she can let down the walls that had kept her so isolated. This has allowed her to rebuild her self-esteem.

There is also some consensus among these women that their lesbian experience has profoundly impacted on their sense of identity in some way. For Paula, Sandra, Eileen, and Nancy, this is clearly an issue phrased in the language of identity. For Ann, on the other hand, seeing herself as lesbian has "become a sense of identity" over time, but not one which fundamentally defines her sense of self. For Joan, to be a lesbian is an experience she cannot have alone. It requires the presence of others, perhaps to "mirror" her self back to herself. Nancy has had to pay a heavy price to finally claim her lesbian identity, but this seems to have helped her gain a more integrated sense of herself. In addition, Ann's and Joan's different strategies for maintaining a separate identity (which remind me of Esther Harding's comments about the difficulties women face in maintaining a sense of separateness while in relationships) make clear the consciousness which must be brought to this project.

For each of these women, there was some struggle over sexual expression which led her to incorporate her experience of loving women into her overall sense of identity or into her sense of herself as a woman capable of expanding her self by engaging in sexual intimacies with other women. There also seems to be a sense among these women that they can have meaningful relationships only with those to whom they can come out. The implications of this for each are clear: She cannot be all of her "self" with others unless they know this about her. I understand this to be another indication of the link between lesbian experience and one's sense of self. It also gives evidence of the role of the political dimension in the formation of a self in that the decision to come out is not an entirely personal one but has impact on, and is impacted by, various levels beyond the strictly personal.

5 Sense of community

Another factor common to all of these women is the shared sense of feeling for women as a group. I am not speaking here of a feminist consciousness necessarily, but of an identification with other women and a concern for the welfare of women in general. This shared identification is based in a recognition that women partake in a common ground of experience. That is, women share something with each other as women in this culture that men cannot be privy to. This seems to make possible, perhaps even to constellate, a set of particular feelings toward women, for example: a higher level of trust, a profound sense of connection and empathy, an immediate perception of commonalities, a belief that one is better understood by women than by men, an experience of being touched at a level not accessible through men. This experience of community seems to provide lesbians with a sense of continuity, as if we have a history that gives context to our feelings, helps thwart potential isolation, and furnishes a container within which we can more safely individuate.

6 Desire for acceptance

Each of these women expressed a desire to be accepted for her choices and for who or how she sees herself to be. Paula's desire to be accepted seems to be satisfied through the acceptance of family and friends. Ann and Eileen have turned to the lesbian community seeing it as the environment which offers them a sense of security and recognition. Sandra seems to be at the center of a series of concentric or overlapping circles which form her world. As she engages in the process of establishing a sense of lesbian identity, she pushes into the next circle in terms of coming out and seems determined, so far, to not let anything stop her. Joan has made decisions about coming out on the basis of where she feels safe and what feels most important to her. Her desire for acceptance is probably most visible in her outspoken and public defense of others. Although Nancy has a supportive family, she seems to long for acceptance in other areas of her life. She is not quite ready to risk everything again for it, but with each positive experience of acceptance by people she cares about, she grows stronger within herself.

Clearly even those who experience their lesbianism with a sense of pride and self-acceptance, are affected by the various social forces which seem to conspire against those in the margins. As noted already, some of these women are happy to be in the margin. They see it, in effect, as a site of resistance. Others would like to be in the mainstream – but, as lesbians, they do not really have that choice.

RE-VISITING SOME OF MY HORIZONS AND HUNCHES

I started out with a set of hunches that I discussed in detail in Chapter 3. The objective of the interviews was not to prove these hunches "right." Rather, I hoped that these hunches would help illuminate whatever came out of the interviews. My intent through-out has been simply to better understand my subject matter. I hoped that lesbian experience, interpreted through these hunches/ horizons, would emerge as a meaningful phenomenon. I feel that I have succeeded in this – or, more accurately, that the phenomena of lesbianisms have succeeded in revealing themselves through the disclosures of each interviewee. I believe that all of my hunches have found some expression in these narratives.

Consensus gentium

The themes discussed above – as well as perhaps those which have been left unsaid – hint at a common ground of lesbian experience that can serve as the basis for a sense of a community of lesbians without phrasing this in the language of identity. Although each of the women interviewed had a different attitude toward the idea of community and felt differently about how important the lesbian community is to her, each recognized some need for a community of women. Both Ann and Eileen seem to feel that the ability to live as part of a lesbian couple requires the support of a lesbian community. For Paula and Sandra, to be "out" and in a community of other lesbian women seems to offer the potential for a more personal unfolding, an image of a container within which the possibilities seem unlimited. For Joan, who sees other aspects of her identity as having a higher priority than her being gay, the idea of a lesbian community is primarily a category of politics. Nancy, who had once relied on the Navy as her community of choice, is now building a network of lesbian friends who have provided her with invaluable support in her healing process and in coming to realize that there is nothing "wrong" with her.

All of these women, to one extent or another, seem to feel a sense of connection with other lesbians. Their *consensus gentium* comprises a shared experience of loving women, of withstanding the external forces arrayed against them (whether from family, society, or the government), and of being marginalized. All of these experiences seem to have both internal and external aspects, or subjective and objective levels, ranging from deep internal struggles with sexuality to external events like being "outed." Ann and Eileen understand even their internal struggles in political terms, recognizing that these are the direct result of external pressures that they share with other lesbians. Although Nancy realizes that internalized homophobia contributed to her struggles, she feels it is incumbent upon her to stand up for herself and to live more honestly in spite of the negative forces working to keep her down. Sandra, who has felt marginalized all of her life in various ways, sees her lesbianism as a site of resistance and community that she has chosen for herself. Joan's sense of community requires that she be politically active, a doer not just a talker. Although each of these women comes to the experience of community with different needs, they all seem to see community as a necessary aspect of being "out." Without a sense of community, their ability to live a full life would be severely diminished and lacking a container.

Personal and collective individuation

That the experiences of these particular lesbians are a movement in service to the individuation process is reflected in their frequent use of the language of individuation, words like: core, whole, center, self, struggle, choices. This was, of course, my overarching hunch – that women who choose to follow a lesbian path are responding to what Jung said was an urge or instinct to individuate. Esther Harding's work provided me with a way to stay rooted in a very Jungian frame while still coming to understand something about the experience of loving another woman. I have tried to show how some of her work, when read from a particular set of horizons, can point the way toward a new Jungian paradigm in relation to lesbian experience. I wondered, but knew, how Jungians could overlook the implications of her idea that to love another woman is to respond to a psychological need which has priority over our species' biological need to procreate. Certainly, Harding hedged her ideas in disclaimers and caveats. But, in the end, who could not see what courage it would require to follow this call. What could make a woman want to do that? Some of the answers to this question can be found in the stories that have been told, but some of them, I believe, are still a mystery. It is this mysterious element which continues both to intrigue and to feed me – like an archetypal image pointing me toward something more and inspiring me to keep trying to understand. All the while, however, I know that we never will discover the whole "truth" – and I do not even want to because then this symbol would lose its magic and be "*dead*" (Jung CW6: 816). Therefore, in a sense, my greatest "finding" is the mystery of lesbianism itself and the power that loving another woman has to propel some of us through life and toward a sense of self that we did not, could not, grasp in any other way.

Jungians tend to emphasize Jung's talk of individuation as "a natural necessity" (CW6: 758) as if it were a smooth and flowing journey toward the goal of "integration." Only when it is convenient do most Jungians remember Jung's admonition that individuation is also work *contra naturam*, that is, "against nature." It is hard work, work that goes against the grain, work performed from a site of resistance. And so it has been for the women I interviewed. Each has paid a price to live as a lesbian. In the classical Jungian view, individuation is also framed as a movement toward "wholeness" that requires some sort of *coniunctio* between the opposites, especially between the "masculine" and the "feminine" aspects of the personality. This reliance on the idea of contrasexuality as central to the individuation process makes Jungian theory problematic for all women, not just for lesbians. But, if individuation requires an anatomically "opposite" Other, then what is a lesbian to do? While things might be changing in the world around us, "the articulated voice of theory" in depth psychology "is dominantly heterosexual" (O'Connor and Ryan 1993: 265) – and, I would add, sexist.

When Harding proposes that lesbian relationships serve a collective purpose by their focus on the psychological aim of individuation (versus the biological aim of the species), she is pointing, by implication, to the great courage required to follow the call of the unfolding psyche. Of course, she is also implying that the biological aim can be served only heterosexually, that it is inextricably tied to reproduction, thus continuing the heterosexist fantasy that "anatomy is destiny." The example of Ann works very much against this fantasy. Ann made deliberate decisions twice in her life to conceive a child while in a relationship with another woman. Certainly, it was modern technology which gave her the option to follow the biological aim while simultaneously pursuing her own sense of her individuation process. But, as I see it, it was also her determination to follow her own individuation process which gave her the courage to refuse to be so dominated by the biological aim that she would sacrifice the psychological in exchange. Lesbianism was her site of resistance. Others came to this kind of decision later in life. Sandra, for example, already had two children when her attraction to another woman overcame her. We could say that the biological aim had been satisfied for her, but that the psychological aim had not – though this might not be the only way to interpret this.

Finally, I am mindful particularly of Ann's insight that the very absence in contemporary times of stereotypical roles in a lesbian relationships actually forces some level of individuation because lesbians are required to self-define their roles without recourse to pre-established or socially constructed roles. This does not necessarily stimulate more conflict than heterosexual couples face, but any conflicts or negotiations that may occur around this issue of roles takes place for lesbians without a sense of socially-sanctioned appropriateness. That is, there are no safe cultural containers for these decisions.

A refusal to be possessed by normalcy

That the experiences of these particular lesbians challenge the concept of "normalcy" is reflected in their refusal to submit to the officially authorized path with its view of what is "normal." Most of the women I interviewed either sought or were drawn to being in lesbian relationships because they feel free in these relationships to reject conventional gender role expectations in both their personal and public lives. This refusal to be bound by stereotypical roles is effectively a refusal to be bound by heterosexual definitions of "woman" or "feminine." If there is "a yawning gulf between conscious and unconscious" in us, as Jung says (CW7: 121), it is certainly exacerbated by the culturally constructed gulf between the definitions of "man" and "woman." Many lesbians in past decades had felt unconsciously possessed by these definitions and saw no option but to choose between "butch" or "femme." But the women we have met in these interviews have refused to be drawn into this. In fact, in virtually all cases, their very reason for choosing to be sexually and emotionally involved with another woman has been in the context of resisting these kinds of pressure. In other words, lesbianism, for them, is a "site of resistance" from the margin and against the concept of "normalcy" that rules as the center of mainstream culture.

All of this has made me wonder how psychological theory might change if, instead of seeing lesbians as "abnormal," we were to theorize that it is heterosexuals who are "abnormal" or possessed, for example, by the archetype of "normalcy". I am not proposing this as fact, but as a way of breaking these categories. What if there is no such thing as "normalcy"? What if Eileen's "sense of rightness" – her sense that this is about what feels "appropriate" to her – is what life is really about? What if we were to see a woman's desire for another woman as a contribution toward a collective individuation process (i.e. toward the process of differentiating individual characteristics versus collective standards, making possible the formation of a community of individuals instead of a mob)? Would that not allow heterosexuals, too, to begin looking at and reflecting upon their own choices, seeing their lives as meaningful rather than just "normal"? Would that not lead to enormous changes in psychological theory?

An expression of the transcendent function

Lesbians (and others) challenge the concept of "gender certainty" as Andrew Samuels has described it (1989b: 75). That we do so in the spirit of the transcendent function is reflected in our refusal to be limited to the qualities ascribed to our assigned gender without (Freud and Jung not withstanding) wanting to be perceived as the other gender. The transcendent function "facilitates a transition from one attitude to another" (Jung CW6: 828). It could be argued that the capacity of lesbianism to transcend (i.e. bridge) two arbitrary sets of qualities qualifies lesbianism to be a symbol whose meaning "inherent in the raw material itself" (ibid.) is to help us make the transition from gender certainty to gender uncertainty.

In addition, as noted above, we have the issue of the biological and psychological aims. Ann made a decision to fulfill both aims with women and Sandra, having satisfied her biological aim first, chose then to satisfy her psychological aim. In both cases, we see how the choice to live as a lesbian may be an expression of the transcendent function. The two seemingly "opposite" aims identified by Esther Harding have been bridged in such a way that the work of individuation is furthered. The aims are not merged as they are in heterosexual relationships. They must be consciously lived out. Thus the image of the lesbian mother presents itself as an expression of lesbianism which, in Jung's words, becomes "a way of attaining liberation by [her] own efforts and of finding the courage to be [her]self" (CW8: 193).

It also becomes clear if we read these stories attentively that there is no single archetypal image or discrete set of images that emerge to represent lesbian experience. We could probably tell each of these stories through the eyes of various archetypal images of either gender – or, better still, create genderless images. Lesbian experience is not, cannot, and should not be categorized in ways that would limit its many particular expressions. That is limiting and borders on an attempt to explain ourselves. An analysis that wishes to incorporate mythological themes would do better to keep such accounts forever open and non-definitive.

Embodied souls

When Esther Harding talks about how the sexual component of relationships between women must be accepted frankly and honestly in order for "a more fundamental rapport" to emerge between the women involved, she is hinting (in spite of herself, perhaps) at the experiences reported by several participants: to be sexually involved with a woman touches a level of the psyche so deep that each has felt somehow transformed. The many references made by most of my interviewees to words like "core," "self," "center," and "fundamental" point clearly to this depth of engagement. In addition, there was a general consensus that although sex is not the most essential feature of a lesbian relationship as such, it is pivotal to the transformative aspect of the experience in that it involves the body in ways that relationships with men did not, that there was a sense of being drawn to something that is both "beyond" *and* inclusive of sex and sexuality, something akin to what Downing implies with the phrase "embodied souls" (1989: 110).

Eileen, for example, spoke eloquently of the power of her sexual attraction to women, how it serves (whether acted upon or not) as the bonding element in her relationships with women. Sex with men, while physically satisfactory, has had no more impact on her than "a highly pleasurable athletic event." It never had a spiritual component for her and it never brought the "more fundamental rapport" she has found with women, or the "sort of revelation" she has experienced in the erotic presence of women. For most, the attraction to another woman has such a strong physical component that it could not be resisted. Sandra, for example, spoke of letting her body lead her since her intellect was resisting. This seems to echo Carrington's phrase about "the fulfillment of an ancient cellular longing" (1990: 64).

In addition, however, each of my participants indicated that the value of her relationships with other women cannot be reduced to sex. Eileen, for example, felt that to love another woman involves "something beyond sex." Eileen, Nancy, and Sandra, to some extent, describe this as a kind of experience that seems possible only in the presence of enormous trust, much of it based on the sense that when one is with another female one is in the presence of someone with whom one shares a common set of experiences and that there is therefore an almost automatic sense of "mutuality." Joan phrases it as a requirement that her lover be a feminist, i.e. that she have a conscious recognition of the meaning and consequences of this shared experience.

The power of the erotic that Lorde describes is also obvious in these accounts. I am thinking especially of Nancy who risked and lost what was most important to her at the time (her career) because she could not deny her attraction to women even though she had not yet been with a woman. But the same is true for the others as well, though not in so dramatic a form. Each took great risks in order to be free to act on this mysterious attraction. And each continues daily to take risks since, as we know, coming out is a process that we repeat daily, in every new situation, with every new person who comes into our lives – and this is done in the context of a culture which often seems fueled by hate.

The "masculine" and other irrelevancies

That the experiences of these particular lesbians give evidence that "the masculine" and related concepts are irrelevant is reflected in their willingness to defy the limits of gender roles, either as "women" or as role-playing lesbians, and in their refusal to attribute their lesbianism to their experiences with men. When Harding suggests that "friendships" between women challenge the standard heterosexual form of relationship with its anima-animus dynamics, she is essentially (and in spite of her own ambivalence) undermining the Jungian reliance on contrasexuality. When the women I talked with repeatedly returned to the sense of self they have discovered in their relationships with women (and not in their relationships with men), they were essentially undermining this construct as well. The animus (which Lyn Cowan has effectively dismantled intellectually) is clearly not a factor here; it is effectively made irrelevant by the experiences of these lesbians. Consequently, it is no longer possible to pretend that the choice to live in a lesbian relationship is not related to an individuation process and it must be clear, to anyone who listens carefully, that this is happening not in the presence of "the masculine" – inner or outer – but in opposition to the idea that an "opposite" other is a requirement of individuation.

For example, Paula can say that in a lesbian relationship she feels free to be herself because there is "more core available" to her in this relationship. She does not feel limited by "all the trappings of [role] expectations." That is, she is not required or expected to project her animus (qualities allowed only to males in our culture) onto her "other." It is not that lesbian relationships are free of projections; it is just that whatever is projected is not pre-ordained by cultural definitions of what is appropriate to one's (constructed) gender. But Paula is also very aware of the price she has paid in the face of cultural sanctions against this kind of love. She has had to resist the ingrained idea that she was in search of "Mr. Right." To be with a woman would mean the end of "living a duplicitous life." No more hiding. She insisted on making her site of resistance visible at least to her family and friends.

As we have seen, Esther Harding points out that some women need to separate themselves from men in order to individuate, that friendships between women enjoy certain qualities not available in heterosexual relationships, and that heterosexually married women have very little incentive to develop their personalities. Here Harding foreshadows perhaps the tendency seen among my interviewees to contrast their experiences of loving other women with their experiences of being with men. It is clear that women who have chosen to love other women have given careful and conscious consideration to how their experiences with women are different from what they experienced with men. Their relationships with men have been found wanting. I sensed no hostility from any of these women toward men as a whole. For them, men as a category are simply irrelevant – although individual men might be important figures in their lives. There was simply a recognition, in various forms and in various languages, that men as partners are insufficient and that any relationships they had had with men simply did not promote their individuation processes.[1]

A *coniunctio* of likes

The focus of lesbian relationships is on working out a *coniunctio* of likes, of resisting the idea that a *coniunctio* requires "opposites." The experience of such a *coniunctio* is repeated throughout these interviews and reflected in the alchemical transformations described therein. If we listen carefully and with open minds to the interviewees we have met, we hear the language of *coniunctio*. We hear these lesbians talk of seeing themselves as reflected in their same other and of feeling free with women to withdraw certain projections or to take down walls. In Jungian terms, it is not the animus they are projecting; it is the self, a genderless sense of "core." There is again no need to conceptualize an animus here. The concept of the animus is merely a tool of Jungian heterosexism.

REVISITING SOME OF MY PERSONAL CONFESSIONS

Concerning my hope to deconstruct heterosexism in Jungian theory

As a somewhat fanatical Jungian, I was determined to make some contribution to "the Jungian project," especially in the area of Jung's failure to understand homosexual experience and his participation in heterosexism and homophobia. And I was intent on responding to Samuels' call for a "program of renewal" (1989a) within analytical psychology in a way that would address an area where "the flaw" of its founder is particularly evident: Jung's theoretical constructs related to "contrasexuality" and his emphasis on the *coniunctio* of "opposites."

I believe that the hunches I presented in Chapter 3, together with the material gathered from and with my interview participants, effectively impeach the standard interpretations of Jungian theory. Rather, let us see Jung as the radical he often truly was. It is time for those of us who have been influenced and moved by Jung to not simply follow him blindly, marching in step to the master's voice, with unexamined acceptance. It is time for us to do something about the mess he helped create by undertaking a truly radical revisioning of Jungian theory.

Demaris Wehr has written about the dismay she felt when she

first discovered the sexism embedded in Jung's psychology. His work had meant so much to her that coming to discover this flaw in him led her to feel betrayed, disappointed, and angry. Eventually, however, her anger "dissipated in the recognition of [Jung's] humanness" (Wehr 1987: ix). She came to realize that this "god" was fallible. She became convinced that it was possible to revise Jung without altogether dismissing him and she set out to make a contribution to this effort by building "a bridge between Jung and feminism" (ibid.: x). I, too, am into building bridges – but a network of them. I have had it in mind to connect up feminism, lesbian studies, Gadamerian hermeneutics, and analytical psychology. This has turned out to be a huge undertaking and this book is just a first step. There is a lot more to be done. I hope I will not be alone in doing it.

Concerning my quest for a methodology

No one in the Jungian world, to my knowledge, has seriously addressed the question of methodology, though several have attempted to prove that Jung was a hermeneut or a phenomenologist. I set out wanting to know what that really meant in practical terms. Whatever one thinks research is, how does a hermeneut do it? What are the basic principles involved? Are there any guidelines?

I hope I have accomplished some of this, theoretically in Chapter 11 and practically in the interviews. I feel quite passionately about the benefits of bridging Jung and Gadamer, of making Jungians more conscious of how integral hermeneutics is to Jung's psychology. However, this task, too, is just begun. Jungian resistance to philosophy is in need of being rehabilitated. If we are to do our work as depth psychologists, we must be willing to look into the philosophical containers that thinkers like Gadamer bring to the borders and margins of psychology. If we really want to make our contribution to postmodern life, we must broaden our view – taking a lesson from feminism – and see that the life of the psyche is, in a manner of speaking, interdisciplinary. As contemporary "psychology" is being led down a soul-less path toward managed care, brief therapies, and credentials dictated by third party payers, it is incumbent upon those who see depth psychology as a refuge from this insanity, to speak up and out. A methodology that marries Jung's respect for psyche with feminism's insistence on context and

Gadamer's demand for dialogue is a powerful methodology indeed – and, I believe, a tool for social change whether in the consulting room or in the world at large.

Concerning the social relevance and political value of this project

Rarely, if ever, has Jung been accused of being overtly political. Most often, and with few exceptions, he is perceived as being so committed to the development of the individual personality that his work is usually dismissed as being irrelevant to social theory and as having no potential impact on political life.[2] Yet, Jung's work is filled with psychological reflections on the state of the world which give clear evidence of his deep interest in world affairs and demonstrate his understanding of how psyche and psychology are relevant, in fact essential, to a meaningful analysis and understanding of our world and culture. Roger Brooke indirectly implies this when he declares that "the central thrust of Jung's whole cultural therapeutic endeavour . . . was to reawaken for modern humanity a sense of soul in the world of things" (Brooke 1991: 7). I believe that my insistence on maintaining a Jungian perspective grounded in Gadamerian hermeneutics is about more than merely sketching out a methodology. I believe it speaks to the sense of urgency voiced by both Jung and Gadamer that the world is in trouble and that each of us has some responsibility in that.

For Gadamer, this is expressed as a plea that we apply ourselves to the task of achieving more self-understanding and a greater sense of community. In the context of an appeal for cooperation among nations and amid his grave concerns about "our over-stimulated . . . technological civilization" and the fate of non-Western cultures, Gadamer issues the following challenge:

> We are still a far cry from a common awareness that this is a matter of the destiny of everyone on this earth and that the chances of anyone's survival are . . . small . . . if humanity . . . does not learn to rediscover out of need a new solidarity. No one knows how much time we still have.
>
> (1981: 85)

Gadamer hopes that humanity will, if slowly, come "to know itself as humanity, for this means knowing that it belongs together for better or for worse and that it has to solve the problem of its life on this planet" (ibid.: 86). When Gadamer argues for the fusion of horizons and mutual agreement, he has in mind the big picture in which all of us, as partners in conversation,

> come under the influence of the truth of the object and are thus bound to one another in a new community. To reach an understanding in a dialogue is not merely a matter of putting oneself forward and successfully asserting one's own point of view, but being transformed into a communion in which we do not remain what we were.
>
> (1960/1993: 379)

For Jung, all of this is often phrased as a warning: "Truly we can no longer afford to underestimate the importance of the psychic factor in world affairs" (1953/1970: 168). In a passage written in 1916, Jung issues a kind of wake up call to the individual, emphasizing how the world is created by all of us. In reflecting on the lessons of "the current war," Jung notes the destructive consequences which result when we try to make someone else, our neighbor, responsible for our own "evil qualities":

> The psychology of the individual is reflected in the psychology of the nation. What the nation does is done also by each individual, and so long as the individual continues to do it, the nation will do likewise. Only a change in the attitude of the individual can initiate a change in the psychology of the nation. The great problems of humanity were never yet solved by general laws, but only through regeneration of the attitudes of individuals. If ever there was a time when self-reflection was the absolutely necessary and only right thing, it is now, in our present catastrophic epoch.
>
> (CW7: 4)

Jung's insistence that we focus on the life of the individual and his notorious distrust for groups should not distract us from his message about the individual's social responsibilities:

> It is, unfortunately, only too clear that if the individual is not truly regenerated in spirit, society cannot be either, for society is the sum total of individuals in need of redemption. . . . the salvation of the world consists in the salvation of the individual soul.
>
> (CW10: 536)

> If a man is capable of leading a responsible life himself, then
> he is also conscious of his duties to his community.
>
> (CW18: 1351)

Jung's views, it seems to me, are not unrelated to Gadamer's. My intentions in taking note of all of this is mainly to dispel the fallacy that Jung's work is socially or politically irrelevant and to point out an additional link between them in terms of their respective concerns for the fate of humanity. Both see the only salvation to lie in the individual's ability to achieve greater consciousness and to take on responsibility for community life. These comments might be addressed as well to the community of those involved in psychology who seem to believe that their attitudes and work are unrelated to politics. Nothing could be further from the truth, as Samuels (1993) has gone to great lengths to show us.

IN CONCLUSION

In conclusion, I want to reiterate the importance of the philosophical and theoretical pieces that came together for me in the common ground between Gadamer and Jung. There, in that location, and from my feminist horizon, I found a space from which to look meaningfully at lesbian experience. I experienced a fusion of horizons that emerged from a dialectical process (between me and my participants, between the ideas of Gadamer and Jung, between me and them, between me and others) and which gave me a new appreciation for language, both verbal and imaginal. I have come to understand my subject matter "better" than I did before and to value the role of my own preunderstanding and self-understanding in making that possible. I have come to feel open to "the other" in ways I had never thought possible. I have come to learn the meaning of "the priority of the question" and the overriding necessity for more partnerships of conversation. I have emerged from this process transformed, sometimes painfully, at every level of experience – personal, interpersonal, social, political, and professional. I can only hope that my readers, too, will be touched by the experience of these lesbianisms revealed.

Ultimately, it seems to me that the phenomena of women loving women give evidence of our capacity for "soul-making" (Hillman 1975: 3) and our willingness to follow the call to individuate wherever it takes us and in spite of internal conflicts and external

oppositions. Hillman says that what our world needs is "a fundamental shift of perspective out of that soulless predicament we call
modern consciousness" (ibid.). I agree with him. I believe that the
stories which form the core of this book speak precisely to that.

NOTES

1 PERSONAL CONFESSIONS

1 In keeping with Jungian custom, references to Jung's *Collected Works* are to volume and paragraph number, except in those unusual situations where certain sections are not marked by paragraph numbers (for example, the forward to a particular edition of a volume). References in those cases are to page numbers and are preceded by "p."
2 All quotes on pp. 11–13 are from the tape recording of that lecture.

3 FOREGROUNDING MY HORIZONS

1 Let me be clear here: I do not intend to be reductive or to "equate" all oppressed people. However, I do intend to acknowledge that we all share space in the margin – which remains marginalized no matter how crowded and internally differentiated it is. Nor is this an attempt to co-opt, universalize, or diffuse the focus of hooks' work, but rather to acknowledge the leadership role of black voices in explicating oppression.
2 In spite of all of this, I must acknowledge that Fuss raises some important questions about the usefulness of thinking in terms of inside/outside, center/margin. For example, she challenges the assumption that the outside is a privileged place of radicality and that the inside always implies cooptation.
3 Of course, one could argue that Harding is just now (in 1933) noticing such friendships among women although they have existed all along, even if they often were not acknowledged for what they were. However, it has been only within this century that the sexual component of such relationships has been admitted and only within the last couple of decades that lesbians have begun to coalesce into a community. It is in this context that I find Harding's analysis to be particularly noteworthy. [4]She relates this to "the awkwardness of an adolescent civilization changing from childhood to adult life" (1933/1970: 96). She tries to be sympathetic: "the instinctual frustration with its inevitable suffering,

which these individuals have to bear, must be considered the growing pains of society" (ibid.). The sacrificial quality that Harding evokes here raises for me the image of the scapegoat, an image which has some appeal. Its origins can be traced to ancient rituals in which the scapegoat took the role of a "healing agent" and was seen as critical to the spiritual life of the collective, functioning "to bring the transpersonal dimension to aid and renew the community" (Perera 1986: 8). However, to imagine lesbian/gay experience this way is also to buy into a definition that serves only collective purposes and that does not have meaning in its own right since it is defined strictly according to what has been excluded (from the mainstream). This, of course, is problematic and prone to falling into the Jungian trap of complementarity. In addition, Harding's inability to associate "the growing pains of a society" with anything but adolescence is clearly an assumption (no matter how well-meaning) that simply reflects Jungian prejudices about homosexuality.

5 I will not pursue the biological route here either. But it seems important to take note of Harding's admission that the biological significance of women's relationships is a part of our evolution, not antithetical to it. This stands in direct opposition to the usual homophobic arguments that inevitably include some appeal to "reproduction," as if the need to reproduce the species can be meaningful only at the literal level, as if life is the product of biological reproduction, and as if humanity can be defined and contained within the realm of biology.

6 I am not implying that this would be Harding's view. She is clear in her judgement: "From the biological standpoint this movement toward friendship must be considered a regressive phase of civilization, for on account of it many potential wives and mothers have remained unmarried" (1933/1970: 119).

7 This could also be seen as a more sympathetic variation on the scapegoat complex discussed in note 4 above.

8 I was brought to this idea in conversation with Randi Koeske.

9 Take, for example, Haddon's efforts in *Body Metaphors* (1988). While she creatively challenges established definitions of "masculine" and "feminine" by demonstrating how much they effectively mirror rather than oppose each other, she then fails to use her analysis to deconstruct the categories themselves because she is so attached to the idea that women's bodies are literally capable of giving birth.

5 DEBATES FROM LESBIAN LITERATURE

1 Phelan, citing Fuss, makes a similar point: "essentialism is linked to oppression" (1993: 773). While this strategy is "understandable," oppression, she insists, will not be undermined by holding on to "such essentialized identities." We must be willing to accept "that perhaps there is no single core to lesbian identity and thus that our identities rely on politics rather than ontology – indeed, that ontology is itself an effect of politics" (ibid.).

2 Butler makes a similar point: "The effort to identify the enemy as singular in form [i.e. "the masculinist signifying economy"] is a reverse-discourse that uncritically mimics the strategy of the oppressor instead of offering a different set of terms" (1990: 13).

7 SAME-SEX LOVE IN DEPTH PSYCHOLOGY

1 Others have also critiqued the concept of androgyny. Samuels refers to "the illusion of androgyny" and describes it as an attempt to uphold the two categories of gender (1989b: 105), although he does think it might have some value as a "challenge to the heterosexist frame" (1993: 146). Cowan argues that the image of the androgyne is really just an attempt on the part of a "desperate" psyche "to escape from the tyranny" imposed by a culture obsessed with "genderism" (1994: 48). Caroline Stevens points out that the concept of androgyny "obscures recognition of the fact that 'masculine' and 'feminine' qualities are *not* valued as equal in our culture" and that its use can allow us to ignore this "imbalance of power" (1992: 191).

2 On the whole, this book is tremendously impressive for its exhaustive treatment of everything Jung and Jungians have ever said about "the feminine" and the animus. However, while Douglas' critiques of Jung are sometimes scathing, they are also sometimes limited and apologetic. She does not confront any of the problematic and underlying assumptions of Jungian theory, but rather attempts to redeem some outmoded concepts, sometimes in ways that make me cringe. For example, she says: "What needs to be kept is the assumption that there *is* a difference between the masculine and the feminine and between men's and women's psychology" even though "what these differences are and how they arise remains unclear and needs further investigation" (1990: 149). She does question the assumption that "the feminine" and "the masculine" are opposite and complementary and the tendency to define them stereotypically. Yet, I cannot help but wonder: If women are not to be limited to "the feminine," why bother even to have something called "the feminine"?

3 It is not my intent to provide a thorough review of the writers in each category since Downing and Hopcke have done this between them. I intend only to hit some highlights as a way of describing the category rather than everyone in it.

4 In a recent interview with Scott Wirth, Henderson, while implying that homosexuality is "arrested development" (Wirth 1993b: 231), also goes on to admit that "If the homosexual patient in analysis successfully meets the conflict of the opposites . . . then the person becomes mature" (ibid.: 236).

5 Representative essays by these authors (except Stevens) can be found in Schwartz-Salant and Stein (1992). Roger Payne (1990) believes that there is something encouraging in the work of Anthony Stevens. I cannot agree. For example, in his book on archetypes, Stevens links homosexuality to the boy who has not been initiated "into the

masculine world" and who is therefore "doomed irredeemably to languish under the dominance of his mother complex" (1982:117).

6 Elsewhere, Young-Eisendrath (1992) also has written in defense of contrasexuality. I include her as a Reformulator because of her feminist stance. However, I find her analyses to be very mixed. While she often argues from a feminist perspective, she also often, in the end, comes to extremely conservative conclusions.

7 What does this say about "the feminine"? What can be so "feminine" about something that "most females" supposedly have such trouble accessing? And why would we need to be led to "the feminine" by special males (Dionysus, Jung, Bosnak, etc.)? Doesn't this challenge the very concept of "the feminine principle"? This continued tendency among Jungians to hold on to gender-based language and constructs is part of what keeps Jungian theory in a closet, sitting in the dark and afraid of its own shadow. It really is time to turn the light on and open the door before we go blind or suffocate. Certainly we can do better than this as post-Jungians.

8 This paper remains unpublished, having been labeled by a potential publisher as "too vinegary" (from a private conversation with Cowan).

9 "Power and Possibility in the Structure of Gender Relations," October 29, 1993. Part of a conference sponsored by the C. G. Jung Institute of Chicago and entitled "Who Do We Think We Are?: The Mystery and Muddle of Gender."

10 Of course, Downing's book (1989) is also an excellent source of reflections on Freud's views of homosexuality.

9 WEAVING A RESEARCH DESIGN: FEMINISM, GADAMERIAN HERMENEUTICS, AND JUNGIAN PRACTICE

1 For example, Sandra Harding's (1987b) three categories of feminist epistemologies; Nielsen's (1990) account of the evolution of feminist inquiry into the various feminist postempirical strategies; Margrit Eichler's four epistemological principles of feminist research (referred to in Stanley and Wise 1990: 38); Cook and Fonow's attempt at defining "five basic epistemological principles" of feminist research (1986/1990: 72–73); and the suggestions offered in Honderich (1995: 242).

2 Being mindful of Butler's complaint that various positions are often "conflated" under the label "postmodern" (1992: 4), I will only note that there are substantial differences among these various perspectives, even though they might be seen as having close and even evolutionary links.

3 Many have discussed the complications of establishing a relationship between feminism (which arguably is a modernist movement rooted in liberal humanistic urges toward emancipation) and postmodernism (which radically opposes all modernist thinking and has neglected the analysis of categories such as gender; for example, Brennan (1989), Butler (1992), Cole (1993), Flax (1990b), Hekman (1990), Nicholson

(1990), Nye (1995), Phelan (1993), Singer (1992). As I see it, the participants in this debate are scattered along a continuum. Some, like Butler, practice a feminism which is radically informed by the various postmodern discourses. Others, like Hekman, recognize "the uneasy relationship" between these two sets of ideas, but propose that they are really "complementary and mutually corrective" (1990: 2, 8). Some, like Flax, are guarded about postmodernism, yet claim that feminist theory "properly belongs in the terrain of postmodern philosophy" since it cannot be totally contained within the terms of modernity (1990b: 183). Others, like Cole, Di Stefano, Harding, and Stanley and Wise, are extremely suspicious of postmodernism and doubt whether it can provide a viable epistemology for feminism.

11 HERMENEUTICS AS METHODOLOGY

1 For various takes on the often uneasy relationship between hermeneutics and deconstruction, see, for example, Michelfelder and Palmer (1989) and Silverman (1994).
2 Actually, Gadamer often expresses himself in terms which even sound Jungian. For example, he echoes Jung's idea of the self-regulating psyche when he notes a "fundamental insight" of hermeneutics: "that life always discovers some kind of equilibrium and that there also pertains to this equilibrium a balance between our unconscious drives and our conscious human motivations and decisions" (1981: 109).
3 We might extrapolate from this that a concept of reliability which requires repeatability could be harmful to human beings since it excludes the reality of one's individual facts.
4 "Indeed," Jung once wrote parenthetically, "language itself is only an image" (CW9i: 271).
5 See, for example, Lockhart (1983) and Humbert (1988) who both address this, though differently.
6 Of course, this also confronts us with the teleological aspect of Jung's thinking. Hermeneutics is said not to be teleological because it "does not progress toward any complete revelation of the thing" (Weinsheimer 1985: 250). I would argue, however, that although Gadamer may not speak the same language as Jung, Gadamer's faith in the outcome of the dialectic process is evidence of some teleological belief.
7 Gadamer (in translation, at least) has used several phrases to convey this idea of agreement: "mutual agreement" (1989e: 56), "mutual understanding" (1960/1993: 180), "a common ground" (1989c: 94), and "a common language" (1960/1993: 378). Others have used additional English terms to explicate Gadamer's idea: Warnke refers to "consensus" (1987: 107), Weinsheimer talks about "a shared meaning" (1985: 138), and Shusterman alludes to a "strategy for shared understanding" (1989: 217).
8 Quoted from personal correspondence received from Dr Palmer and dated September 17, 1993. Although I have not followed Palmer's Thirty Theses methodically, I believe their spirit permeates my own thinking.

13 "FINDINGS" AND REFLECTIONS

1 In fact, I sense much more hostility toward men from heterosexual women and other men than from lesbians. For example, when I look out at the cultural images around me, at TV sitcoms, films, magazines, I feel sad and I cannot help but wonder how little boys survive the onslaught – or do they?

2 One recent exception, however, is Samuels (1993).

REFERENCES

Aylesworth, Gary E. (1991) "Dialogue, Text, Narrative: Confronting Gadamer and Ricoeur," in Hugh J. Silverman (ed.) *Gadamer and Hermeneutics: Science, Culture, Literature*, pp. 63–81, New York: Routledge.

Banister, Peter, Burman, Erica, Parker, Ian, Taylor, Maye, and Tindall, Carol (1994) *Qualitative Methods in Psychology*, Buckingham: Open University.

Barnaby, Karin and D'Acierno, Pelligrino (eds) (1990) *C. G. Jung and the Humanities: Toward a Hermeneutics of Culture*, Princeton: Princeton University Press.

Beebe, John (1993) "Toward an Image of Male Partnership," in Robert H. Hopcke, Karin Lofthus Carrington, and Scott Wirth (eds) *Same-Sex Love and the Path to Wholeness: Perspectives on Gay and Lesbian Psychological Development*, pp. 151–169, Boston: Shambhala.

Bleicher, Josef (1980) *Contemporary Hermeneutics: Hermeneutics as Method, Philosophy and Critique*, London: Routledge.

Bosnak, Robert (1993) "Individuation, Taboo, and Same-Sex Love," in Robert H. Hopcke, Karin Lofthus Carrington, and Scott Wirth (eds) *Same-Sex Love and the Path to Wholeness: Perspectives on Gay and Lesbian Psychological Development*, pp. 264–272, Boston: Shambhala.

Brennan, Teresa (ed.) (1989) *Between Feminism and Psychoanalysis*, London: Routledge.

Brooke, Roger (1991) *Jung and Phenomenology*, New York: Routledge.

Brown, Laura (1989) "New Voices, New Visions: Toward a Lesbian/gay Paradigm for Psychology," *Psychology of Women Quarterly* 13, 4: 445–458.

Butler, Judith (1990a) "Gender Trouble, Feminist Theory, and Psycho-analytic Discourse," in Linda Nicholson (ed.) *Feminism/Postmodernism*, pp. 324–340, New York: Routledge.

—— (1991) "Imitation and Gender Insubordination," in Diana Fuss (ed.) *Inside/Out: Lesbian Theories, Gay Theories*, pp. 13–31, New York: Routledge.

—— (1992) "Contingent Foundations: Feminism and the Question of 'Postmodernism,'" in Judith Butler and Joan Scott (eds) *Feminists Theorize the Political*, pp. 3–21, New York: Routledge.

—— (1993) *Bodies That Matter: On the Discursive Limits of "Sex"*, New York: Routledge.

229

Carrette, Jeremy R. (1992) "Review of *Jung and Phenomenology*," *Harvest* 38: 204–209.

Carrington, Karin Lofthus (1990) "The Alchemy of Women Loving Women," *Psychological Perspectives* 23: 64–82.

Casey, Edward (1990) "Jung and the Postmodern Condition," in Karin Barnaby and Pelligrino D'Acierno (eds) *C. G. Jung and the Humanities: Toward a Hermeneutics of Culture*, pp. 319–324, Princeton: Princeton University Press.

Cole, Eve Browning (1993) *Philosophy and Feminist Criticism*, New York: Paragon.

Cook, Judith A. and Fonow, Mary Margaret (1986/1990) "Knowledge and Women's Interests," in Joyce M. Nielsen (ed.) *Feminist Research Methods: Readings from the Social Sciences*, pp. 69–93, Boulder, CO: Westview.

Cowan, Lyn (1994) "Dismantling the Animus," lecture originally delivered October 1991 and later revised and expanded into an unpublished paper. Page numbers cited refer to the most recent version of this paper, a copy of which was given to me by the author.

Davies, Bronwyn (1990) "Women's Subjectivity and Feminist Stories," in Carolyn Ellis and Michael G. Flaherty (eds) *Investigating Subjectivity: Research on Lived Experience*, pp. 53–76, Newbury Park, CA: Sage.

Decker, Beverly (1995) "How to Have Your Phallus and Be It Too," in Judith Glassgold and Suzanne Iasenza (eds) *Lesbians and Psychoanalysis: Revolutions in Theory and Practice*, pp. 63–89, New York: The Free Press.

de Lauretis, Teresa (1990) "Eccentric Subjects: Feminists Theory and Historical Consciousness," *Feminist Studies* 16, 1: 115–150.

Donleavy, Pamela (1996) "Tracks in the Wilderness of Dreaming: An Interview with Robert Bosnak," *The Round Table Press Review* 3, 3: 1, 4–9.

Douglas, Claire (1990) *The Woman in the Mirror: Analytical Psychology and the Feminine*, Boston: Sigo.

Downing, Christine (1989) *Myths and Mysteries of Same-Sex Love*, New York: Continuum.

—— (1992) *Women's Mysteries: Toward a Poetics of Gender*, New York: Crossroad.

—— (1995) "An Archetypal View of Lesbian Identity," in Judith Glassgold and Suzanne Iasenza (eds) *Lesbians and Psychoanalysis: Revolutions in Theory and Practice*, pp. 265–285, New York: The Free Press.

Duggan, Lisa (1993) "The Trials of Alice Mitchell: Sensationalism, Sexology, and the Lesbian Subject in Turn-of-the-Century America," *Signs* 18, 4: 791–812.

Faderman, Lillian (1981) *Surpassing the Love of Men*, New York: William Morrow.

Ferguson, Ann (1981) "Patriarchy, Sexual Identity and the Sexual Revolution," in "On 'Compulsory Heterosexuality and Lesbian Existence': Defining the Issues," in Nannerl O. Keohane, Michelle Z. Rosaldo and Barbara C. Gelpi (eds) *Feminist Theory: A Critique of Ideology*, pp. 147–161, Chicago: University of Chicago Press.

—— (1990) "Is There a Lesbian Culture?" in Jeffner Allen (ed.) *Lesbian Philosophies and Cultures*, pp. 63–88, Albany: State University of New York Press.

Fischer, Constance (1987), "The Quality of Qualitative Research," *Theoretical and Philosophical Psychology* 7, I: 2–11.

Flax, Jane (1990a) "Postmodernism and Gender Relations in Feminist Theory," in Linda Nicholson (ed.) *Feminism/Postmodernism*, pp. 39–62, New York: Routledge.

—— (1990b) *Thinking Fragments: Psychoanalysis, Feminism, and Postmodernism in the Contemporary West*, Berkeley: University of California Press.

Foucault, Michel (1980) *Power/Knowledge: Selected Interviews and Other Writings, 1972–1977*, (Colin Gordon, ed.), New York: Pantheon.

Fraser, Nancy and Nicholson, Linda (1990) "Social Criticism without Philosophy: An Encounter between Feminism and Postmodernism," in Linda Nicholson (ed.) *Feminism/Postmodernism*, pp. 19–38, New York: Routledge.

Frye, Marilyn (1983) *The Politics of Reality: Essays in Feminist Theory*, Trumansburg, NY: Crossing.

Fuss, Diana (ed.) (1991) "Inside/Out," in *Inside/Out: Lesbian Theories, Gay Theories*, pp. 1–10, New York: Routledge.

Gadamer, Hans-Georg (1960/1993) *Truth and Method* (2nd edn) (Joel Weinsheimer and Donald G. Marshall, trs), New York: Continuum.

—— (1976) *Philosophical Hermeneutics*, (David E. Linge, tr. and ed.), Berkeley: University of California.

—— (1981) *Reason in the Age of Science*, (Frederick G. Lawrence, tr.), Cambridge, MA: MIT.

—— (1989a) "Destruktion and Deconstruction," (Geoff Waite and Richard Palmer, trs), in Diane P. Michelfelder and Richard E. Palmer (eds) *Dialogue and Deconstruction*, pp. 102–113, Albany: State University of New York Press.

—— (1989b) "Hermeneutics and Logocentrism," (Richard Palmer and Diane Michelfelder, trs), in Diane P. Michelfelder and Richard E. Palmer (eds) *Dialogue and Deconstruction*, pp. 114–125, Albany: State University of New York Press.

—— (1989c) "Letter to Dallmyr, 1985," (Richard Palmer and Diane Michelfelder, trs), in Diane P. Michelfelder and Richard E. Palmer (eds) *Dialogue and Deconstruction*, pp. 93–101, Albany: State University of New York.

—— (1989d) "Reply to Jacques Derrida," (Diane Michelfelder and Richard Palmer, trs), in Diane P. Michelfelder and Richard E. Palmer (eds) *Dialogue and Deconstruction*, pp. 55–57, Albany: State University of New York Press.

—— (1989e) "Text and Interpretation," (Dennis J. Schmidt and Richard Palmer, trs), in Diane P. Michelfelder and Richard E. Palmer (eds) *Dialogue and Deconstruction*, pp. 21–51, Albany: State University of New York Press.

Glassgold, Judith M. and Iasenza, Suzanne (eds) (1995) *Lesbians and Psychoanalysis: Revolutions in Theory and Practice*, New York: The Free Press.

Goldenberg, Naomi (1979) *Changing of the Gods: Feminism and the End of Traditional Religions*, Boston: Beacon.

Goldner, Virginia (1991) "Toward a critical relational theory of gender," *Psychoanalytic Dialogues* 3, 1: 249–272.

Grondin, Jean (1991/1994) *Introduction to Philosophical Hermeneutics* (Joel Weinsheimer, tr.), New Haven: Yale University Press.

Haddon, Genia Pauli (1988) *Body Metaphors: Releasing God-Feminine in Us All*, New York: Crossroad.

Hall, Nor (1980) *The Moon and the Virgin: Reflections of the Archetypal Feminine*, New York: Harper and Row.

Harding, M. Esther (1933/1970) *The Way of All Women*, New York: Harper and Row (Colophon).

Harding, Sandra (1987a) "Introduction: Is There a Feminist Method?," in Sandra Harding (ed.) *Feminism and Methodology*, pp. 1–14, Bloomington: Indiana University Press.

—— (1987b) "Conclusion: Epistemological Questions," in Sandra Harding (ed.) *Feminism and Methodology*, pp. 181–190, Bloomington: Indiana University Press.

—— (1990) "Feminism, Science, and the Anti-Enlightenment Critiques," in Linda Nicholson (ed.), *Feminism/Postmodernism*, pp. 83–108, New York: Routledge.

Hekman, Susan J. (1990) *Gender and Knowledge: Elements of a Postmodern Feminism*, Boston: Northeastern University Press.

Hewison, D. S. (1995) "Case History, Case Story: An Enquiry into the Hermeneutics of C. G. Jung," *Journal of Analytical Psychology* 40, 3: 383–404.

Hillman, J. (1975) *Re-Visioning Psychology*, New York: Harper Colophon.

—— (1981) "The Imagination of Air and the Collapse of Alchemy," in the *Eranos Yearbook* 50: 273–333, Dallas: Spring.

Hoagland, Sarah L. (1988) *Lesbian Ethics: Toward New Value*, Palo Alto: Institute of Lesbian Studies.

Holt, David (1992) *The Psychology of Carl Jung: Essays in Application and Deconstruction*, Lewiston, NY: Edwin Mellen.

Honderich, Ted (ed.) (1995) *The Oxford Companion to Philosophy*, Oxford: Oxford University Press.

hooks, bell (1990a) "Choosing the Margin as a Space of Radical Openness," in *Yearning: Race, Gender, and Cultural Politics*, pp. 145–153, Boston: South End Press.

—— (1990b) "Postmodern Blackness," in *Yearning: Race, Gender, and Cultural Politics*, pp. 23–31, Boston: South End Press.

Hopcke, Robert (1989) *Jung, Jungians, and Homosexuality*, Boston: Shambhala.

—— Carrington, Karin Lofthus, and Wirth, Scott (eds) (1993) *Same-Sex Love and the Path to Wholeness: Perspectives on Gay and Lesbian Psychological Development*, Boston: Shambhala.

Humbert, Elie (1988) *C. G. Jung: The Fundamentals of Theory and Practice*, (Ronald G. Jalbert, tr.), Wilmette, IL: Chiron.

Jarrett, James L. (1992) "Jung and Hermeneutics," *Harvest* 38: 66–84.

Johnston, Jill (1973) *Lesbian Nation: The Feminist Solution*, New York: Simon and Schuster.

Jung, C. G. (1933/1970) "Introduction," in M. Esther Harding, *The Way of All Women*, New York: Harper and Row (Colophon).
—— (1953/1970) *Psychological Reflections* (Jolande Jacobi and R. F. C. Hull, eds), Princeton: Princeton University Press.
—— (1953–1979) *The Collected Works of C.G. Jung* (Vols 1–20), Princeton: Princeton University Press. References are to CW by volume and paragraph number.
—— (1961) *Memories, Dreams, Reflections*, New York: Pantheon.
—— (1970) "Two Posthumous Papers," Spring: 168–175.
—— (1973) *C.G. Jung Letters*, vol. 2: 1951–1961, (Aniela Jaffe, ed.; R. F. C. Hull, tr.), Princeton: Princeton University Press.
—— (1974) *The Freud/Jung Letters: The Correspondence between Sigmund Freud and C. G. Jung*, (William McGuire, ed.; Ralph Manheim and R. F. C. Hull, trs), London: The Hogarth Press and Routledge & Kegan Paul.
Kelsey, Morton T. (1991) "Jung as Philosopher and Theologian," in Renos K. Papadopoulos and Graham S. Saayman (eds) *Jung in Modern Perspective*, pp. 182–192, Bridport: Prism.
Kitzinger, Celia (1987) *The Social Construction of Lesbianism*, London: Sage.
—— (1995) "Social Constructionism: Implications for Lesbian and Gay Psychology," in Anthony R. D'Augelli and Charlotte J. Patterson (eds) *Lesbian, Gay, and Bisexual Identities Over the Lifespan: Psychological Perspectives*, New York: Oxford University Press.
Kolodny, Annette (1980) "Dancing through the Minefield: Some Observations on the Theory, Practice and Politics of a Feminist Literary Criticism," *Feminist Studies* 6, 1: 1–25.
Lather, Patti (1986) "Research as Praxis," *Harvard Educational Review*, 56, 3: 257–277.
Lauter, Estelle and Rupprecht, Carol Schreier (1985) " Introduction," in Estelle Lauter and Carol Schreier Rupprecht (eds) *Feminist Archetypal Theory: Interdisciplinary Re-Visions of Jungian Thought*, Knoxville: University of Tennessee Press.
Lawrence, Frederick G. (tr.) (1981) "Translator's Introduction," in *Hans-Georg Gadamer: Reason in the Age of Science*, pp. ix–xxxiii, Cambridge, MA: MIT.
Lerner, Gerda (1977) *The Female Experience: An American Documentary*, Indianapolis: Bobbs-Merrill.
Linge, David E. (ed. and tr.) (1976) "Editor's Introduction," in *Hans-Georg Gadamer, Philosophical Hermeneutics*, pp. xi–lviii, Berkeley: University of California Press.
Lockhart, Russell A. (1983) *Words as Eggs: Psyche in Language and Clinic*, Dallas: Spring.
Lorde, Audre (1984a) "Use of the Erotic: The Erotic as Power," in *Sister Outsider*, pp. 53–59, Freedom, CA: Crossing.
—— (1984b) "The Master's Tools Will Never Dismantle the Master's House," in *Sister Outsider*, pp. 110–113, Freedom, CA: Crossing.
McKenna, W. and Kessler, S. (1985) "Asking Taboo Questions and Doing Taboo Deeds" in K. J. Gergen and K. E. Davis (eds) *The Social Construction of the Person*, New York: Springer-Verlag.
Madison, Gary B. (1991) "Beyond Seriousness and Frivolity: A Gadamerian

to Deconstruction," in Hugh J. Silverman (ed.) *Gadamer and Hermeneutics: Science, Culture, Literature*, (pp. 119–148), New York: Routledge.

Magee, Maggie and Miller, Diana C. (1996) "Psychoanalytic Views of Female Homosexuality," in Robert P. Cabaj and Terry S. Stein (eds) *Textbook of Homosexuality and Mental Health*, pp. 191–206, Washington: American Psychiatric Press.

Marcus, Jane (1982) "Storming the Toolshed," in Nannerl O. Keohane, Michelle Z. Rosaldo, and Barbara C. Gelpi (eds) *Feminist Theory: A Critique of Ideology*, pp. 217–235, Chicago: University of Chicago Press.

Michelfelder, Diane P. and Palmer, Richard E. (eds) (1989) "Introduction," in *Dialogue and Deconstruction: The Gadamer–Derrida Encounter*, pp. 1–18, Albany: State University of New York Press.

Monick, Eugene (1987) *Phallos: Sacred Image of Masculinity*, Toronto: Inner City.

Monick, Eugene (1993) "Mirroring Affirmation: With Special Reference to Psychoanalysis and to Men," in Robert H. Hopcke, Karin Lofthus Carrington, and Scott Wirth (eds) *Same-Sex Love and the Path to Wholeness: Perspectives on Gay and Lesbian Psychological Development*, Boston: Shambhala.

Monk, Ray (1990) *Ludwig Wittgenstein: The Duty of Genius*, New York: Penguin.

Moustakas, Clark (1994) *Phenomenological Research Methods*, Thousand Oaks: Sage.

Mudd, Peter (1992) "Jung and the Split Feminine," unpublished paper.

Nagy, Marilyn (1991) *Philosophical Issues in the Psychology of C. G. Jung*, Albany: State University of New York Press.

Nicholson, Linda (ed.) (1990) *Feminism/Postmodernism*, New York: Routledge.

Nielsen, Joyce M. (1990) "Introduction," in Joyce M. Nielsen (ed.) *Feminist Research Methods: Readings from the Social Sciences*, pp. 1–37, Boulder, CO: Westview.

Nye, Andrea (1995) *Philosophy and Feminism: At the Border*, New York: Twayne.

O'Connor, Noreen and Ryan, Joanna (1993) *Wild Desires and Mistaken Identities: Lesbianism and Psychoanalysis*, New York: Columbia University Press.

Packer, Martin J. and Addison, Richard B. (eds) (1989) *Entering the Circle: Hermeneutic Investigation in Psychology*, Albany: State University of New York Press.

Palmer, Richard E. (1969) *Hermeneutics: Interpretation Theory in Schleiermacher, Dilthey, Heidegger, and Gadamer*, Evanston, IL: Northwestern University Press.

Papadopoulos, Renos K. and Saayman, Graham S. (eds) (1991) *Jung in Modern Perspective: The Master and His Legacy*, Bridport: Prism.

Payne, Roger (1990) "Some Reflections on Homosexuality," *Harvest* 36: 155–163.

Pellauer, Mary D. (1985) "Moral Callousness and Moral Sensitivity," in Barbara H. Andolsen, Christine E. Gudorf, and Mary D. Pellauer (eds),

234

Women's Consciousness, Women's Conscience: A Reader in Feminist Ethics, pp. 33–50, San Francisco: Harper and Row.

Penelope, Julia (1992) *Call Me Lesbian: Lesbian Lives, Lesbian Theory,* Freedom, CA: Crossing.

Peplau, Letitia Anne and Conrad, Eva (1989) "Beyond Nonsexist Research: The Perils of Feminist Methods in Psychology," *Psychology of Women Quarterly* 13, 4: 379–400.

Perera, Sylvia Brinton (1981) *Descent to the Goddess: A Way of Initiation for Women,* Toronto: Inner City.

—— (1986) *The Scapegoat Complex,* Toronto: Inner City.

Phelan, Shane (1989) *Identity Politics: Lesbian Feminism and the Limits of Community,* Philadelphia: Temple University.

—— (1993) "(Be)Coming Out: Lesbian Identity and Politics" *Signs* 18, 4: 765–790.

Ponce, Charles (1988) "On the Possession of Consciousness," in *Working the Soul: Reflections on Jungian Psychology,* pp. 139–177, Berkeley: North Atlantic.

Rauhala, Lauri (1991) "The Basic Views of Jung in the Light of Hermeneutic Metascience," in Renos K. Papadopoulos and Graham S. Saayman (eds) *Jung in Modern Perspective,* pp. 34–53, Bridport: Prism.

The Reader's Digest Great Encyclopedic Dictionary (1975), Pleasantville, NY: Reader's Digest Association, Inc.

Reinharz, Shulamit (1992) *Feminist Methods in Social Research,* New York: Oxford.

Rich, Adrienne (1980) "Compulsory Heterosexuality and Lesbian Existence," *Signs* 5, 4: 631–660.

Ricoeur, Paul (1973) "Human Sciences and Hermeneutical Method: Meaningful Action Considered as Text," in D. Carr and E. Casey (eds) *Explorations in Phenomenology,* pp. 13–46, The Hague: Martinus Nijhoff.

—— (1980) "Existence and Hermeneutics," (Kathleen McLaughlin, tr.), in Josef Bleicher, *Contemporary Hermeneutics: Hermeneutics as Method, Philosophy and Critique,* pp. 236–256, London: Routledge.

—— (1981) *Hermeneutics and the Human Sciences* (John B. Thompson, ed. and tr.), Cambridge: Cambridge University Press.

Rychlak, Joseph F. (1991) "Jung as Dialectician and Teleologist," in Renos K. Papadopoulos and Graham S. Saayman (eds) *Jung in Modern Perspective,* pp. 34–53, Bridport: Prism.

Samuels, Andrew (1985) *Jung and the Post-Jungians,* London: Routledge and Kegan Paul.

—— (1989a) "Jung, Anti-Semitism, and the Fuehrerprinzip" (Cassette Recording 4.2.89), Pittsburgh, PA: Pittsburgh Jung Society.

—— (1989b) *The Plural Psyche: Personality, Morality and the Father,* London: Routledge.

—— (1992) "Men under Scrutiny," *Psychological Perspectives* 26: 42–61.

—— (1993) *The Political Psyche,* London: Routledge.

Sandner, Donald (1993) "The Role of the Anima in Same-Sex Love Between Men" in Robert H. Hopcke, Karin Lofthus Carrington, and Scott Wirth (eds) *Same Sex Love and the Path to Wholeness: Perspectives on Gay and Lesbian Psychological Development*, pp. 219–230, Boston: Shambhala.

Schott, Robin (1991) "Whose Home is it Anyway? A Feminist Response to Gadamer's Hermeneutics" in Hugh J. Silverman (ed.) *Gadamer and Hermeneutics: Science, Culture, Literature*, pp. 202–209, New York: Routledge.

Schwartz-Salant, Nathan and Stein, Murray (eds) (1992) *Gender and Soul in Psychotherapy*, Wilmette, IL: Chiron.

Sedgwick, Eve Kosofsky (1990) *Epistemology of the Closet*, Berkeley: University of California.

Shusterman, Richard (1989) "The Gadamer-Derrida Encounter: A Pragmatist Perspective," in Diane P. Michelfelder and Richard E. Palmer (eds) *Dialogue and Deconstruction: The Gadamer-Derrida Encounter*, pp. 215–221, Albany: State University of New York Press.

Silverman, Hugh J. (1994) *Textualities: Between Hermeneutics and Deconstruction*, New York: Routledge.

Singer, Linda (1992) "Feminism and Postmodernism," in Judith Butler and Joan Scott (eds), *Feminists Theorize the Political*, pp. 3–21, New York: Routledge.

Squire, Corinne (1989) *Significant Differences: Feminism in Psychology*, New York: Routledge.

Stanley, Liz and Wise, Sue (1990) "Method, Methodology and Epistemology in Feminist Research Processes," in Liz Stanley (ed.) *Feminist Praxis: Research, Theory and Epistemology in Feminist Sociology*, pp. 20–60, London: Routledge.

—— (1993) *Breaking Out Again: Feminist Ontology and Epistemology*, (2nd edn), London: Routledge.

Steele, Robert (1982) *Freud and Jung: Conflicts of Interpretation*, London: Routledge and Kegan Paul.

Stein, Edward (ed.) (1990) *Forms of Desire: Sexual Orientation and the Social Constructionist Controversy*, New York: Routledge.

Stevens, Anthony (1982) *Archetypes: A Natural History of the Self*, New York: Quill.

Stevens, Caroline T. (1991) "Lesbian Family, Holy Family: Experience of an Archetype," in Christine Downing (ed.) *Mirrors of the Self: Archetypal Images That Shape Your Life*, pp. 144–150, Los Angeles: Tarcher.

—— (1992) "What is the Animus and Why Do We Care?," in Nathan Schwartz-Salant and Murray Stein (eds) *Gender and Soul in Psychotherapy*, pp. 185–201, Wilmette, IL: Chiron.

Walker, Mitchell (1991) "The Double: Same-Sex Inner Helper," in Christine Downing (ed.) *Mirrors of the Self: Archetypal Images That Shape Your Life*, pp. 48–52, Los Angeles: Tarcher.

Warnke, Georgia (1987) *Gadamer: Hermeneutics, Tradition and Reason*, Stanford, CA: Stanford University Press.

Weaver, M. I. Rix (1982) "An Interview with C.G. Jung: 1955," in Ferne Jensen and Sidney Mullen (eds) *C.G. Jung, Emma Jung and Toni Wolff: A Collection of Remembrances*, pp. 90–95, San Francisco: Analytical Psychology Club of San Francisco.

Wehr, Demaris (1987) *Jung and Feminism: Liberating Archetypes*, Boston: Beacon.

Weinrich, J. (1990) "Reality or Social Construction?" in Edward Stein (ed.) *Forms of Desire: Sexual Orientation and the Social Constructionist Controversy*, New York: Routledge.

Weinsheimer, Joel C. (1985) *Gadamer's Hermeneutics: A Reading of Truth and Method*, New Haven: Yale University Press.

Westkott, Marcia (1979/1990) "Feminist Criticism of the Social Sciences," in Joyce M. Nielsen (ed.) *Feminist Research Methods: Readings from the Social Sciences*, pp. 58–68, Boulder, CO: Westview.

Williams, Patricia J. (1991) *The Alchemy of Race and Rights*, Cambridge, MA: Harvard University Press.

Wirth, Scott (1993a) "Not 'A One-Sided Sexual Being': Clinical Work with Gay Men from a Jungian Perspective" in Robert H. Hopcke, Karin Lofthus Carrington, and Scott Wirth (eds) *Same-Sex Love and the Path to Wholeness: Perspectives on Gay and Lesbian Psychological Development*, pp. 186–218, Boston: Shambhala.

—— (1993b) "Reflections on Homosexuality: An Interview with Joseph Henderson" in Robert H. Hopcke, Karin Lofthus Carrington, and Scott Wirth (eds) *Same-Sex Love and the Path to Wholeness: Perspectives on Gay and Lesbian Psychological Development*, pp. 231–245, Boston: Shambhala.

Woodman, Marion (1982) *Addiction to Perfection: The Still Unravished Bride*, Toronto: Inner City.

—— (1985) *The Pregnant Virgin: A Process of Psychological Transformation*, Toronto: Inner City.

Woolger, Jennifer B. and Woolger, Roger J. (1987) *The Goddess Within: A Guide to the Eternal Myths that Shape Women's Lives*, New York: Fawcett Columbine.

Young-Eisendrath, Polly (1992) "Gender, Animus, and Related Topics," in Nathan Schwartz-Salant and Murray Stein (eds) *Gender and Soul in Psychotherapy*, pp. 151–177, Wilmette, IL: Chiron.

Young-Eisendrath, Polly and Wiedemann, Florence (1987) *Female Authority: Empowering Women Through Psychotherapy*, New York: Guilford.

Zita, J. N. (1981) "Historical Amnesia and the Lesbian Continuum," in "On 'Compulsory Heterosexuality and Lesbian Existence': Defining the Issues," in Nannerl O. Keohane, Michelle Z. Rosaldo and Barbara C. Gelpi (eds) *Feminist Theory: A Critique of Ideology*, pp.161–176, Chicago: University of Chicago Press.

Zuckert, Catherine H. (1996) *Postmodern Platos: Nietzsche, Heidegger, Gadamer, Strauss, Derrida*, Chicago: University of Chicago Press.

INDEX

INDEX

Honderich, Ted 139
hooks, bell 28–9, 30, 32, 74, 76, 77, 78, 84
Hopcke, Robert 94–8, 99, 102, 103, 114
horizons 140, 141, 145, 146, 148, 161, 173, 180, 182, 187, 188, 190, 191, 202, 206, 209, 210, 221; defined 24–5; fusion of 24, 128, 133, 146, 159, 179–82, 183, 187, 220, 221; in interviews 145, 148, 156; philosophical 7, 27–35; researcher's 140–2; theoretical 7, 36–59, 190; *see also* foregrounding
Humbert, Elie 177
Husserl, Edmund 159, 164–5

Iasenza, Suzanne 113, 117–18
identification 47, 51, 52, 55, 75–6, 78, 96, 97, 101–2, 114, 116, 207
identity 95, 113, 118, 122, 123, 155; black 76–7; construction of 70, 77, 95, 136; cultural 74; ego- 109; as narrative 79; politics 10, 68–79, 84; myth of 38; self-identification 15, 80, 82, 83, 84; -sign 74; *see also* lesbian(s): identity
image 171; *see also* archetypal
individual, the 26, 37, 39, 47, 48, 51, 59, 71, 135, 162, 169, 173, 174, 175, 177, 220–1; as collectively constituted 135
individualism 70, 139
individuality 39, 44, 47, 65, 78, 162, 169, 182
individuation 10, 21, 44, 51–2, 55, 56, 58, 92, 95, 109, 119, 181, 213, 216, 217, 221; collective 39–51, 55, 210–12, 213; homosexual 95, 96, 97; lesbian 39–52 *passim*, 104, 105, 210–12
inside/outside rhetoric 29–31, 73
"integrate"/"integration" 21, 33, 57, 70, 95, 106, 107, 211
interactionists/synthesizers 68, 71
interpretation(s) 23, 25, 26–7, 35, 78, 107, 133, 142, 143, 144, 148, 159, 162, 164, 168, 169, 171, 174, 182, 184 –7 *passim*, 189, 190, 209; of dreams 26–7; of experience 90, 92, 121; of symbols 20, 21; of tradition 174; *see also* text interpretation
interpreter, the 24–5, 27, 171–2, 174, 180
interpretive inquiry 132–4, 149, 165, 185; evaluation of interpretive

accounts 187–91; question of validity and reliability 186–7, 188, 191
interpretive inquiry criteria: coherence 189, 190; consensus 189, 190; external evidence 189, 190; inconcludability 188; indexicality 188; practical implications 189, 190; reflexivity 188
interview themes: contrasting experience of loving women to experience of loving men 205–6; desire for acceptance 208; desire to provide a context 203–4; impact on sense of self 206–7; sense of community 207–8; view of lesbian experience as a series of choices 204–5
interviewee(s) 139, 144–7, 186, 190, 192, 204, 209, 213, 216–17; as text 148–9; *see also* interviews
interviewer 143, 144, 148, 217; as not "the expert" 142, 187
interviews 4, 6–7, 187, 188, 190, 209; as method 142–9; my experience of 127–8, 200–1; selection of participants 84, 144–5; process of 146; setting 18, 20, 60, 119, 150, 166, 168, 190, 192; *see also* Ann; Eileen; interviewees; Joan; Nancy; narratives; Paula; question(s); Sandra

Jarrett, James L. 165–6, 175
"Joan" 150–7, 203, 204, 206–10 *passim*, 215
Johnston, Jill 45
Jung, C. G. 1, 2, 7, 9, 10, 11, 16, 19, 24, 32–5 *passim*, 39, 40, 48, 49, 51–5 *passim*, 98, 99, 100, 103, 105–11 *passim*, 114, 129, 143, 148, 149, 160, 161, 162, 164–6 *passim*, 168, 169, 172, 173, 181, 182, 206, 210–14 *passim*, 217, 218, 219, 221; on agreement and horizons 181–2; and anti-Semitism 11–13; *Collected Works* 16, 162–3, 223n1; concern with politics 219–21; on confession 9; on *consensus gentium* 37; on the dialectical character of understanding 168–9, 181; and feminism 14–15, 106; as "flawed" 13, 14, 217–18; and Gadamer 26–7, 166–84; and Heidegger 35; as hermeneut 218; on hermeneutics

241

INDEX